MIGRATION, WORK AND CITIZENSHIP IN THE ENLARGED EUROPEAN UNION

Law and Migration

Series Editor
Satvinder Singh Juss, King's College London, UK

Migration and its subsets of refugee and asylum policy are rising up the policy agenda at national and international level. Current controversies underline the need for rational and information debate of this widely misrepresented and little understood area.

Law and Migration contributes to this debate by establishing a monograph series to encourage discussion and help to inform policy in this area. The series provides a forum for leading new research principally from the Law and Legal Studies area but also from related social sciences. The series is broad in scope, covering a wide range of subjects and perspectives.

Other titles in this series:

Refugee Law and Practice in Japan
Osamu Arakaki
978-0-7546-7009-4

International Migration and Global Justice
Satvinder Juss
978-0-7546-4671-6 (Hbk)
978-0-7546-7289-0 (Pbk)

Migration, Work and Citizenship in the Enlarged European Union

SAMANTHA CURRIE
University of Liverpool, UK

ASHGATE

Published by

Ashgate Publishing Limited
Wey Court East
Union Road
Farnham
Surrey GU9 7PT
England

Ashgate Publishing Company
Suite 420
101 Cherry Street
Burlington, VT 05401-4405
USA

www.ashgate.com

British Library Cataloguing in Publication Data

Currie, Samantha
Migration, work and citizenship in the enlarged European Union. - (Law and migration)
1. Alien labor - Legal status, laws, etc. - Great Britain
2. Labor market - Great Britain 3. Aliens - Great Britain - Social conditions 4. Great Britain - Emigration and immigration
I. Title
344.4'10162

Library of Congress Cataloging-in-Publication Data

Currie, Samantha, 1982-
Migration, work, and citizenship in the enlarged European Union / by Samantha Currie.
p. cm. -- (Law and migration)
Includes bibliographical references and index.
ISBN 978-0-7546-7351-4 (hardcover) 1. Citizenship--European Union countries. 2. Freedom of movement--European Union countries. 3. Labor policy--European Union countries. 4. Migrant labor--European Union countries. 5. Alien labor --Great Britain. 6. Migrant labor--Europe, Eastern. I. Title.
KJE5124.C87 2008
342.2408'3--dc22

2008029387

ISBN 978-0-7546-7351-4

Mixed Sources
Product group from well-managed forests and other controlled sources
www.fsc.org Cert no. SA-COC-1565
© 1996 Forest Stewardship Council
FSC

Printed and bound in Great Britain by
MPG Books Ltd, Bodmin, Cornwall.

Contents

List of Tables

List of Cases

Judgments of the European Court of Justice

Case 267/83 *Aissatou Diatta v Land Berlin* [1985] ECR 567
Case C-268/99 *Aldona Malgorzata Jany and Others v Staatssecretaris van Justitie* [2001] ECR I-8615
Case C-281/98 *Angonese v Cassa di Risparmio di Bolzano SpA* [2000] ECR I-4139
Case 32/75 *Anita Cristini v Société nationale des chemins de fer français* [1975] ECR 1085
Case 379/87 *Anita Groener v Minister for Education and the City of Dublin Vocational Educational Committee* [1989] ECR 3967
Case 235/87 *Annunziata Matteucci v Communauté française of Belgium and Commissariat général aux relations internationales of the Communauté française of Belgium* [1988] ECR 5589
Case C-356/98 *Arben Kaba v Secretary of State for the Home Department* [2000] ECR I-2623
Case C-466/00 *Arben Kaba v Secretary of State for the Home Department* [2003] ECR I-2219
Case C-413/99 *Baumbast and R v Secretary of State for the Home Department* [2002] ECR I-7091
Case C-308/93 *Bestuur van de Sociale Verzekeringsbank v J.M. Cabanis-Issarte* [1996] ECR I-2097
Case 24/86 *Blaizot v University of Liège* [1988] ECR 379
Case 36/74 *B.N.O. Walrave and L.J.N. Koch v Association Union cycliste internationale, Koninklijke Nederlandsche Wielren Unie et Federación Española Ciclismo* [1974] ECR 1405
Case C-214/94 *Boukhalfa v Germany* [1996] ECR I-2253
Case C-138/02 *Brian Francis Collins v Secretary of State for Work and Pensions* [2004] ECR I-2703
Case C-148/02 *Carlos Garcia Avello v État belge* [2003] ECR I-11613
Case 316/85 *Centre public d'aide sociale de Courcelles v Marie-Christine Lebon* [1987]
Case C-147/03 *Commission of the European Communities v Austria* [2005] ECR I-5969
Case C-216/94 *Commission of the European Communities v Belgium* [1995] ECR I-2155
Case C-278/94 *Commission of the European Communities v Belgium* [1996] ECR I-4307
Case 65/03 *Commission of the European Communities v Belgium* [2004] ECR I-6427

Case C-35/97 *Commission of the European Communities v France* [1998] ECR I-5325

Case C-285/00 *Commission of the European Communities v France* [2001] ECR I-3801

Case 249/86 *Commission of the European Communities v Germany* [1989] ECR 1263

Case C-185/96 *Commission of the European Communities v Greece* [1998] I-6601

Case C-365/93 *Commission of the European Communities v Greece* [1995] ECR I-499

Case 305/87 *Commission of the European Communities v Hellenic Republic* [1989] ECR 1461

Case C-388/02 *Commission of the European Communities v Ireland* [2003] ECR I-2173

Case 63/96 *Commission of the European Communities v Italy* [1988] ECR 29

Case C-337/97 *C.P.M. Meeusen v Hoofddirectie van de Informatie Beheer Groep* [1999] ECR I-3289

Case 274/96 *Criminal proceedings against Horst Otto Bickel and Ulrich Franz* [1998] ECR I-7637

Case 207/78 *Criminal proceedings against Gilbert Even et Office national des pensions pour travailleurs salariés* [1979] ECR 2019

Case 137/84 *Criminal proceedings against Mutsch* [1985] ECR 2681

Case 66/85 *Deborah Lawrie-Blum v Land Baden-Württemberg* [1986] ECR 2121

Case 53/81 *D.M. Levin v Staatssecretaris van Justitie* [1982] ECR 1035

Case 9/74 *Donato Casagrande v Landeshauptstadt München* [1974] ECR 773

Cases 389 and 390/87 *Echternach and Moritz v Minister van Onderwijs en Wetenschappen* [198] ECR 723

Case C-49/98 *Finalarte Sociedade de Construção Civil Ld*[a] [2001] ECR I-7831

Case C-413/01 *Franca Ninni-Orasche v Bundesminister für Wissenschaft, Verkehr und Kunst* [2003] ECR I-13187

Case 65/81 *Francesco Reina and Letizia Reina v Landeskreditbank Baden-Württemberg* [1982] ECR I-33

Case 293/83 *Françoise Gravier v City of Liège* [1985] ECR 593

Case 43/75 *Gabrielle Defrenne v Société anonyme belge de navigation aérienne Sabena* [1978] ECR 1365

Case C-164/94 *Georgios Aranitis v Land Berlin* [1996] ECR I-135

Case C-406/04 *Gérald De Cuyper v Office national de l'emploi* [2006] ECR I-694

Case C-212/05 *Gertraud Hartmann v Freistaat Bayern* (judgment of 18 July 2007)

Case C-57/96 *H. Meints v Minister van Landbouw, Natuurbeheer en Visserij* [1997] ECR I-6689

Case C-224/02 *Heikki Antero Pusa v Osuuspankkien Keskinäinen Vakuutusyhtiö* [2004] ECR I-5763

Case C-76/05 *Herbert Schwarz and Marga Gootjes-Schwarz v Finanzamt Bergisch* Gladbach (judgment of 11 September 2007)

Case C-238/98 *Hugo Fernando Hocsman v Ministre de l'Emploi et de la Solidarité* [2000] ECR I-6623
Case C 340/89 *Irène Vlassopoulou v Ministerium für Justiz, Bundes-und Europaangelegenheiten Baden-Württemberg* [1991] ECR 2357
Case C-438/05 *International Transport Workers' Federation and Finnish Seamen's Union v Viking Line ABP and OÜ Viking Line Eesti* (judgment of 11 December 2007)
Case C-208/05 *ITC Innovative Technology Center GmbH v Bundesagentur für Arbeit* (judgment of 11 January 2007)
Case 48/75 *Jean Noël Royer* [1976] ECR 497
Case C-237/94 *John O'Flynn v Adjudication Officer* [1996] ECR I-2617
Case C-25/02 *Katharina Rinke v Ärztekammer Hamburg* [2003] ECR 8349
Case C-302/97 *Klaus Konle v Republik Österreich* [1999] ECR I-3099
Case C-162/00 *Land Nordrhein-Westfalen v Beata Pokrzeptowicz-Meyer* [2002] ECR I-1049
Case C-341/05 *Laval un Partneri Ltd v Svenska Byggnadsarbetareförbundet, Svenska Byggnadsarbetareförbundets avdelning 1, Byggettan and Svenska Elektrikerförbundet* (judgment of 18 December 2007)
Case 118/75 *Lynne Watson and Alessandro Belmann* [1976] ECR 1185
Case C-85/96 *María Martínez Sala v Freistaat Bayern* [1998] ECR I-2691
Case C-224/98 *Marie-Nathalie D'Hoop v Office national de l'emploi* [2002] ECR I-6191
Case C-60/00 *Mary Carpenter v Secretary of State for the Home Department* [2002] ECR I-6279
Case 76/72 *Michel S. v Fonds national de reclassement social des handicapés* [1973] ECR 457
Case C-456/02 *Michel Trojani v Centre public d'aide sociale de Bruxelles* [2004] ECR I-7573
Case C-291/05 *Minister voor Vreemdelingenzaken en Integratie v R. N. G. Eind* (judgment of 11 December 2007)
Case 59/85 *Netherlands v Ann Florence Reed* [1986] ECR 1283
Case C-447/93 *Nicolas Dreessen v Conseil National de l'Ordre des Architectes* [1994] ECR I-4087
Case C-258/04 *Office national de l'emploi v Ioannis Ioannidis* [2005] ECR I-8275
Case C-164/99 *Portugaia Construções Ld*[a] ECR I-787
Case 181/84 *Queen, ex parte Man v Intervention Board for Agricultural Produce* [1985] ECR 2889
Case C-292/89 *R v Immigration Appeal Tribunal, ex parte Antonissen* [1991] ECR I-745
Case 139/85 *R. H. Kempf v Staatssecretaris van Justitie* [1986] ECR 1741
Case C-11/06 *Rhiannon Morgan v Bezirksregierung Köln* (judgment of 23 October 2007)
Case C-90/97 *Robin Swaddling v Adjudication Officer* [1999] ECR I-1075
Case C-184/99 *Rudy Grzelczyk v Centre public d'aide sociale d'Ottignies-Louvain-la-Neuve* [2001] ECR I-6193

Case C-113/89 *Rush Portuguesa v Office national d'immigration* [1990] ECR I-1417
Case C-109/01 *Secretary of State for the Home Department v Hacene Akrich* [2003] ECR I-9607
Case 197/86 *Steven Malcolm Brown v The Secretary of State for Scotland* [1988] ECR 3205
Case 39/86 *Sylvie Lair v Universität Hannover* [1988] ECR 3161
Case C-192/05 *Tas-Hagen and Tas v Raadskamer WUBO van de Pensioen-en Uitkeringsraad* [2006] ECR I-10451
Case C-331/88 *The Queen v Minister of Agriculture, Fisheries and Food and Secretary of State for Health, ex parte Fedesa* [1994] ECR I-48663
Case C-209/03 *The Queen (on the application of Dany Bidar) v London Borough of Ealing and Secretary of State for Education and Skills* [2005] ECR I-2119
Case 196/87 *Udo Steymann v Staatssecretaris van Justitie* [1988] ECR 6159
Cases 64/96 and 65/96 *Uecker and Jacquet v Land Nordrhein-Westfalen* [1997] ECR I-3171
Case 222/86 *Union nationale des entraîneurs et cadres techniques professionnels du football (Unectef) v Georges Heylens* [1987] ECR 4097
Case C-415/93 *Union Royale Belge des Sociétés de Football Association (ASBL) v Bosman* [1995] ECR I-4921
Case C-357/89 *V. J. M. Raulin v Minister van Onderwijs en Wetenschappen* [1992] ECR I-1027
Case 249/83 *Vera Hoeckx v Openbaar Centrum voor Maatschappelijk Welzijn, Kalmthout* [1985] ECR 973
Case 63/76 *Vito Inzirillo v Caisse d'allocations familiales de l'arrondissement de Lyon* [1976] ECR 2057
Case 213/05 *Wendy Geven v Land Nordrhein-Westfalen* (judgment of 18 July 2007)
Case C-1/05 *Yunying Jia v Migrationsverket* [2007] ECR I-0001

UK Cases

Brook Street Bureau (UK) Ltd v Decas [2004] EWCA Civ 217
Bruce v Postworth Ltd [2005] IRLR 557
Cable & Wireless plc v Muscat [2006] IRLR 354
Decas v Brook Street Bureau (UK) Ltd [2006] IRLR 354
Franks v Reuters Ltd [2003] IRLR 423
Ironmonger v Movefield Ltd [1998] IRLR 461
James v Greenwich London Borough Council [2007] ICR 577
McMeehan v Secretary of State for Employment [1997] I.C.R. 549
Montgomery v Johnson Underwood Ltd [2001] IRLR 269
Motorola Ltd v Davidson [2001] IRLR 4
Nessa v Chief Adjudication Officer [1999] 4 All E.R. 677
O'Kelly v THF plc [1983] IRLR 369
Putans v Tower Hamlets BC [2006] EWHC 1634 (Ch)

R (on the application of H and D) v Secretary of State for Work and Pensions [2004] 3 CMLR 11
Ready Mixed Concrete (South East) Ltd v Minister of Pension [1968] 2 QB 497
Stevenson, Jordan and Harrison Ltd v Macdonald and Evans [1952] 1 TLR 101
Wickens v Champion Employment [1984] ICR 365
Zalewska v Department for Social Development [2007] NICA 17

List of UK Legislation

Acts of Parliament
Civil Partnership Act 2004, C.33
National Minimum Wage Act 1998, C.39
Employment Rights Act 1996, C.18
Housing Act 1996, C.52
Employment Agencies Act 1973, C.35
Immigration Act 1971, C.77

Statutory Instruments

Allocation of Housing and Homelessness (Eligibility) (England) Restrictions 2006, SI 2006/1294
Immigration (European Economic Area) Regulations 2006 SI 2006/1003
Accession (Immigration and Worker Authorization) Regulations 2006 SI 2006/3317
Accession (Immigration and Worker Registration) Regulations 2004, SI 2004/1211
Social Security (Habitual Residence) Amendment Regulations 2004, SI 2004/1232
Tax Credit (Residence) (Amendment) Regulations 2004, SI 2004/1243
Child Benefit (General) (Amendment) Regulations 2004, SI 2004/1244
Allocation of Housing and Homelessness (Amendment) England Regulations 2004, SI 2004/123
Conduct of Employment Agencies and Employment Business Regulations 2003, SI 2003/3319
State Pension Credit Regulations 2002, SI 2002/1792
Immigration (European Economic Area) Regulations 2000, SI 2000/2326
Homelessness (England) Regulations 2000, SI 2000/701
Working Time Regulations 1998, SI 1998/1833

List of European Union Materials and Community Legislation

Treaties

Treaty Establishing the European Community (consolidated version)
Treaty on European Union (consolidated version)
Treaty of Lisbon [2007] OJ C306/01
Treaty of Accession 2005 [2005] OJ L157/11 (Bulgaria and Romania)
Act concerning the conditions of accession of Bulgaria and Romania [2005] OJ L157/203
Treaty of Accession 2003 [2003] OJ L236/17
Act concerning the conditions of accession of the Czech Republic, Estonia, Cyprus, Latvia, Lithuania, Hungary, Malta, Poland, Slovenia and the Slovak Republic [2003] OJ L236/33
Treaty of Accession 1985 [1985] OJ L302/23 (Portugal and Spain)
Treaty of Accession 1979 [1979] OJ L 291/5 (Greece)

Agreements with Third Countries

Europe Agreement establishing an association between the European Communities and their Member States, of the one part, and the Republic of Poland, of the other part, [1993] OJ L348/3
Agreement on the European Economic Area [1994] OJ L001/3
Agreement between the European Community and its Member States and the Swiss Confederation on the Free Movement of Persons [2002] OJ L114/6

EC Regulations

Regulation 864/2007 of the European Parliament and of the Council of 11 July 2007 on the law applicable to non-contractual obligations (Rome II) [2007] OJ L199/40
Regulation 883/2004/EC of the European Parliament and of the Council of 29 April 2004 on the coordination of social security systems [2004] OJ L200/1
Regulation 1408/71/EEC on the application of social security schemes to employed persons and their families moving within the Community, last consolidated text published [1997] OJ L28/1

Regulation 1251/70/EEC on the right of workers to remain in the territory of a Member State after having been employed in that State [1970] OJ Sp. Ed. L143/24

Regulation 1612/68/EEC on free movement of workers within the Community [1968] OJ L257/2

EC Directives

Directive 2005/36/EC of the European Parliament and of the Council of 7 September 2005 on the recognition of professional qualifications [2005] OJ L255/22

Directive 2004/38/EC of the European Parliament and of the Council of 29 April 2004 on the right of citizens of the Union and their family members to move and reside freely within the territory of the Member States [2004] OJ L158/77

Directive 2003/109/EC of 25 November 2003 concerning the status of third-country nationals who are long-term residents [2004] OJ L16/44

Directive 2003/86/EC of 22 September 2003 on the right to family reunification [2003] OJ L251/12

Directive 99/42/EC of the European Parliament and of the Council of 7 June 1999 establishing a mechanism for the recognition of qualifications in respect of the professional activities covered by the Directives on liberalisation and transitional measures and supplementing the general systems for the recognition of qualifications [1999] OJ L201/77

Directive 99/70/EC of 28 June 1999 concerning the framework agreement on fixed-term work [1999] OJ L175/43

Directive 96/26/EC of 29 April 1996 on admission to the occupation of road haulage operator and road passenger transport operator and mutual recognition of diplomas, certificates and other evidence of formal qualifications intended to facilitate for these operators the right to freedom of establishment in national and international transport operations [1996] OJ L223/15

Directive 96/71/EC of the European Parliament and of the Council of 16 December 1996 concerning the posting of workers in the framework of the provision of services [1996] OJ L18/1

Directive 93/96/EEC of 29 October 1993 on the right of residence for students [1993] OJ L317/59

Council Directive 93/16/EEC of 5 April 1993 to facilitate the free movement of doctors and the mutual recognition of their diplomas, certificates and other evidence of formal qualifications [1993] OJ L165/1

Directive 92/51/EEC of 18 June 1992 on a second general system for the recognition of professional education [1992] OJ L209/25, as amended by Directive 2001/19/EC [2001] OJ L206/1 on a second general system for the recognition of professional education and training to supplement Directive 89/48

Directive 93/104/EC of 23 November 1993 concerning certain aspects of the organisation of working time [1993] OJ L307/18

Directive 90/364/EEC of 28 June 1990 on the right of residence [1990] OJ L180/26

Directive 90/365/EEC of 28 June 1990 on the right of residence for employees and self-employed persons who have ceased their occupational activity [1990] OJ L180/28

Directive 89/48/EEC of 21 December 1988 on a general system for the recognition of higher-education diplomas awarded on completion of professional education and training of at least three years' duration [1989] OJ L19/16

Directive 86/457/EEC of 15 September 1986 on specific training in general medical practice [1986] OJ L267/26

Directive 85/384/EEC of 10 June 1985 on the mutual recognition of diplomas, certificates and other evidence of formal qualifications in architecture, including measures to facilitate the effective exercise of the right of establishment and freedom to provide services [1985] OJ L223/15

Directive 85/432/EEC of 16 September 1985 concerning the coordination of provisions laid down by Law, Regulation or Administrative Action in respect of certain activities in the field of pharmacy [1985] OJ L253/37

Directive 80/155/EEC of 21 January 1980 concerning the coordination of provisions laid down by Law, Regulation or Administrative Action relating to the taking up and pursuit of the activities of midwives [1980] OJ L33/8

Directive 78/687/EEC of 25 July 1978 concerning the coordination of provisions laid down by Law, Regulation or Administrative Action in respect of the activities of dental practitioners [1978] OJ 233/10

Directive 78/1027/EEC of 18 December 1978 concerning the coordination of provisions laid down by Law, Regulation or Administrative Action in respect of the activities of veterinary surgeons [1978] OJ L362/7

Directive 77/486/EEC of 25 July 1977 on the education of the children of migrant workers [1977] OJ L199/139

Directive 77/453/EEC of 27 June 1977 concerning the coordination of provisions laid down by Law, Regulation or Administrative Action in respect of the activities of nurses responsible for general care [1977] OJ L176/8

Directive 75/363/EEC of 16 June 1975 concerning the coordination of provisions laid down by law, regulation or administrative action in respect of activities of doctors [1975] OJ L167/14

Directive 64/221/EEC of 25 February 1964 on the co-ordination of special measures concerning the movement and residence of foreign nationals which are justified on grounds of public policy, public security or public health [1964] OJ 850/64

EC Decisions

Council Decision of 15 August 1987 adopting the European Community Action Scheme for the Mobility of University Students (Erasmus) [1987] OJ L166/20

Miscellaneous

Rome Convention of 1980 on the law applicable to contractual obligations [1980] OJ L266/1

Council of Ministers of Education Resolution [1976] OJ C38/1

Preface

The law is stated as it was in January 2008.

The Treaty of Lisbon amending the Treaty on European Union and the Treaty establishing the European Community, was signed at Lisbon on 13 December 2007 ([2007] OJ C306/01).

Assuming that ratification progresses the Treaty will enter into force on 1 January 2009, the Treaty of Lisbon will amend the Treaty on European Union and the Treaty establishing the European Community. The latter will be renamed the Treaty on the Functioning of the European Union (TFEU). In addition, a table of equivalences annexed to the Treaty undertakes a large-scale renumbering of the Articles in both Treaties.

This book uses the pre-Lisbon Treaty numbering. Where it is felt necessary and appropriate, however, reference is made to the numbering and provisions as they *would* stand post-ratification and *after* the entering into force of the Treaty of Lisbon. Such references are based on the text signed in December 2007 and the table of equivalences annexed to it.

Acknowledgments

I owe a tremendous amount of thanks to a number of people who have helped me along the way as I prepared this book. My colleagues in Liverpool – especially Helen Stalford, Fiona Beveridge and Michael Dougan – have provided invaluable early-career support, encouragement and guidance. I am also grateful to Dora Kostakopoulou (Manchester) for the interest she has taken in my work.

I am hugely indebted to all of the research participants who agreed to give up their time to be interviewed and showed genuine enthusiasm for the research and its aims. Without their openness and readiness to inform others about the project the book would not have been possible. Thanks must also go to the Socio-Legal Studies Association for providing a research grant which enabled additional empirical work to be carried out in Poland.

I am very grateful to a number of colleagues who have taken time out of their busy schedules to read and comment on various chapters – Michael Dougan, Fiona Beveridge, Arianna Andreangeli, Liz Oliver and Keleigh Coldron. The rigorous efforts of Sonia Hadj Ayed in preparing this book for publication are also particularly appreciated. Thanks must also go to Catriona Sangster for her attention to detail!

Heartfelt thanks go to my family and friends for their unwavering support and humour – in particular, to my mum for always having faith in me. Finally, I need to thank Darren for his love and support and for putting up with me (and the mess!) whilst I worked on this project.

List of Abbreviations

CAI	Citizens Advice International
CEE accession states	The Central and Eastern European Member States that acceded in either 2004 or 2007
CEE	Central and Eastern Europe
CIS	Commonwealth of Independent States
EAT	Employment Appeal Tribunal
ECAS	European Citizen Action Service
ECHR	European Convention on Human Rights
ECJ	European Court of Justice
EU	European Union
EU2	The Central and Eastern European Member States that acceded to the EU in 2007 (Romania and Bulgaria)
EU8	The Central and Eastern European Member States that acceded to the EU in 2004 (Czech Republic, Estonia, Hungary, Latvia, Lithuania, Poland, Slovakia and Slovenia)
EU15	The Member States that formed the EU prior to 1 May 2004 (Austria, Belgium, Denmark, Finland, France, Germany, Greece, Ireland, Italy, Luxembourg, Netherlands, Portugal, Spain, Sweden and United Kingdom)
EU25	The Member States that formed the EU prior to 1 January 2007 (EU8, EU15, Malta and Cyprus)
EURES	European Employment Services
IOM	International Organization for Migration
NCVQ	National Council for Vocational Qualifications
NGO	Non-Governmental Organization
NVQ	National Vocational Qualification (in the UK)
REC	Recruitment and Employment Confederation
SAWS	Seasonal Agricultural Workers' Scheme
SBS	Sectors Based Scheme
TEU	Treaty on the European Union
TFEU	Treaty on the Functioning of the European Union
TGWU	Transport and General Workers' Union
TUC	Trades Union Congress
TAW	Temporary Agency Work
WRS	Workers' Registration Scheme

In memory of Nannar

Chapter 1

Introduction

In the early part of the twenty-first century, the European Union's membership has transformed from a club of 15 'western' European countries to an alliance of 27 that also encompasses ten post-communist central and eastern European (CEE) countries. For a significant period of time during the twentieth century these CEE countries sat far-beyond the political reach of the 'western world'. The iron curtain detached east from west, not only from an ideological perspective, but also physically: movement of persons between the two regions of Europe was severely restricted.

With the accessions of the Czech Republic, Estonia, Hungary, Latvia, Lithuania, Poland, Slovenia and Slovakia (along with Malta and Cyprus) in May 2004, the EU's population increased by 28 per cent to more than 500 million people (Vaughan-Whitehead 2003, 31). In January 2007 this figure rose by a further 29 million as the EU enlarged again to take in Romania and Bulgaria (Lanzieri 2007, 1). Thus, the fifth and sixth rounds of enlargement are regarded as significant due to the scale on which they occurred. Clearly though, these rounds of expansion also hold much broader symbolic and political significance for the post-communist CEE countries involved. For example, some of the discussions surrounding the 2004 enlargement in particular were couched in rather emotive terms about the 'return' of these eight CEE countries to their rightful place in Europe (Kengerlinsky 2004; Maas 2002).

Despite the positive emphasis in the literature on the unification of Europe, the existence of various transitional arrangements in both the 2003 and 2005 Treaties of Accession[1] has meant that, in reality, accession did not occur overnight, but instead, is being staged over a number of phases.[2] One of the most notable areas subject to such initial phasing-in is the free movement of persons. The 15 established Member States (the EU15)[3] are entitled to derogate from the *acquis* on the free movement of workers in respect of nationals of the eight 2004 CEE

---

1 Treaty of Accession 2003 [2003] OJ L 236/17; Treaty of Accession 2005 [2005] OJ L157/11.

2 For example such transitional arrangements exist in relation to, *inter alia*, the free movement of workers, the Common Agricultural Policy and the free movement of capital. See Inglis 2004; Hillion 2004.

3 Austria, Belgium, Denmark, Finland, Germany, Greece, Ireland, Italy, Luxembourg, the Netherlands, Portugal, Spain, Sweden and the United Kingdom.

accession states (the EU8), and nationals of Romania the Bulgaria (the EU2), for a maximum period of seven years.[4]

The existence of transitional mobility restrictions contradicts the EU's established policy of promoting internal labour migration. The desire to encourage free movement has been the driving force behind long-established legal developments, such as the mutual recognition of qualifications and the extension of social rights and family reunification entitlements to EU nationals exercising rights of free movement. Traditionally, such initiatives have been adopted as part of the overriding economic objective to establish a Common Market with mobile factors of production.[5] More recently, however, there have also been moves at EU level to highlight the professional, cultural and linguistic benefits of working in another Member State. For example, the European Commission designated 2006 the European Year of Workers' Mobility (European Commission 2005c) and put in place various schemes and projects designed to emphasize the benefits of geographic mobility and to provide key, practical information about rights to work abroad.[6] It is perhaps somewhat ironic that such positively-framed mobility projects have been put in place during a period within which a significant proportion of EU nationals experience free movement restrictions.

The primary aim of this book is to explore the legal status and experiences of migrant workers from the CEE accession states during the operation of the transitional arrangements. Furthermore, as the right to free movement is closely associated with the notion of citizenship under EU law, an objective is to analyse the relevance of the Union citizenship status for this group.[7] Previously, academic research has analysed the position and rights of those EU nationals who have exercised mobility rights flowing from the free movement provisions to work in another Member State (Golynker 2006; Ackers 1998).[8] Similarly, the status

---

4 Cyprus and Malta, also 2004 accession states, are not subject to such transitional restrictions.

5 Despite such initiatives it is widely acknowledged that rates of intra-Community migration have remained low. For example recent Eurobarometer surveys indicate that only 4 per cent of EU nationals have taken up residence in another Member State. See European Commission 2006b.

6 For example, an online European job portal with details of EU-wide vacancies was put in place: <http://europa.eu.int/eures/home.jsp> (last accessed 17 January 2008). Similarly, a European job fair was held 29-30 September 2006. The European Citizen Action Service also set up a free movement telephone hotline in 2006 (ECAS, 2006) <http://www.ecas.org/file_uploads/1179.pdf> (last accessed 17 February 2008).

7 Articles 17 and 18 EC. Following the entering into force of the Treaty of Lisbon ([2007] OJ C306/01), scheduled for 1 January 2009, these provisions will be renumbered as Articles 20 and 21 TFEU (assuming ratification progresses smoothly). Should the Treaty of Lisbon ([2007] OJ C306/01) enter into force these provisions will be renumbered as Articles 20 and 21 TFEU (assuming ratification progresses smoothly). On the notion of Union citizenship see, *inter alia*, Fries and Shaw 1998; Shaw 1998; Everson 1995; O'Leary 1996; Faist 2001; Kostakopoulou 2001.

8 In relation to workers the primary Treaty provision is Article 39 EC (after the Lisbon Treaty enters into force, Article 45 TFEU). Secondary legislation clarifies the contingent

of third-country nationals in the EU, particularly following the introduction of the Treaty of Amsterdam which inserted Title IV on 'visas, asylum and immigration' into the EC Treaty, is an issue that has received the attention of academic researchers (Kostakopoulou 2002a, 2002b; Barratt 2003; Guild and Harlow 2001).

During the transitional periods,[9] CEE accession nationals are clearly not granted complete access to the rights of free movement accorded to 'ordinary' internal EU migrants; therefore, the citizenship status they occupy is not immediately analogous to that of EU15 nationals. Neither is the status of EU8 and EU2 nationals equivalent to that of most third-country nationals as they are, as nationals of EU Member States, citizens of the Union in spite of the imposition of transitional mobility restrictions. Consequently CEE accession migrants occupy a unique status under Community law.[10] They may be Union citizens by formal definition but, in practical terms, their repertoire of rights is limited. The ability to move as a worker to another EU Member State is one of the key free movement rights available to those with Member State nationality. As a result of the limitations placed on this right by the transitional arrangements, the recent 'eastward' enlargements provide an interesting lens through which issues of labour migration and the citizenship status of migrant workers can be examined.

The following chapters explore CEE accession nationals' legal rights to access work in the EU15, their experiences of such work, and their access to and engagement with broader family and social entitlement during the transitional period(s). In that sense, citizenship, is conceptualized not merely as a bundle of rights but as a practice; a real 'lived' experience. The citizenship status of CEE accession migrants is shaped by formal legal entitlement, law in action (as it is implemented by the Member Sates and 'accessed' by the migrants), and social and cultural perceptions and experiences 'on the ground'. The interaction of this group with the various aspects of legal provision is measured against the position of EU15 migrants (and by extension migrants from Malta and Cyprus) who are not subject to any transitional mobility restrictions. The juxtaposition of formal legal status and practical experience throughout the various chapters aims to provide a representation of the overall status and employment experience of CEE accession migrants. In adopting this approach, however, the aim is not only to critique the specific status granted to the migrants, but also to reflect more generally on the notion of Union citizenship as expressed formally in the EC Treaty. In particular, the discussion challenges the perception of citizenship as a universally applicable concept and demonstrates how certain types of free movement, exercised by particular kinds of migrant citizen, are valued to a greater extent than others.

employment, family and social rights; in particular Regulation 1612/68 [1968] OJ L257/2 and now Directive 2004/38 [2004] OJ L158/77.

9 2004–2011 in respect of the EU8; 2007–2014 in respect of the EU2.

10 As the Treaty of Lisbon merges the pillars of the European Union it may be more suitable simply to refer to European Union law as opposed to Community law in future (should ratification proceed in all Member States).

Empirical Research

The research on which this book is based was of a socio-legal nature and, therefore, combined analysis of the formal legal framework that shapes the status of CEE accession migrants with empirical investigation of the migrants' practical experiences. As yet, there is no agreed definition of the term socio-legal, but it is generally understood to refer to approaches that are multi or interdisciplinary in nature:

> Our theoretical perspectives and methodologies are informed by research undertaken in many other disciplines. Traditionally socio-legal scholars have bridged the divide between law and sociology, social policy and economics (Socio-Legal Studies Association).[11]

Essentially, socio-legal scholars endeavour to take legal study outside of the legal 'office' to investigate 'law-in-society' (Bradshaw 1997, 99). Importantly, this often involves evaluating the law and its operation by applying some form of data collection techniques to the phenomenon under consideration.

The research that informs this book was carried out between 2004 and 2007 and focused specifically on the status of EU8 migrants in the aftermath of the 2004 enlargement. This book also incorporates, where appropriate, the accession of Bulgaria and Romania and particular considerations pertaining to the 2007 enlargement. An empirical element is incorporated to both complement and contextualize the more black letter exploration of the law by providing some tangible examples of how the law shapes the migration process and experience.

In order for an in-depth picture of the formal legal status of CEE migrants to emerge the analysis was carried out on a number of levels, taking into consideration the various layers of regulation impacting on the free movement rights of the migrants. At the supranational level, the Treaties of Accession and the detail of the transitional arrangements were the obvious focal point. In order to consider this in a more meaningful context, the details of the transitional rules were analysed in the light of provisions of EU law on free movement and citizenship that govern the rights of EU nationals generally. At the national level, the EU15 Member States' implementation of transitional arrangements was considered. Such domestic implementation also has a significant impact on the extent of CEE accession migrants' entitlement, experience and status, as the design of the transitional arrangements bestows a considerable degree of discretion upon the implementing Member States. The research, while adopting EU law as a wider frame of reference, focused on the specific context of the UK legal framework put in place to regulate EU8 migration following enlargement. In this respect, the research represents an attempt to challenge and move beyond the media-projected images of EU8 workers (Polish in particular) that have dominated the debate in

---

[11] As quoted on the Socio-Legal Studies Association website <http://www.slsa.ac.uk> (last accessed 9 November 2007).

the UK since the decision was taken by the government to extend labour market access rights to EU8 nationals in 2004.[12]

The empirical research focussed on labour migration from Poland to the UK and the experiences of Polish migrants. Therefore, the empirical research essentially provided a case study of Polish migrants who worked in the UK in the post-accession environment. Throughout the chapters of this book, findings from the case study on Polish workers complement the legal analysis which applies more broadly to the wider category of EU8 migrant workers (and, in some instances, also to migrant workers from Romania and Bulgaria). Semi-structured, qualitative interviews and focus groups were conducted with Polish migrants working in the UK in 2004 and 2005. These respondents had either moved within the year leading up to the date of the 2004 enlargement (that is, from May 2003) or following Poland's accession in May 2004. In order to add a cross-national element to the empirical work, and to gain a greater understanding of the complexities relating to post-accession migration from Poland, further qualitative interviews were carried out in Poland (in August 2005) with return migrants who had moved to the UK (during the same time period as those workers mentioned above) but who had since returned to Poland.

The research supporting this publication aimed to gain a (qualitative) insight into the phenomenon of post-EU enlargement migration from the perspective of the migrants themselves. The objective was to reveal some of the human consequences of migration that are often hidden behind migration statistics. Migration research has largely been dominated by studies that rely on statistical data. Indeed, Singleton (1999, 156) has pointed to the 'positivist imperative' whereby researchers continue to favour a quantitative approach over others. This study attempted to 'get behind the numbers' and look at the impact of the legal framework(s) on the ground from the perspective of those the law seeks to address.

Notwithstanding the overall commitment to a qualitative approach, the value of quantitative based analyses is also recognized and statistical secondary data is utilized throughout the book to contextualize the more qualitative examples. The main secondary source relied on in this respect is the Accession Monitoring Report which details the statistical data connected to the operation of the UK Workers' Registration Scheme (WRS). The report has been published quarterly by the UK government since the May 2004 EU enlargement and provides details

---

12 The attitude of the British press has varied since the 2004 enlargement. Initially the UK government was heavily criticized after making the decision to allow EU8 nationals to work in the UK, for example: Smith 2004; *Daily Mail* 2004. Accusations and suspicions of 'benefit tourism' against EU8 migrants have also been present in the press coverage of the issue, for example, Hall 2006. There has, though, also been some recognition of an apparent good work ethic demonstrated by Polish migrant workers and celebration of the idea that they have been working in occupations not filled by UK nationals (Righter 2006; Foggo and Habershon 2006). Although, as the accession of Bulgaria and Romania drew near, the tone of the debate on accession migration in the tabloid press appeared to become a little more strained. For example, Nicolson 2006; Ingham 2006.

about those EU8 nationals that have registered as workers under the WRS.[13] It has been an invaluable source of information on the employment activity of EU8 migrants across various occupations (including hours of work and wages), the characteristics of the EU8 workers in the UK (in terms of factors such as age, gender and percentage of those with dependents in the UK), and the extent to which EU8 workers have sought access to certain welfare benefits in the UK. In spite of the value of this information there are certain methodological features of the data included in the Accession Monitoring Report that need to be acknowledged. First, the data covers only those EU8 workers who have formally registered their employment on the WRS since 1 May 2004. It does not include within its ambit the (unknown) number of EU8 migrants who have taken up work in the UK without fulfilling this registration requirement. Neither does it measure the number of EU8 migrants who do not fall within the category of 'employed' (such as the self-employed). It does, however, include some students as EU8 migrant students who work part-time are not exempt from the registration requirement. Furthermore, the data from the WRS is by no means an estimate of net migration to the UK from the EU8 Member States as it only presents a cumulative figure of those that have applied to the scheme from the date of accession. It does not measure, to any extent, the outflow of EU8 migrants as there is no requirement for those who leave to 'de-register' from the scheme.

The findings from the empirical work are drawn upon throughout the book to highlight particular experiences of Polish migrant workers in the UK and to emphasize how the legal framework and the formal status they are granted shapes these experiences. This sample does not claim to present a representative picture of the overall experience of the population of post-accession Polish workers in the UK, but to provide an interesting and rich qualitative insight into the experiences of some of those that moved in the aftermath of the 2004 EU enlargement. Furthermore, some broader conclusions can be drawn when the experience of the sample is coupled with the available and relevant statistical information.

In terms of how the research progressed, the empirical work preceded the analysis, or 'theory building', at the conceptual-abstract level; therefore the reasoning was inductive in nature (DeVaus 2001, 6). The qualitative interviews did not set out to 'test' any predetermined theory regarding the impact of the EU legal framework on free movement and migration. Rather the data was used to construct a theory; the theory was 'grounded' in the data collected. Glaser and Strauss (1967), the pioneers of grounded theory, stress the importance of developing analytical interpretations of data throughout the research process and of refining the developing theoretical analysis. Important facets of the grounded theory approach include simultaneously collecting and analysing data, coding, using comparative methods, memo writing and sampling to refine the emerging theoretical ideas:

13 For the latest report see Home Office Border and Immigration Agency 2007. The reports from the series can be accessed at <http://www.ukba.homeoffice.gov.uk/sitecontent/documents/aboutus/reports/accession_monitoring_report/> (last accessed 17 February 2008).

> Grounded theory methods do not detail data collection techniques; they move each step of the analytic process toward the development, refinement, and interrelation of concepts. (Charmaz 2003, 251)

A demonstration of how this grounded approach was applied in the present study is provided by the use of purposive or theoretical sampling. For example, during the interviews in the UK many of the migrant respondents mentioned that they had enlisted the services of an employment agency to help them find work. As a result, the decision was taken to also interview representatives from a small number of such agencies in Poland. These interviews were designed to explore further the role played by agencies in facilitating the movement of Polish nationals. 'Key informant' interviews were carried out at various points throughout the course of the research when it was felt that the research could benefit from such additional input. One such interview was with a manager of a transport company that had recruited a high number of Polish workers; another was with a legal practitioner with experience of advising migrants from the CEE region; and a further key informant had worked on a project in Poland that ran a telephone helpline designed to provide information about the post-accession regulatory system in the UK.

The research, in striving to apply a genuinely interdisciplinary methodology, drew upon approaches and concepts that span different disciplines in order to develop a more holistic understanding of the status and experiences of CEE migrant workers. This approach is incorporated into the book. The concern of doctrinal legal studies is to analyse and critique the general legal position, whereas the sociological interest is represented by the study of the individuals' experiences and their engagement with the host society.

The Structure of the Book

The following chapters seek cumulatively to contribute to a more theoretical analysis of the legal and social structure that lay the foundations of the research and to detail the key findings. Extracts from the respondents' accounts are integrated into the analysis to highlight the personal impact of migrating from the CEE Member States in the post-accession climate.

Chapter 2 provides an overview of the legal framework that sets the parameters of the new migration space which has emerged since the 2004 and 2007 EU enlargements. In doing so, it seeks to analyse the potential for CEE nationals to qualify for the status of migrant worker during the period when transitional restrictions on the free movement of persons apply. First, the provisions of EU law governing CEE nationals' ability to access work in the EU15 Member States are discussed. Principally, this involves analysis of the transitional arrangements on the free movement of persons contained in the 2003 and 2005 Treaties of Accession. Details are also given of the various national policies implemented across the Member States in the aftermath of the recent accessions in order that the differentiated nature of free movement entitlement can be emphasized. Finally, changes in the tone of the debates on migration and enlargement between 2004 and 2007 are charted.

Chapter 3 considers, in more detail, the UK's Workers' Registration Scheme put in place to regulate post-accession labour migration from the EU8 Member States. In addition to the detail of the legal provisions, the chapter explores some of the practical strategies migrants have utilized to access work in the UK; notably, agencies, employer-organized schemes and informal social/familial networks. The discussion exposes how the particular legal regime in the UK, and the confusion that has surrounded it, appears to have encouraged and entrenched reliance on such migration 'facilitators'. Consequently, this in turn has had the effect of increasing exposure to exploitative employment relationships for some EU8 migrants. Employment agencies, both in the CEE region and the UK, are playing a particularly prominent role in facilitating post-accession labour migration. This chapter considers the nature of the different legal relationships that can emerge under such agency arrangements.

Chapter 4 extends the analysis undertaken in Chapter 3 by moving on from the discussion about how EU8 nationals access employment to analyse their status and experiences of working in the UK. The chapter begins by outlining the labour market profile of post-accession CEE migrants in the UK. The concept of de-skilling is explored and considered in the context of this category of migrants. In particular, aspects of the regulatory framework contributing to the devaluation of the migrants' skills and qualifications are highlighted and examined: first, the UK's regulatory system (the Workers' Registration Scheme) and, secondly, the EU's mutual recognition of qualifications regime. The chapter then explores the gender-dimension of skill-degradation and the particular (professional) consequences of migration for female Polish migrants. Specifically, the discussion considers the differential gender-impact of formalized employer-driven migration schemes which tend to operate in traditionally male-dominated sectors. The chapter concludes by questioning whether the devalued position typically occupied by new accession migrants in the UK may have any long-term consequences for the migrants' labour market activity and professional progression. It does so by speculating on the potential for re-skilling should the migrants remain in the UK or return to their home state. As the analysis progresses, there is consideration of whether the EU is concerned about the 'type' of mobility it wishes to encourage. The apparent 'brain waste' from the CEE region in the aftermath of enlargement stands in contradiction to recent initiatives, tied in to the Lisbon Agenda, aiming to increase intra-Community 'knowledge circulation' by promoting highly-skilled mobility.

Chapter 5 moves on from the employment experience of CEE migrant workers to examine how moving to the UK for the purposes of work can impact on the family lives of migrants. Migration, either for a temporary period or long-term, is often a household strategy utilized to enhance the family unit's prosperity. The objective here is to explore the implications of such migration decisions for family units. The entitlement of accession migrant workers' family members to join the worker in the UK is detailed and, further, the wider social entitlement of the family unit is considered. The ability to access certain welfare benefits in the host state may be important for sustaining the family and its members. The EU free movement provisions are the primary frame of reference when discussing the experience of (re)unified families but, in the case of CEE migrants, this entitlement must be considered in the light of certain aspects of the transitional restrictions on the free movement of persons and placed within the specific context of the UK. The model of family reunification espoused by the free movement of persons provisions has not reflected patterns of migration from the CEE Member States in the initial period following enlargement. The archetypal mover has been a single worker spending temporary periods of time abroad, perhaps receiving assistance from extended relatives and kin who have settled in the host state, but with any immediate family remaining in the home state. The chapter considers how this apparent culture of family separation has characterized the family lives of many recent migrants. In essence, the notion of the transnational family might better reflect CEE migrants' post-accession experience of family life. It does appear, though, that family reunification and the establishment of family life in a host state is becoming increasingly important for post-accession migrants and the chapter incorporates this more recent evidence.

Chapter 6 builds on the discussions in the previous chapters by examining the relevance of the concept of Union citizenship to CEE migrants. Given that mobility rights and the contingent social entitlement of workers and their families flowing from the free movement of persons provisions are a central facet of Union citizenship, the chapter explores the impact of the restricted mobility rights on the citizenship status of nationals from the CEE accession countries. It opens with a discussion of the meaning of Union citizenship and the significance of free movement to the concept. Then there is examination of the impact of the transitional restrictions on the, traditionally privileged, category of economic migrant workers who, inevitably, occupy a downgraded citizenship status during the transitional period. The discussion moves on to look at the potential significance of Article 18 EC and the broader free movement rights that flow from it to EU8 and EU2 nationals. In examining the links between the citizenship status of CEE nationals and the different sites of free movement in the EC Treaty, there is also scope to trace the development of Union citizenship from a predominantly market-based status to a more inclusive and social conception, with greater scope for economically inactive migrants to gain a degree of access to the status and the valuable rights that append to it. Finally, the chapter links with earlier parts of the book by focussing specifically on the UK as a frame of reference. There is analysis of the potential impact of the developing law on citizenship on the status of EU8 migrants who are not economically active in the UK. Thus, the UK's post-accession rules, which seek to deny new arrival work seekers and former workers rights of residence and equal treatment, are considered in the light of developments in the citizenship and free movement *acquis*. Overall, the analysis highlights the discrepancy between the objective of bringing Europe 'closer to it citizens' and the exclusion of the new citizens from the full package of citizenship entitlement.

Chapter 7, the concluding chapter, draws together the material and analysis from the preceding chapters to emphasize how the complexity endemic in the legal framework has translated to the migrants' practical experience of living and working in the UK. As a result of the interaction between the various layers of legal context considered throughout the book (the transitional arrangements contained in the Accession Treaty; the free movement of persons and formal citizenship provisions as interpreted by the Court of Justice; the domestic implementation of transitional rules; and the migrants' engagement with various actors connected to the system), CEE migrants are experiencing a novel typology of citizenship in the aftermath of the 2004 and 2007 enlargements. Primarily, the self-interest of EU15 Member States, employers and agencies has been a principal determinant of this group's status and experience. The discussion also ponders the potential for the transitional arrangements to have a longer-term impact on the citizenship status and identity of those they address even beyond the expiry of the transitional period.

Chapter 2

Transitional Rules in the Accession Treaties and National Implementation throughout the EU

Introduction

This chapter seeks to highlight the legal rules, at EU and domestic level, which set the parameters of CEE accession nationals' formal rights to work in the EU15 Member States during the transitional period. The central aim of the discussion is to analyse the potential of accession nationals to qualify as migrant workers in the aftermath of enlargement when transitional restrictions on the free movement of persons apply. These temporary restrictions, enshrined in the Accession Treaties, allow the EU15 Member States to derogate from elements of the free movement *acquis*. The effect of the transitional rules is to deny CEE accession nationals full access to the (usually far-reaching) EU law right to move to and reside in another Member State for the purposes of work; instead, the national law of the EU15 initially governs EU8 and EU2 nationals' labour market access.[1]

The free movement of persons proved to be one of the most controversial topics to be negotiated in the run-up to the signing of the Treaty of Accession in 2003, 'since in most Member States the possible influx of workers from the Acceding Countries remain[ed] unpopular among the general public' (Farkas and Rymkevitch 2004, 369). Some of the older Member States were concerned about what impact migration of the new 'less-privileged' EU citizens would have within their own territories (Dougan 2004; Kvist 2004); essentially, the transitional arrangements on the free movement of persons represent a compromise negotiated into the Accession Treaties.[2] The first part of this chapter looks at the background

---

[1] It is noteworthy that in the case of the EU2 the newer EU8 Member States are also entitled to implement transitional mobility restrictions.

[2] Treaty of Accession 2003 [2003] OJ L236/17. Article 24, Act of Accession [2003] OJ L236/33 refers to a series of Annexes that contain details of the transitional arrangements in respect of each accession Member State (Annexes V-XIV). For example, in relation to Poland see Annex XII [2003] OJ L236/875. An analogous regime applies to the EU2 under the 2005 Accession Treaty and Act of Accession (Treaty of Accession 2005 [2005] OJ L157/11; Act concerning the conditions of accession of Bulgaria and Romania [2005] OJ L157/203). Each transitional regime concerning the EU8 and EU2 has been negotiated

and rationale behind the imposition of transitional mobility restrictions in the aftermath of the 2004 (and, by extension, the 2007) enlargement. In the second part the provisions themselves, as included in the Accession Treaties, are examined and in the third part the national implementation of transitional restrictions is considered.

The Rationale behind Temporary Mobility Restrictions

Preparations for the accession of a group of CEE Member States considered as 'poor' in comparison to the old and 'wealthy' EU15 forced the EU institutions and the old Member States to grapple with the complex prospect of migration in an enlarged European Union with significant economic disparities between east and west. In the years leading up to the 2004 enlargement reservations centred on the possibility of increased migration flows to the EU15 from the CEE accession states in the light of the new citizens being granted rights to free movement. Kvist (2004, 305) summarizes the (economic) argument as such:

> Comparatively less wealth in acceding countries is seen as a push factor for migration, and the higher wealth of older member states as a pull factor.

High east-west wage differentials combined with high unemployment rates in (some) of the CEE accession states gave way to fears that an 'influx' of accession nationals would head to the EU15. By way of example, in 2004 monthly minimum wages in Poland and the Czech Republic were €177 and €207 respectively; whereas in the UK and France the relevant figures were €1083 and €1173 (Paternoster 2004, 2).[3] Given that the respective 2004 monthly minimum wages in Romania and Bulgaria were €69 and €61, apprehension about migration from the EU2 was also pronounced (ibid.).

Concerns were expressed in the older Member States about the potential for disruption to occur in the national labour markets. For example, German trade unions lobbied extensively for transitional arrangements on free movement, arguing that the arrival of workers from the CEE Member States would lead to a reduction in wages in the territory and entrench further the problematic unemployment rate (Jileva 2002, 694). Furthermore, the potential for social dumping, with businesses benefiting financially from establishing their offices in the CEE region where the cost of premises and wages are significantly lower than in the EU15, was another adverse consequence predicted prior to

---

in the same way and the arrangements concerning free movement of persons are found in Part 2 of each annex. The term 'Annexes' will be used from herein when referring to the transitional arrangements that apply to the EU8 and EU2.

3 In 2003 the average unemployment rate in the EU15 was 8.1 per cent whereas in the new CEE Member States it was 14.5 per cent. In some Polish regions, however, the unemployment rate was above 20 per cent (in particular, Kujaw sko-Pomorskie, Lubuskie and Zachodniopomorskie), see Mladý 2004, 2–3.

enlargement (Kvist 2004, 305; Dougan 2004, 112). The notion of social tourism was also prevalent in the debates. It was suggested that differences between social welfare systems in the old and new Member States would encourage migration by people primarily motivated by the desire to claim generous social benefits while making little contribution to the host society in return (Kvist 2004, 306). Migrant workers are perceived to be a particular threat in this respect due to the relatively low threshold, set by the Court of Justice, which must be reached in order to activate the principle of non-discrimination on the ground of nationality in the area of social advantages.[4] To qualify as a worker exercising a right to free movement under Article 39 EC,[5] and thus be eligible for protection on the basis of the non-discrimination principle, one must be classed as undertaking effective and genuine work, under the direction of an employer, for which one receives remuneration.[6] Crucially for those that subscribe to the argument that welfare tourism is a likely consequence of EU eastward expansion, the Court has held that those working part-time, those carrying out work that falls below a state's minimum subsistence level and those claiming benefits in conjunction with employment can still constitute 'workers' under Article 39 EC.[7] Furthermore, the type of welfare benefits available to workers is extremely inclusive due to the wide definition assigned to the concept of 'social advantage' in Article 7(2) of Regulation 1612/68;[8] essentially, it has come to be understood as referring to almost any form of social welfare available to the state's own nationals.[9]

The recent enlargements were not the first time such concerns of mass migration to 'the west' have been voiced; indeed, similar fears were expressed in the aftermath of the fall of the Berlin Wall in 1989. Thränhardt (1996, 227) points out how various researchers, journalists and politicians in western Europe and the United States predicted 'Russian floods' of up to 25 million migrants. Movement on such a large scale, however, did not occur from Russia or from other parts of the Commonwealth of Independent States (CIS) (Mayhew 1998). Instead it seems that certain European countries, such as Germany, actively recruited from the region in the early 1990s in order to fill labour shortages (Thränhardt 1996, 228–30).[10] In addition to these east-west fears, apprehension regarding increased flows of migrants – and the perceived likelihood of welfare tourism and labour market disruption – also surrounded the 'southern' accessions

---

4 Pursuant to Article 7(2), Regulation 1612/68 [1968] OJ L257/2.

5 Should the Treaty of Lisbon ([2007] OJ C306/01) enter into force the relevant provision will Article 45 TFEU.

6 For example, Case 66/85 *Lawrie-Blum* [1986] ECR 2121; Case 196/87 *Steymann* [1988] ECR 6159; Case C-456/02 *Trojani* [2004] ECR I-7573.

7 See Case 53/81 *Levin* [1982] ECR 1035; Case 139/85 *Kempf* [1986] ECR 1741; Case C-357/89 *Raulin* [1992] ECR I-1027.

8 Case 207/78 *Even* [1979] ECR 2019.

9 For example, Case 32/75 *Fiorini v SNCF* [1975] ECR 1085; Case 65/81 *Reina* [1982] ECR I-33; Case 59/85 *Netherlands v Reed* [1986] ECR 1283.

10 A trend that appears to have continued post-accession with the EU15 allegedly 'cherry picking' highly-skilled workers from the EU8, see Vaughan-Whitehead 2003, 441.

of Greece (1981) and Portugal and Spain (1986). Like the EU8 and EU2, these Member States, which also had comparatively lower wage levels,[11] were subject to a transitional period throughout which the mobility entitlement of their nationals was restricted.[12] Greek migrant workers were subject to a six year transitional arrangement whereas Spanish and Portuguese nationals initially faced a seven year restriction on mobility. However, as no significant movement occurred, this transitional period came to an end slightly earlier than was originally anticipated (after five years) (Vaughan-Whitehead 2003, 413). Hence in these cases the anxiety was unfounded. Moreover, in all three of the southern Member States that acceded in the 1980s the overwhelming trend was for emigration rates to other EU Member States to fall in the years following enlargement. All three quickly became, and remain, countries of immigration as opposed to countries of emigration (Kraus and Scwager 2003, 169–71).

Academic opinion has diverged on the issue of whether the 2004 and 2007 EU expansions can be compared to the experience of Spain, Greece and Portugal. For example Orłowski and Zienkowski (cited in Kaczmarczyk 2004, 71), despite recognizing certain cultural and social differences, accept that the accessions of Greece, Spain and Portugal provide an adequate model for projecting patterns of migration from the CEE Member States due to the economic similarities. Additionally, these authors point out that significant numbers of workers from the southern European accession countries had already moved to EU Member States prior to accession, establishing the basis for networks which can help facilitate further mobility. The same is true of nationals from the CEE region. If this reasoning is accepted, it would appear that the transitional arrangements have not responded to any real threat of large scale migration and instead only pander to unfounded fears in the EU15. In actual fact, based on the southern experience, it would appear that the CEE accession states can expect flows of in-migration to increase following accession as a result of movement by both return and new migrants. Furthermore, EU membership may actually deter emigration as the economic prospects of the region begin to show signs of prosperity and as more comprehensive social legislation is introduced, leading to improved social conditions (Ardittis 1994, 5; Jileva 2002).

On the other hand, Vaughan-Whitehead (2003, 419–22) has argued it is misleading to extrapolate experience from the previous EU enlargements, citing a number of factors. First, while the southern accession states did have lower levels of economic development than the rest of the EU Member States at the time of accession, the CEE accession states' economies lag behind the EU15 to a more significant extent:

---

[11] Though income differences between the old Member States and Greece, Spain and Portugal were not as great as the differences between EU15 and EU8 in 2004 (Tamas and Münz 2006a).

[12] Treaty of Accession 1979 [1979] OJ L291/5 (Greece); Treaty of Accession 1985 [1985] OJ L302/23 (Portugal and Spain).

> At the time of entering the EU in the early 1980s, the Southern countries had attained about two-thirds of average EU per capita income, well above the countries of central and eastern Europe, which have reached about one-third of the EU average.[13] This is a substantial difference that could lead to completely different migration behaviour, and in particular to a different scale. (Ibid., 420)

Secondly, the 2004 and 2007 enlargements were on a larger scale than previous accessions as collectively they created 104 million new Union citizens. When Greece joined in 1981 the EU's population increased by 10.5 million and in 1986 Spain and Portugal had a combined population of 49.4 million (Henderson 2000, 1). Arguably the greater number of people involved injects a different dynamic into the most recent enlargements that was not present in previous accessions, particularly as many of the accession countries are even more geographically proximate to EU15 Member States (Germany and Austria in particular) and share common borders. From this perspective comparisons are less useful and, as migration patterns from the EU8 and EU2 are more difficult to predict, transitional restrictions can perhaps be viewed as more justifiable. Furthermore, there is a marked political and cultural disparity between the CEE accession Member States and those southern accession countries. The comparatively weaker social and political infrastructure of the EU8 and EU2, as a consequence of their post-communist status, is perceived as another factor that would prompt a greater incidence of migration. In any event, it is this viewpoint which prevailed despite the report by Boeri and Brücker (2000), carried out at the European Commission's request, concluding that there would be no substantial increase in migration towards the western states following the granting of mobility rights to accession state nationals and that fears of 'swamping' were unfounded.[14] In reality, concerns about negative public reaction to the immediate extension of mobility rights to CEE accession nationals appear to have been the primary factor motivating the inclusion of the transitional restrictions in the Accession Treaties rather than any convincing evidence of probable labour market disruption and welfare tourism.

The following section moves on to the detail of the transitional arrangements but, first, it is helpful to provide some further context by briefly mentioning the EU's input into the system that governed migration between the CEE accession states and the EU15 prior to enlargement. Before acceding to the EU the EU8, along with Romania and Bulgaria, had concluded Europe Association Agreements with

---

13 This data relates to 2003.

14 Prior to enlargement numerous studies, using a variety of methodologies each with their own strengths and weaknesses, attempted to predict the future extent of migration from the EU8 to the EU15. Some researchers (such as Boeri and Brücker 2000) used economic, model-based studies whereas others designed studies based on surveys of EU8 nationals (for example Wallace 1998). For a comprehensive overview see Kaczmarczyk 2004; Vaughan-Whitehead 2003, 414–18. For discussion of the evidence emerging post-accession see Tamas and Münz 2006a; 2006b; Boeri and Brücker 2005.

the Community (and the Member States).[15] The aim of the Europe Agreements was to facilitate the development of free trade with the associate countries. They were very much a stepping stone to the eventual accession of the EU8 and EU2 countries, and they helped to shape the rights of migrants from the region within the EU (Mayhew 1998). Each Agreement included a Title IV which dealt with the movement of workers, establishment and supply of services. While EU8 and EU2 nationals were able to establish businesses in the EU Member States on the same basis as nationals,[16] the Agreements did not create any right of entry for workers. Rather, they provided that those lawfully admitted to the labour market under national law were entitled to protection from nationality-based discrimination in the areas of working conditions, remuneration or dismissal.[17] This extended valuable protection to those CEE nationals in work, especially given that the ECJ held the provision to be directly effective,[18] but the Agreements did not positively facilitate the movement of workers and in reality offered relatively modest commitments[19] to CEE nationals seeking to work in the pre-enlarged EU (Hedemann-Robinson 2001, 571). Jileva (2002, 692) argues that by framing the Europe Agreements in this way the EU Member States effectively safeguarded themselves against labour migrants from the CEE countries. It is quite pertinent then, but perhaps not surprising, that the older Member States have sought to continue to 'protect themselves' from migratory movements from the CEE region following the accession of the EU8 and EU2.

The Detail of the Transitional Arrangements

The transitional arrangements operate by permitting the already established Member States to derogate from Articles 1–6 of Regulation 1612/68 for a maximum period of seven years in respect of EU8 and EU2 nationals.[20] By granting entitlement to EU nationals to access the labour markets of other Member States, these provisions are the main source of an EU migrant worker's mobility and employment rights. EU15 Member States are not, therefore, entitled to control migration in general from the CEE accession states during the transitional period. They are, however, permitted to decide the conditions under which EU8 and EU2 nationals access employment in their territories. Once that access is

---

[15] For example, Europe Agreement establishing an association between the European Communities and their Member States, of the one part, and the Republic of Poland, of the other part, [1993] OJ L348/3.

[16] Article 44(3), Europe Agreement with Poland [1993] OJ L348/2.

[17] Article 37(1), Europe Agreement with Poland [1993] OJ L348/2. This effectively afforded those who did work in the EU15 the same *in-work* protection as EU migrant workers under Article 39 EC and Regulation 1612/68 [1968] OJ L257/2.

[18] Case C-162/00 *Pokrzeptowicz-Meyer* [2002] ECR I-1049.

[19] Article 41 did *encourage* Member States to improve the existing facilities of access to employment accorded under bilateral agreements.

[20] The transitional period runs from 1 May 2004–30 April 2011 in the case of the EU8 and from 1 January 2007–31 December 2013 in the case of the EU2.

secured, host Member States are not entitled to restrict any of the benefits which flow from the employment status. For example, EU8 and EU2 nationals who do find work are entitled to equal treatment with nationals in respect of terms and conditions of employment,[21] access to housing[22] and, importantly, to social and tax advantages.[23] CEE migrants in the EU15 are also be able to utilize the provisions on the aggregation and exportability of social security benefits under Regulation 1408/71,[24] as these measures are not subject to any transitional rules.

Nationals of Cyprus and Malta, despite acceding to the EU at the same time as the EU8 states, were accorded full free movement rights immediately upon accession. The smaller size of these countries combined with their geographic positioning and (alleged) higher standard of living have been used as justification for the distinction made between them and the CEE accession states.[25] Precisely because of its small size, Malta is entitled to impose its own safeguards if it suspects large-scale movement into its territory by nationals of other Member States.[26] The EU8 and EU2 states, under the terms of the transitional arrangements in the Accession Treaties, have the right to retaliate against the EU15 by adopting reciprocal restrictive measures as regards access to their labour markets by nationals of the old Member States.[27]

Clearly, the permitted derogations focus predominantly on workers as a category of migrant citizen (those whose status flows primarily from Article 39 EC) and leave unscathed the mobility rights of EU8 and EU2 self-employed persons (whose rights flow from Article 43 EC).[28] Consequently, the distinction between workers and self-employed persons is of the upmost importance during the transitional period as those classified as having established in an EU15 Member States are able to access full free movement entitlement.[29] This can be a problematic distinction to make as modern patterns of employment often involve

---

21 Article 7(1) Regulation 1612/68.

22 Article 9 Regulation 1612/68.

23 Article 7(2), Regulation 1612/68. There is an abundance of case law on the issue of 'social advantages' and the Court has stressed the concept should be interpreted broadly: Case 207/78 *Even* [1979] ECR 2019. 'Social advantages' has been held to include discretionary benefits: Case 65/81 *Reina* [1982] ECR I-33, and benefits granted after employment has been terminated: Case C-57/96 *Meints* [1997] ECR I-6689. It also covers benefits not directly linked to employment, such as a right to be accompanied by an unmarried partner, Case 59/85 *Netherlands v Reed* [1986] ECR 1283.

24 Regulation 1408/71, last consolidated text published [1997] OJ L28/1.

25 Although Hillion (2004b, 597) has questioned whether the standard of living of (reunited) Cyprus would be higher than that of Slovenia.

26 Para. 2, Annex XI (Malta).

27 Para. 13, Annexes.

28 This will later be enshrined in Article 49 TFEU if the Treaty of Lisbon is ratified and enters into force.

29 If a migrant works under the direction of another in return for payment they qualify as a worker within the scope of Article 39 EC, see *inter alia* Case 196/87 *Steymann* [1988] 6159. Those that are self-employed operate independently outside a relationship of subordination, under their own responsibility, and in return for remuneration paid to

people moving from a status of employment to one of self-employment (and back again) regularly (Chalmers et al. 2006, 701). There have been claims that in some instances CEE accession nationals have registered in a EU15 Member State in a self-employed capacity in an attempt to circumvent the restrictions on workers despite, in fact, being employees (Tamas and Münz 2006a).

The free movement rights of EU8 and EU2 nationals providing or receiving services in the EU15 on the whole remain intact during the transitional period.[30] Austria and Germany, however, are entitled to restrict the provision of services in certain regions because of the potential for serious labour market disturbances to occur in sensitive sectors, such as construction and industrial cleaning.[31] In addition, the transitional arrangements leave intact the ability of EU8 and EU2 nationals to exercise rights of free movement as economically inactive migrants pursuant to Article 18 EC.[32] Self-sufficient CEE nationals are able to reside in an EU15 Member State on the basis of Article 18 EC and, hence, will be entitled to non-discriminatory treatment in respect of matters falling within the scope of the Treaty, under Article 12 EC.[33] It is sufficient to note at this stage that economically inactive migrants, such as students, who exercise rights of free movement as citizens under Article 18 EC enjoy a much less secure status in a host state than do traditional 'economic' migrants. Crucially the right to reside is subject to the conditions of having sufficient financial resources and comprehensive medical insurance.[34] The focus in this chapter, however, is limited to those that move in order to work as the aim here is to examine how accession nationals gain access to the status of migrant worker during the transitional period. Essentially, the concern at this stage is to explore the climate within which EU8 and EU2 migrant workers have had to operate as a result of the interaction between EU law (in the form of the transitional arrangements on free movement) and the implementing domestic law.

The transitional arrangements last for a maximum of seven years and the system works on a 2+3+2 basis.[35] For the first two years (2004–2006 for the EU8;

---

them directly (it is for the national court to decide if these conditions are satisfied). See, *inter alia*, Case C-268/99 *Aldona Malgorzata Jany* [2001] ECR I-8615.

30 Article 49 EC; to be renumbered as Article 56 TFEU should the Treaty of Lisbon enter into force.

31 Para. 13, Annexes.

32 To be renumbered as Article 21 TFEU should the Treaty of Lisbon enter into force.

33 Case C-85/96, *Martínez Sala* [1998] ECR I-2691. The self-sufficiency requirement is subject to the principle of proportionality: Case C-184/99 *Grzelczyk* [2001] ECR 6193. The entitlement of CEE migrants under the general right to free movement in Article 18 EC is considered further in Chapter 6. Under the Treaty on the Functioning of the European Union, the principle of non-discrimination on grounds of nationality would be enshrined in Article 18.

34 Article 7, Directive 2004/38 [2004] OJ L158/77; previously Directive 90/364 [1990] OJ L180/26, Article 1. The self-sufficiency requirement is subject to the principle of proportionality: Case C-184/99 *Grzelczyk* [2001] ECR 6193.

35 Paragraphs 2–12 of the Annexes provide details of how the transitional arrangements operate in practice. See also European Commission 2002a.

2007–2009 for the EU2) the implementing Member States are able to govern migration from the EU8 and EU2 through 'national measures' or through rules stemming from bilateral agreements.[36] Essentially, national immigration law can continue to regulate labour migration from the CEE states during this time period. This is, however, subject to the standstill clause which provides that any national measures put in place should not be more restrictive than those in force on the day of the signature of the Accession Treaty.[37] After the initial two-year period the implementing Member States then decide, again unilaterally, whether they are to continue with these national measures or grant full labour market access to CEE accession nationals for the next three years (2006-2009 for the EU8; 2009–2012 for the EU2).[38]

Generally the intention is that after five years, all national measures relating to labour market access will cease and EU8 and EU2 workers enjoy complete mobility rights. However, the implementing Member States are given discretion to continue applying national measures beyond this period for a further two years if they encounter 'serious disturbances' in the labour market *or* 'a threat of serious disturbances'.[39] Finally, after seven years have expired (1 May 2011 for the EU8; 1 January 2014 for the EU2) CEE accession nationals will be extended full free movement of workers entitlement.

Throughout the whole of the transitional period, those Member States that have not continued or, indeed, never implemented national measures and opened up their labour market immediately, continue to have the option of invoking the 'safeguard' clause in the Accession Treaty. This allows the Member State to submit a 'request' to the Commission that the application of Articles 1–6 of Regulation 1612/68 be suspended in its territory and that transitional restrictions on workers' mobility be restored.[40] Member States wanting to make use of this provision should notify the Commission that it 'undergoes or foresees disturbances in its labour market which could seriously threaten the standard of living or level of employment in a given region or occupation'. Strictly, the Member State should await the Commission's formal Decision[41] but in 'urgent and exceptional cases' the Member State can unilaterally suspend the mobility rights and provide a 'reasoned ex-post notification' afterwards.

There are certain CEE nationals who are 'immune' from the transitional provisions: those who have lived and worked in one of the old EU Member States for an uninterrupted period of 12 months or more prior to accession, for example,

---

36 Para. 2, Annexes.

37 Para. 14, Annexes. The prior regime governing EU8 migration was based on the Europe Agreements.

38 Member States must notify the Commission of their intentions before the initial two-year period expires: para. 3, Annexes.

39 Para. 5, Annexes. Again, the Commission must be notified.

40 Para. 7, Annexes.

41 The Commission is obliged to notify the Council of its decision. Within two weeks from the date of the decision any Member State can request the Council to annul or amend the Decision: para. 7, Annexes.

can continue to reside and work in that particular Member State on the same basis as other EU15 workers.[42] This applies also to those who are admitted for 12 months uninterrupted following accession.[43] The rights that these migrants enjoy are strictly limited to the particular Member State that originally granted them access. Thus, although they have continued access to their host state's labour market they cannot then move to another Member State and take up work there. Furthermore, if they 'voluntarily leave' the labour market of the Member State within the initial 12 months, they forfeit the right to reside and work there.[44] An interesting contrast can be drawn here with the position of third-country nationals under the Long Term Residents Directive;[45] third-country national migrants who obtain the status of long-term resident in one Member State are entitled to take up subsequent residence in another Member State and enter employment there.[46] Recent Community initiatives have attempted to promote the integration of third-country nationals within the Member States (Hedemann-Robinson 2001; Kostakopoulou 2002a; 2002b; Barratt 2003; Guild and Harlow 2001).[47] This makes the comparatively exclusionary treatment of the newest Union citizens seem all the more anomalous. There is, however, a clause which obliges the implementing Member States to give preference to EU8 and EU2 nationals over third-country nationals in respect of labour market access.[48] Presumably this classification of third-country nationals is not intended to include the European Economic Area Countries (Iceland, Liechtenstein, and Norway) or Switzerland as nationals of these countries clearly enjoy more favourable mobility rights than EU8 and EU2 nationals during the post-accession transitional period.[49]

The defining feature of the transitional arrangements which apply to the EU8 and EU2 is the almost unlimited discretion enjoyed by the implementing Member States. Prior to enlargement it was suggested that the flexible design of the transitional measures permitted the old Member States to unilaterally adapt the rules to suit their own labour market needs (Vaughan-Whitehead 2003;

42 Para. 2, Annexes.

43 This 12 months can be a mixture of time before and after accession, provided it is continuous.

44 Para. 2, Annexes.

45 Directive 2003/109/EC [2004] OJ L16/44. Ireland, the UK and Denmark are not bound by this Directive. For discussion see Kostakopoulou 2002b.

46 Article 14, Directive 2003/109/EC [2004] OJ L16/44. Subject to the residence conditions set out in Article 15 which includes a provision that allows Member States to require third-country nationals to comply with 'integration measures'.

47 Following the communitarization of parts of the third pillar in the Treaty of Amsterdam, creating Title IV, Part Three, of the EC Treaty in 1997. See Tampere European Council Presidency Conclusions, 15–16 October 1999; see also Directive 2003/86/EC on the right to family reunification [2003] OJ L251/12.

48 Para. 14, Annexes. Thus, the transitional arrangements may negatively impact on the status of third-country nationals in the EU Member States' labour markets.

49 EEA Agreement [1994] OJ L001/3; Agreement between the European Community and its Member States and the Swiss Confederation on the Free Movement of Persons [2002] OJ L114/6.

Adinolfi 2005). The post-accession evidence, limited though it may currently be, appears to support this proposition. Research carried out by Tamas and Münz (2006a; 2006b), for example, suggests that migration from the EU8 to the EU15 following the 2004 enlargement has been predominantly demand-driven with migrants moving to the regions and sectors with labour market shortages.[50] From the perspective of the EU15 Member States, therefore, the flexible design of the transitional arrangements has been a welcome factor and the transitional measures, as a whole, a success. Due to the particular design of the transitional arrangements, EU8 and EU2 nationals do not have uniform entitlement to migrate in search of employment across the EU Member States. A migrant's ability to access the labour market differs across the EU15. Furthermore, in the case of Romanian and Bulgarian nationals, the individual *EU25* Member States have the choice of whether to impose restrictions. The EU8 Member States – whilst still at the receiving end of transitional arrangements themselves – are able to impose limits on the movement of nationals from the EU2. Thus, nationals of the latest accession states have to manage an even more complex geometry of free movement entitlement. The following section examines the national implementation of the transitional arrangements in order to consider how this discretion has been utilized.

National Implementation of Transitional Restrictions

The national context is an important part of any discussion of transitional arrangements since the decision whether to implement restrictions is a unilateral one for each of the implementing Member States and they are given significant discretion regarding the length and scope of any such restrictions. This section first examines the response of the EU15 in the immediate aftermath of the accession of the EU8. It then moves on to look at the approaches adopted subsequently, after the Commission reported on the functioning of the transitional arrangements and the transitional period moved into its second stage (May 2006-April 2009). Finally, an overview of the free movement policies adopted by the Member States following the accession of Bulgaria and Romania is given.

Transitional Free Movement Policies Directed at EU8 Nationals

EU15 labour market policies immediately following EU8 accession In the immediate aftermath of the 2004 enlargement the EU15 Member States could be grouped into four categories in terms of free movement policy. First, Austria and Germany, the two Member States that had been the most ardent supporters of transitional restrictions, adopted a strict stance from the outset. These Member States had also taken it upon themselves in the lead up to accession to steer the EU-level debate on transitional mobility restrictions by promoting their inclusion in the Accession Treaty. For example, former German Chancellor, Gerhard

---

50 This is discussed further below in relation to the national implementation of transitional restrictions.

Schröder, had sought to steer the debate on the need for implementation of transitional arrangements as far back as 2000:

> Many of you are concerned about expansion of the EU ... The German Government will not abandon you with your concerns ... We still have 3.8 million unemployed, the capacity of the German labour market to accept more people will remain seriously limited for a long time. We need transitional arrangements with flexibility for the benefit of both the old and the new member states. (Schmid 2000)

Germany and Austria can be labelled as the 'shepherds' who guided the debate at EU level. Continuing with this analogy, it follows that the second group can be categorized as the 'sheep'. This category was comprised of those Member States that did not initially intend to impose mobility restrictions but decided later to implement protectionist measures, effectively following the example set by the 'shepherds' and, indeed, each other or, more appropriately, the 'flock'.[51] As more states made policy U-turns and announced that transitional measures would be implemented, those still resisting found themselves under increased national pressure to follow suit. In the months running up to enlargement transitional restrictions spread across the EU15 in the manner of a domino effect producing what was essentially a 'race to the bottom'. During this period the Member States imposing transitional periods adopted various regimes based on their national systems. Tamas and Münz (2006a, 2) point to the existence of work permits, annual quotas, bilateral agreements, seasonal permits or permits giving EU8 migrant labour access only to a particular sector. In particular, these authors point out that Austria maintained national restrictions but issued temporary work permits to EU8 nationals on the basis of labour market-based needs tests and discretionary decisions of the government. Germany continued to apply its bilateral seasonal labour agreements which are often utilized by Polish nationals. Thus, even the two Member States who most ardently supported transitional restrictions were content to turn to EU8 migrant workers in order to sustain their own labour markets.

The UK constituted the third category. It resisted calls to impose transitional restrictions, at least in the manner of those enshrined in the Accession Treaty, opting instead to grant labour market access to EU8 nationals provided they registered on a Workers' Registration Scheme. However, this 'open' free movement policy was accompanied by changes to the test determining entitlement to various welfare benefits[52] and restrictions on the residence entitlement of EU8 migrants who, for whatever reason, cease to be employed. The common perception is that open labour market access is tantamount to a liberal or even generous policy. In actual fact the UK system applicable to EU8 migrant workers, which has remained in force for a number of years now, is not as liberal as it might appear and is

---

[51] The EU15 Member States that fall into this category are: Belgium, Denmark, Finland, France, Greece, Italy, Luxembourg, the Netherlands, Portugal and Spain.

[52] Benefit claimants in the UK are required to be both habitually resident and 'lawfully resident' (which, for EU8 nationals, means they must either currently be in work or have built up a year of continuous work). The is discussed further in Chapters 3 and 6.

arguably one of the more exploitative post-accession free movement regimes to have emerged such that this Member State may be best described as a 'wolf in sheep's clothing'.[53] By denying EU8 migrant workers full access to the rights and benefits that normally accrue to migrant workers after an employment relationship has expired under EU law, the UK profits from the national insurance and tax contributions paid by EU8 workers (Gilpen et al. 2006), who are often situated in sectors of the labour market with 'hard-to-fill' jobs, but does not shoulder responsibility for their welfare, in return, should they later fall on hard times.

Ireland, which held the EU Presidency at the date of enlargement, and Sweden implemented the most liberal transitional free movement regimes. Both allowed immediate and unrestricted free movement of labour from the EU8 without any concomitant requirement to register (as in the UK). Initially, though, it looked as though Sweden would implement transitional restrictions; the Swedish government had prepared a proposal whereby EU8 nationals would have been required to have an open-ended job waiting for them in Sweden (European Industrial Relations Observatory 2004). However, these proposals were defeated by the Swedish Parliament just two days before accession. These two Member States, therefore, applied Community free movement law unreservedly in the initial two-year period (Chow 2006).[54]

Initial labour market effects and EU15 policies after 1 May 2006 In accordance with the requirements of the Accession Treaty, in April 2006 the Commission produced a report on the functioning of the transitional arrangements (European Commission 2006c). The Commission confirmed that during the initial two years diverse national measures had been put in place across the EU15 resulting in legally different regimes existing for access to the labour markets of the Member States (ibid, 4). Consequently, the lack of uniformity created a complex and, arguably, confusing state of affairs for any EU8 nationals seeking to migrate to the EU15.

In the report the Commission stressed that migration flows between the EU8 and the EU15 in the initial two year period had been limited and were not significant enough to have adversely affected the EU labour market (ibid, 13). Interestingly, the report concluded that transitional arrangements were not

---

53 The exploitative nature of the UK's post-accession regime is a theme which emerges throughout the book. In Chapter 3, the UK rules are explored in greater detail. In addition, Chapter 4 looks at the work undertaken by EU8 migrants in the UK and suggests that often the workers' skills are devalued in the labour market despite the jobs they do contributing positively to the UK economy. Chapter 5 examines the family life of EU8 migrants and suggests that restricted welfare entitlement in the UK may have prevented some EU8 workers from having their family members join them. Chapter 6, on Union citizenship, suggests that the UK's denial of welfare assistance to EU8 work-seekers and former workers may be in contravention of Community law.

54 Ireland did introduce a habitual residence test in respect of non-contributory social assistance: Chow 2006. However, as this test applies to EU8 nationals on the principle of equal treatment as regards Irish (and EU15) nationals this does not appear contrary to Community law.

the primary determinant of mobility flows into the EU15, but rather that the individual Member State's labour market conditions were the principal factor influencing migration:

> There is no evidence to show a direct link between the magnitude of mobility flows from the EU10 Member States and the transitional arrangement in place. Ultimately, mobility flows are driven by factors related to supply and demand conditions. (Ibid., 14)[55]

Further, the report emphasized the positive effect that EU8 migrants, and the work carried out by them, was having on the economies of the EU15; in particular, how migrants from the accession countries were helping to alleviate skills bottlenecks in EU15 labour markets (ibid., 13–14).[56] This explains why even the most zealous supporters of transitional arrangements continue to operate temporary migration schemes in various sectors in an attempt to fill vacant positions and, again, emphasizes how the flexible design of the transitional measures have worked for the benefit of EU15 Member States. EU8 migrant workers appear to have been playing a complementary role in the labour market by carrying out work nationals have neither the desire nor the skills to do. Despite fears of overcrowding and labour market disruption, the experience of those Member States that immediately opened up their labour markets suggested that the extension of mobility rights to EU8 nationals did not impact negatively on the employment rates of nationals (ibid., 14).[57]

This notion of demand-driven migration resonates with the market-based migration theory devised by Favell and Hansen (2002). This theory contends that the market is, and has been, the primary driver behind migration processes in the EU and its Member States:

> Despite the nation-state's continued attempt to define migration as a political phenomenon – controlled by categories of 'legal' and 'illegal' migration, the granting (or not) of nationality and citizenship rights, and so forth – migration in Europe is in fact beginning to resemble more the scenario of labour market theorists, who point to self-regulating supply and demand factors as the ultimate determinants of why people move and where they end up. (Ibid., 597)

From this perspective the existence of transitional arrangements will have little impact on migration flows because the ultimate dynamic shaping mobility patterns will be the market economy and the labour markets within. Furthermore, it appears that many of the Member States that did impose transitional restrictions encountered increased numbers of EU8 migrants working in the irregular, black

55 The demand-driven nature of EU8 migration is confirmed by Tamas and Münz 2006b.

56 Various reports focussing on the UK confirm this, e.g. Gilpin et al. 2006; Home Office et al. 2006.

57 Again, research has confirmed these findings in relation to the UK, see Gilpin et al. 2006.

labour market in the aftermath of enlargement (European Commission 2006a). Arguably, such workers who took up work in the shadow economy were also responding to a demand for low-skilled and flexible labour.

While the transitional arrangements in place may not be the primary determinant of migration patterns into a particular Member State one would obviously expect those Member States with (more) open labour market access to experience greater inflows of migrants. Patterns of migration into Ireland and the UK would appear to support this view. The Commission's report draws on data from the European Labour Force Survey which provides that EU10[58] nationals made up 0.4 per cent of the total working age population in the EU15 in 2005 (as compared to 0.2 per cent prior to accession in 2003).[59] In the case of Ireland, however, in 2005 EU10 nationals accounted for 2 per cent of the working age population.[60] Meanwhile, in the UK the figure rose from 0.7 per cent in 2003 to 1.4 per cent in 2005. Interestingly, there was no such increase in the percentage of EU10 nationals making up the working age population in Sweden (the other EU15 Member State with an 'open' labour market): it remained constant at 0.2 per cent from 2003–2005.[61] Tamas and Münz use this as evidence to support the view that legal labour market access does not automatically lead to large migration flows and that, in fact, demand for labour is a much greater factor (Tamas and Münz 2006a).[62] This view is clearly an influential one. The discussion here has already suggested the UK and Ireland had labour market shortages. Other social factors, however, are likely to also be influential. For example, it is telling that, out of the three Member States which opened their labour markets following the 2004 EU enlargement, the two (predominantly) English-speaking Member States experienced the greater inflows. In addition, in the case of the UK at least, there is a history of migration from Poland which is likely to have led to the creation of migration networks and migration diasporas, helping to facilitate and ease the burdens associated with the migration process.[63]

There is scope here only for a brief sketching of the, still emerging, labour market trends in the aftermath of accession. The general conclusion from the studies thus far is that those pre-accession fears of labour market crowding and welfare tourism have not materialized.[64] Instead, those Member States with open employment access have reported positive results for the labour market

58 The report includes Malta and Cyprus within its ambit and hence refers to the EU10 as opposed to the EU8.

59 All statistics taken from European Commission 2006c, 8–9.

60 No comparable data exists in relation to 2003.

61 Of course, the European Labour Force Survey has methodological drawbacks, particularly as regards comparability as each Member State collects and provides its own data.

62 This also corroborates Favell and Hansen's (2002) argument mentioned above.

63 On migration networks see, *inter alia*, Faist 2000; Waldinger and Lichter 2003; Rees 1966; Choldin 1973; MacDonald and MacDonald 1964.

64 Although at times media commentary in the UK would suggest otherwise. Obviously, it is not clear what would have emerged if transitional arrangements had not been implemented in any EU15 Member State.

and economy in general (Home Office and Department for Work and Pensions 2007a). The remaining chapters of this book, and the qualitative empirical work upon which they are based, support the view that in the UK EU8 migrants have taken jobs in the lower echelons of the labour market that have been left vacant by nationals, despite often being overqualified for these roles, and have demonstrated little desire to claim welfare benefits for themselves or their families. It is also worth noting, however, that in the UK there have been particular concerns regarding the local and regional impacts of the recent migration. This stems from the finding that post-2004 EU8 migrants have found themselves working in regions of the UK that have previously not experienced high levels of immigration.[65] In light of this, it has been suggested that local services (such as schools, health services, housing and language classes) have come under pressure as a direct result.[66] Much of the current discussion on the localized implications relies on anecdotal evidence and media articles as opposed to any rigorous research but, as will be shown below, these ideas have played an important part in influencing the debate on CEE accession migration (Robinson 2007, 98–111).

Following the expiry of the initial two-year phase an even more complex geometry of free movement entitlement has emerged across the EU15. The labour market positions of Germany, Austria, Ireland, the UK and Sweden did not alter significantly after 1 May 2006; therefore, the Member States at opposite ends of the labour market access scale remained stable.[67] Amongst the Member States in the middle group, however, there have been changes in labour market regulation with many of the countries which applied transitional restrictions initially relaxing the rules to allow EU8 nationals greater access to work. Greece, Finland, Portugal and Spain stated early in 2006 that they would allow full labour market access from 1 May 2006. Meanwhile, under Prime Minister Prodi, Italy opened up its labour market in July 2006, reversing the earlier decision of the Berlusconi government. The remaining EU15 Member States – Belgium, France, the Netherlands, Denmark, and Luxembourg – maintain a variety of labour market restrictions, of varying degrees of severity, such as quota systems, work permits and temporary schemes in certain employment sectors (Traser 2006;

65 The distinctive geographical patterns of the recent migration is likely to be shaped by a number of factors but the availability of low-cost air travel (with airlines such as Easyjet and Ryanair flying to regions across the UK) and the prominent role played by agencies in facilitating moves from the EU8 (see Chapter 3) warrant a specific mention. See Stenning et al. 2006.

66 The Local Government Association, which represents councils in England and Wales, has been particularly keen to ensure that such concerns are represented in the debate, see Institute of Community Cohesion 2007. In June 2007 the government convened a panel of public service experts. This Migration Impacts Forum has been given the task of helping to collect evidence on the impact migration is having on housing, health and social care, education, employment and community cohesion.

67 The German government did introduce a slightly more relaxed procedure which allows employers seeking to recruit electrical or mechanical engineers from an EU8 Member State to obtain a work permit without the need to apply for a certificate confirming that they had first sought to appoint an applicant of German nationality.

Tamas and Münz 2006a; 2006b; Mahony 2006; Euractiv 2006a). All of the EU15 Member States are entitled to rely on the safeguard clause until the transitional period fully expires in 2011. In turn, the EU8 are able to maintain reciprocal measures against the EU15.[68]

The case remains that the number of different regimes in place across the EU15 creates a somewhat complex and highly differentiated patchwork of free movement rights. From the perspective of EU8 nationals who wish to explore the migration opportunities available to them in the EU15, comprehensive and accurate information may not be easy to access and the various systems create the potential for confusion. This has been recognized by the European Citizen Action Service (ECAS) which, in August 2006, set up a hotline on free movement rights (European Citizen Advice Service 2006). The initiative, which responds to both emails and telephone calls, was part of the activities ECAS planned in 2006 to coincide with the European Year of Workers' Mobility (European Commission 2005c)[69] and aims to provide migrants and potential migrants with information about exercising mobility rights throughout the EU. Furthermore, the recently established European Employment Services (EURES), a network coordinated by the Commission and involving public employment services, trade union and employers' organizations in all of the Member States, now makes detailed information on the various transitional labour market policies freely available on its website.[70]

The chapter which follows examines the labour market rules in the UK under the transitional regime in greater detail. The primary component of the UK regime is the Worker Registration Scheme and, as will be demonstrated, uncertainty and confusion appear to have accompanied the implementation of this system.

Transitional free movement policies directed towards EU2 nationals EU2 migrants seeking to exercise free movement rights in order to work in another Member States must navigate a different (and further complicated) set of national restrictions. The EU15 Member States' approaches towards Romania and Bulgaria have inevitably been shaped by the repercussions (perceived or genuine) of their policies towards the EU8 from 2004 onwards. While a number of the EU15 Member States have taken steps towards liberalization of their labour markets, as the discussion regarding the post-2006 changes in policy above demonstrates, others – specifically the UK – have sought to impose harsher limits on the mobility rights of nationals from the new Member States. This tendency in the UK is a response to the debate at national level, fuelled by the media, reflecting the view that extremely large numbers (certainly more than predicted) of EU8 migrants

---

[68] Para. 13, Annexes. Writing in January 2008, only Hungary continues to apply such restrictions. Slovenia lifted its reciprocal restrictions on 25 May 2006 and Poland did so on 17 January 2007.

[69] See the Commission's website devoted to the European Year of Workers' Mobility initiative <http://europa.eu.int/comm/employment_social/workersmobility2006/index_en.htm> (last accessed 29 January 2008).

[70] <http://europa.eu.int/eures/> (last accessed 18 January 2008).

have taken the opportunity to work in the UK.[71] Furthermore, EU2 nationals' mobility rights cannot only be restricted by the EU15 but also by the ten Member States that acceded in 2004. The fact that a larger, more socially and economically diverse collection of Member States was able to impose restrictions from 2007 altered the climate within which the transitional rules were implemented.

Eight Member States allowed immediate and complete labour market access to EU2 nationals: the Czech Republic, Poland, Estonia, Latvia, Lithuania, Slovenia and Sweden. A further three liberalized labour market access but with the attached condition that workers register their employment: Cyprus, Finland and Slovakia. It is no surprise that the vast majority of those states without transitional restrictions in place have been on the receiving end of transitional arrangements recently (and in many cases continue to be so). Hungary is the only of the EU8 Member States to have implemented mobility restrictions in the sense of maintaining work permit requirements for EU2 nationals wishing to take up employment in its territory. Sweden is the only EU15 Member State to have offered, in a complete sense, open labour market access from the outset.

The remaining Member States took advantage of the opportunity to impose transitional restrictions on the free movement rights of EU2 nationals from 1 January 2007.[72] Largely, these restrictions have taken form of work permit obligations and, again, suggest that it is not the desire to keep out new Member State nationals *per se* that drives the implementation of mobility restrictions but, rather, the desire to ensure that any migration which does occur is organized in such a way it that suits the needs of the older Member States. Denmark, Malta, Greece, France, Italy, Luxembourg, Belgium, Italy, the Netherlands, Spain, Portugal, Ireland, the UK, Austria and Germany all require Romanian and Bulgarian nationals to hold a work permit, but the rules relating to the issuing of the permits vary in severity depending on the particular aims of the implementing government and the condition of the national labour market. For example, a Greek work permit is issued only if an employer cannot find an EU25 national to fill the vacant post; moreover, to obtain a work permit in Spain an EU2 national must first provide evidence of a job offer and demonstrate an employer's approval of the work permit application. At the other end of the spectrum, Italy does not require EU2 nationals to hold work permits for employment in a number of sectors with shortages of workers (such as agriculture, hospitality, domestic work and construction). Similarly, France has put in place a simplified work permit procedure for a number of occupations with job vacancies.

---

71 A cumulative total of 715,000 EU8 workers registered to work in the UK between May 2004 and September 2007 (to give an example of a yearly figure, in 2006 there were 227,865 registrations) (Home Office Border and Immigration Agency, 2007). Though this should not be read as a representation of net migration due to various methodological considerations connected to the statistics on the Workers' Registration Scheme.

72 The Commission has put together an overview of the current rules on free movement which can be viewed at <http://ec.europa.eu/employment_social/free_movement/enlargement_en.htm> (last accessed 9 February 2008).

The UK's position is interesting in that the extension of the right to work to EU8 nationals has directly contributed to the imposition of work permit requirements on those citizens in the next round of enlargement. It was in October 2006 that the UK government announced that it did not intend to extend the policy of open labour market access to Bulgarian and Romanian nationals following the entry of these countries into the EU. In his statement in the House of Commons at the time, former Home Secretary John Reid reiterated the point that EU8 migration has had positive economic consequences for the UK:

> [The WRS] has been a success. Workers from the new member states have filled skills gaps, including in key public services such as the NHS and social care, and have contributed to UK growth and prosperity. Studies have found no evidence they have taken jobs away from British workers or undercut wages. Employers and customers alike have welcomed their skills. Very few have brought dependents and the proportion attempting to claim out of work benefits has been less than 1 per cent.[73]

After acknowledging the positive economic effect of the EU8 workers, however, the (now former) Home Secretary made reference to the existence of 'some transitional impacts' of the 2004 enlargement, namely: some schools having increased admissions, pressures on language schools providing English tuition, and Local Authorities reporting pressures on the availability of private housing. These infrastructure-related effects, which are clearly linked to the concerns of localized migration pressures described above, obviously resonate with the perception that extremely large numbers of EU8 migrants have taken the opportunity to work in the UK. It is these concerns which influenced the government in imposing limits on the free movement entitlement of EU2 nationals.

In order to work in the UK a Bulgarian or Romanian national must first apply be granted a worker authorization card.[74] Such cards can only be obtained by: those who carry out 'work permit employment' and have been granted a work permit under the national immigration rules;[75] individuals who take up work in an otherwise 'authorised category of employment' (such occupations include domestic workers, nurses and au pairs);[76] or, those who gain a place on a low-skilled migration scheme (such as the Sectors Based Scheme and the Seasonal Agricultural Workers Scheme).[77] Worker authorization cards are only issued in relation to specific jobs, meaning that the worker is effectively 'tied' to the job (and the employer) in order to maintain their status of legality. Furthermore, in most cases (across all categories) at the beginning of the application process an employer

---

73 Hansard, HC, vol. 48, col. 23 (23 February 2004).

74 Pursuant to the rules set out in the Accession (Immigration and Worker Authorization) Regulations 2006 SI 2006/3317.

75 Regulation 11, Accession (Immigration and Worker Authorization) Regulations 2006 SI 2006/3317.

76 Schedule 1, Accession (Immigration and Worker Authorization) Regulations 2006 SI 2006/3317.

77 Regulations 9 and 10, Accession (Immigration and Worker Authorization) Regulations 2006 SI 2006/3317.

must first seek approval of the work arrangement under the work permit system. Only once this approval has been given can an individual apply for an accession worker card (see Home Office Border and Immigration Agency 2007c). Between January 2007 and September 2007, there were 3820 applications by Romanians and Bulgarians for Accession Worker Cards in the UK and 2855 of these were approved (Home Office Border and Immigration Agency 2007b, 3).[78]

Aside from obtaining a worker authorization card, there is one other avenue open to EU2 nationals seeking to migrate to the UK during the transitional period: the Accession (Immigration and Worker Authorization) Regulations 2006 allow 'highly skilled' Bulgarians and Romanians to enter the UK and to work. 'Highly skilled' is defined quite narrowly on the basis of national immigration law rules applicable also to third-country nationals.[79] Given that only 45 EU2 nationals entered the UK on this between July and September 2007 (Home Office Border and Immigration Agency 2007b, 6), it seems this route of entry is not proving to be of benefit to a great many Bulgarians or Romanians.

It is noteworthy that the decision of the UK government to impose transitional mobility restrictions on the nationals of these countries was accompanied by the reservation of all the places on the low-skilled migration schemes for EU2 nationals. This was announced by John Reid when he confirmed the imposition of restrictions on Bulgarian and Romanian nationals:

> From 1 January 2007 we will be phasing out all low-skilled migration schemes from outside the EU. Places on the two low-skilled migration schemes (the seasonal agricultural workers scheme and the sectors based scheme which between them currently have 19,750 places) will now be restricted to nationals from Romania and Bulgaria.[80]

This decision, which reflects the preference clause in the Treaty of Accession's transitional provisions,[81] undoubtedly demonstrates the potential negative impact of EU enlargement on the position of third-country nationals in the Member States. Moreover, it highlights the expectation held by some of the Member States about the role the new EU citizens will fulfil; essentially, they are expected to carry out the low-skilled, low-status and low-paid work.[82]

---

[78] The UK Home Office publishes quarterly statistics on Bulgarian and Romanian nationals in the UK. Available online at <http://www.ukba.homeoffice.gov.uk/sitecontent/documents/aboutus/reports/bulgarianromanian/> (last accessed 19 February 2008).

[79] Regulation 4. 'Highly skilled' also includes those who, within the last 12 months, have obtained (i) a Higher National Diploma or degree awarded by a relevant institution in Scotland; or (ii) a degree with second class honours or above in a subject approved by the Department for Education and Skills for the purpose of participation in the Science and Engineering Graduates Scheme, or a master's degree or doctorate in any subject, awarded by a relevant institution in England, Wales or Northern Ireland.

[80] Hansard, HC, vol. 450, col. 84 (24 October 2006).

[81] Para. 14, Annexes

[82] For further discussion of the experience of EU8 migrants working in the lower echelons of the UK labour market see Currie 2007, 83–116.

Conclusion

This chapter has examined the two tiers of regulation which shape the labour mobility rights of CEE accession nationals: the detail of the Accession Treaty provisions, and the varied implementation of the mobility restrictions by the older Member States. It is apparent that self-interest shrouds both levels of regulation. First, the transitional arrangements by their very nature are designed to protect the interests of the older Member States. They have complete discretion over who they admit to their labour market. Inevitably, therefore, the EU15 are much more inclined to grant mobility rights to those who can fill shortages in specific industries in order to meet labour market demands. The UK, for example, by opening up its labour market after the 2004 enlargement may appear to have acted altruistically but it did so in order to fill job positions that were proving unpopular with the national workforce.[83] The fact that it reversed its policy as regards the free movement entitlement of Romanians and Bulgarians, refusing to extend the open labour market on the basis of equality to the newest citizens, perhaps further evidences the selfishness of the UK. Indeed the tendency of the EU15 Member States has been for their policies towards the EU2 to be either equally as restrictive, or even more so, as they are in relation to the EU8.

Additionally, restrictions on the mobility of a large group of EU citizens does not sit well with the objective of instilling a European 'mobility culture', proclaimed most forcefully through the European Year of Workers' Mobility in 2006 (European Commission 2005c; European Commission 2007). It is ironic that the EU sought to publicize job opportunities and encourage EU15 nationals to work in other Member States during a period where such a large proportion of EU citizens have limited mobility rights. It would seem that only movement by some is currently perceived as desirable.

This chapter provides the foundations for many of the remaining chapters. In addition to examining the legal rules that sit at the heart of the research project it has introduced themes which will be developed further throughout the course of the book.

---

83 The UK's decision to open the labour market instead of 'cherry-picking' in the style of other EU15 Member States was based on the perceived wide-ranging need for labour in 2004 (as opposed to a concentrated number of sectors).

Chapter 3

EU8 Migrants' Access to the UK Labour Market during the Transitional Period

Introduction

It was demonstrated in the previous chapter how, due to the terms of the transitional arrangements, national implementation is an essential part of any discussion of migration in the enlarged EU. The national context is the primary determinant of CEE accession nationals' free movement entitlement during the transitional period(s). This chapter moves on to look specifically at the domestic level rules in the UK that build on the status accorded to EU8 nationals under the Accession Treaties – primarily, the Workers' Registration Scheme (WRS). Although an overview of the various transitional regimes was sketched in the previous chapter, the aim here is to consider how EU8 migrants have gained access to the UK labour market following the 2004 enlargement. The discussion attempts to complement the analysis of the legal framework with exploration of some of the practical methods through which migrants have found work in the UK; most notably, reliance on agencies, employer-organized schemes and kinship networks.

The UK's Post-Accession Regulatory System: the Workers' Registration Scheme

The UK provides an especially interesting framework within which to study migration from the EU8 due to the particular stance it adopted: labour market access rights have been left largely intact (subject to registration) but the legal test governing access to benefits – the habitual residence test – has been modified in an attempt to ensure so-called welfare tourism does not occur. Given the particular focus of this chapter, it is the Worker Registration Scheme's rules that provide the primary basis for the discussion; however, because the UK system links the issues of employment, lawful residence and benefit entitlement there is also some mention of the altered social benefit rules.

The WRS system is problematic in a number of respects. The difficulties relate to the various conditions imposed, in particular, registration deadlines for employees and employers, a 12 month rule for benefit entitlement, and certain other bureaucratic provisions that appear to have culminated in the creation of an atmosphere of uncertainty. The prevailing uncertainty, in turn, has encouraged migrants to seek information about their rights to work in the UK and available job opportunities by relying on various other actors and methods. For example, employment agencies based both in the EU8 and in the UK, appear to have played a prominent role in facilitating migration in the post-accession environment (Ward et al. 2005). Individual employers seeking to benefit from the availability of EU8 workers in order to fill vacant positions have also been active players in the new migration space. Many employers have established recruitment schemes in the EU8 specifically to target workers. In addition to seeking assistance from 'official' sources such as these migrants are continuing to rely on informal migrant networks for information about job opportunities, and life generally, in the host state.

The Background to the UK's Labour Market Policy towards EU8 Migrants

In the lead up to accession a decidedly negative image of potential migrants from the EU8 was portrayed by quarters of the British press. Much emphasis was placed on the 'threat' posed to the benefits system and labour market by migrants.[1] The pressure exerted on the UK government to impose restrictive measures was heightened as the majority of other Member States announced transitional restrictions. The UK, however, was in a different position to many of its EU15 counterparts, notably because the UK economy appeared to be in need of foreign labour across a number of different sectors of the employment market. David Blunkett, then Secretary of State for the Home Department, asserted on 23 February 2004:

> We currently have more than 500,000 vacancies and will benefit from the skills, flexibility and willingness to work of those new migrant workers.[2]

As already mentioned in Chapter 2, this rationale appears to have been justified in the light of post-accession evidence which suggests that EU8 workers have plugged gaps in the UK labour market that would not otherwise be filled by nationals.[3] One of the first instalments of the Accession Monitoring Report series, published by the Home Office, stated that:

> The vast majority of workers are young and single, and many are doing key jobs to support public services … Accession workers are continuing to go where the work is, helping to fill gaps in our labour market. (Home Office et al. 2005a, 2)

---

1 For example, Smith 2004.

2 Hansard, HC, vol. 48, col. 23 (23 February 2004).

3 Clearly, different dynamics have shaped free movement policy post-2007. As discussed in Chapter 2, later reasoning appears to be that the economy may have benefited from the presence of EU8 workers but to continue this policy in respect of the EU2 would place pressure on certain local infrastructures (language training and housing provision for example).

Anderson et al. (2006, 65–70), in their research on central and eastern European migrants working in the UK, report that employers of EU8 migrants had often persistently attempted to recruit UK workers prior to accession without success. Essentially, the authors found that many UK workers were not prepared to accept employment in the type of sectors EU8 migrants have occupied following accession, including hospitality, agriculture and food processing, which are characterized by low wages, long hours and physically-demanding work.[4]

It seems that the UK approach is the result of a political balancing act; the government was keen to allow accession migrants to work in the country to help fill labour shortages but at the same time it wanted to be seen to be responding to concerns connected to the benefit system, to limit political damage. Thus in the same statement Mr Blunkett also stressed the importance of preventing abuse of the welfare system:

> Whether they are plumbers or paediatricians, they are welcome if they come here openly to work and contribute. At the same time, it is clearly not right that people should be able to come here, fail to get a job and then enjoy access to the full range of public services and social security benefits.[5]

The WRS attempts to knit together the issues of employment, legal residence and access to social benefits for EU8 migrants. The effect of the system is to make legal residence dependent upon being in employment and, in turn, access to social benefits is restricted to those legally resident, in other words, those in work. Two statutory instruments implement the system: the Accession (Immigration and Worker Registration) Regulations 2004;[6] and the Social Security (Habitual Residence) Amendment Regulations 2004.[7]

The UK has not restricted the ability of EU8 migrants to access employment in its territory and thus it has not derogated from Articles 1–6 of Regulation 1612/68 as envisaged by the transitional arrangements. However, the WRS does create a legal requirement for EU8 migrants to register their employment. In fact, the employment status of EU8 nationals is only considered to be legal upon registration.[8] Furthermore, the worker registration rules limit the right of residence for EU8 workers to the effect that an EU8 national is only considered to be legally resident when in work and registered on the scheme (at least for the first 12 months of residence). An EU8 national who is unemployed, either as a

---

4 More detail about the type of jobs EU8 migrants have taken in the UK is provided in Chapter 4.

5 Hansard, HC, vol. 48, col. 24 (23 February 2004).

6 Referred to here as 'Worker Registration Regulations', (WRR) SI 2004/121.

7 Referred to here as 'Social Security Regulations', (SSR) SI 2004/1232.

8 Some EU8 nationals are exempt from the requirement to register: those that had leave to enter on 30 April 2004 (reg. 2(2) and (3) WRR); those working legally in the UK for a period of 12 uninterrupted months ending after 30 April 2004 (reg. 2(4)); those family members of an EU15 national already in the UK (reg. 2(6)); and self-employed EU8 nationals (reg. 2(5)).

new arrival work seeker or a former worker, only has a right to reside under UK law if they can demonstrate economic self-sufficiency.[9]

The Registration Process: Obligations of Employees and Employers

With regard to the practicalities of registering on the WRS, once in employment there is a deadline of 30 days within which the EU8 worker must apply to the WRS.[10] To register, the migrant must complete a registration form and provide a letter from an employer as confirmation of the employment relationship.[11] An employer is only an 'authorized employer' if the worker complies with the registration process and applies for a registration certificate,[12] which includes paying an initial registration fee of £90.[13] Therefore, an EU8 national working without registering on the WRS is classified as an illegal worker and as being unlawfully resident. It is important to note that EU8 nationals are required to register on the scheme in respect of every job they take up. If they have more than one job simultaneously they must hold a registration card for each of these jobs.[14]

It is apparent that a significant number of post-accession EU8 migrants have not registered on the WRS. For example, of the 33 respondents who took part in this study and who were required to register, only ten of them had done so.[15] The research on CEE workers by Anderson et al. (2006) confirms this trend for non-registration. Amongst their sample of 217 workers, 75 had not registered (ibid., 97). In some cases, this is the choice of the individual migrant; many of those interviewed for the research upon which this book is based were unhappy with the registration fee which, especially in the initial phase after arrival, was viewed as being very costly. Some also stressed that there was 'no point' in registering as they did not intend to stay longer than a few months and had no interest in accumulating uninterrupted months of lawful employment. For others, non-registration had not been a conscious decision; they were simply not aware about the requirement to register or were misinformed of the applicability of the scheme to them.[16] Anderson et al. (2006, 97) point to the lack of incentives for EU8 migrants to register, in particular the low probability that the UK authorities would actually carry out a deportation against such EU8 nationals (despite this being a theoretical possibility):

---

9 Regulation 4(3), WRR. This is in line with the residence rights of economically inactive migrants under EU law.

10 Regulation 7(2)(b)(i), WRR.

11 Regulation 8(4), WRR.

12 Regulation 5(2) WRR.

13 Regulations 7(2)(b) and 8(4)(a) WRR, respectively. The original fee in May 2004 was £50 and it later rose to £70.

14 Regulation 7(2)(c), WRR.

15 More than 33 respondents took part but those who had worked in the UK for a continuous period of 12 months prior to accession were not required to register (regulation 2(4), WRR).

16 The degree of confusion surrounding the scheme is elaborated on below.

> While working for longer than one month without registration does constitute 'illegal work' the sanctions on workers are ... complex to enforce. It may well be that certain groups of A8 workers, most particularly those who are not intending to stay for very long in the UK, and who are not concerned with claiming benefits at any time in the future are not motivated to register.

On the other hand, it appears that in some instances it is at the employer's (or agency's) insistence that workers do not register. Despite the fact that employers commit an offence by employing unregistered EU8 workers,[17] there are very few checks conducted and enforcement of this law is weak. It is generally the case that levels of prosecution against employers for violations of immigration law are low and this trend is prevalent also in the operation of the WRS (Anderson et al. 2006). This is especially interesting because part of the rationale underpinning the WRS was to eradicate, at least to an extent, the black labour market and to promote legitimacy:

> By taking these measures [implementing the WRS] we will ensure that those arriving in Britain can work for their living openly and honestly and are not drawn into the sub-economy.[18]

The following respondent was aware of the need for EU8 nationals to be educated about their employment rights, but he also gives an example of how unofficial employment can place migrant workers in a weak bargaining position:

> Many employers don't care about rights but we shouldn't give permission for people to treat us like slaves. My friend [who was unofficially employed] started work but after two days the employer said 'you are not enough good for me' and he didn't get any wages. (Interview 001.JK)

Research carried out by Anderson and Rogaly (2005, 7) found that some migrant workers in the UK are subject to such levels of exploitation and control that they fall within the international legal definition of 'forced labour'. Even migrants who can legally work in the UK, such as EU8 nationals, are exploited 'because they are unable to enforce their legal rights because of the power employers often have over them'. Part of their research specifically looked at the position of EU8 nationals in the UK and the report found that some employers had refused to register EU8 workers on the WRS (ibid.). It is likely such employers prefer to keep workers away from the 'legitimacy' associated with registration; after all, it is easier to offer poor work and pay conditions to those who exist outside of the official scheme away from even the most basic checks and balances.[19] The

---

17 Regulation 9(1), WRR.

18 David Blunkett MP, Hansard, HC, vol. 418, col. 25 (23 February 2004).

19 EU8 workers should benefit from the protection of Directive 93/104/EC on the organization of working time [1993] OJ L307/18; as well as from the equal remuneration provisions (Article 7(1), Regulation 1612/68).

empirical data generated for the research which forms the basis of this book would support this assertion; there were a number of examples given by migrant workers of employers who preferred to 'keep the work illegal'. For example the following respondent, who worked in a café, was very aware of her employer's reasoning behind the decision to employ only irregular workers:

> I must confess that it was an illegal job because I didn't pay any insurance or tax or register myself. The money wasn't very good. I worked with a girl from Hungary and a girl from Brazil. It was illegal and I think that a lot of people work like that. Even though now it is legal you know the employers don't want to hire people legally because they can then pay less to workers and in such places there are only foreigners working there because no English people would accept that. It is not nice but they can always say: 'if you don't want a job there are plenty of people who would take your place'. (Interview 304.P)

Employers and their actions were a constant source of enquiries to a telephone helpline in Poland set up by the International Organization for Migration (IOM). The initiative was funded by the UK government under a scheme entitled 'Not All Roads Lead to Britain' which aimed to inform people of the right to work while also highlighting the lack of social assistance available. One of the IOM representatives, who had worked on the helpline, recounted details of experiences that had been repeated to her:

> Some employers took all the documents away from the staff and locked them in a safe, or kept people in very bad conditions in a remote village and made them clean all day. There were clear examples of criminal behaviour. (Interview 102.INFO)

There is also an issue of visibility in relation to employers of EU8 migrants. By providing the necessary confirmation of employment under the WRS, employers identify themselves to the authorities as being responsible for such matters as tax and national insurance contributions. Tamas and Münz (2006a, 15) draw a contrast between Sweden, which is regarded as having particularly strong labour market enforcement, and the UK, which has significantly weaker labour market regulation. Though both have opened up their labour markets to workers from the EU8, albeit with different outcomes in respect of the EU8 migrant inflow, research suggests that instances of employer abuse and irregular work in Sweden have been particularly low, whereas in the UK concern has been expressed – for example by trade unions – that some EU8 workers continue to be exploited by employers in terms of low-paid work, poor safety standards and insufficient enforcement of employment rights.[20]

As EU8 nationals are only legally resident if they are in work and registered within 30 days of arrival it follows that they are technically required to arrange employment before moving to the UK or find work quickly. The practical reality is often quite different. The ability to pre-arrange employment will depend upon

[20] In the UK both the TUC and the TGWU have sought to highlight such cases of abuse: TGWU 2006; TGWU 2005; TUC 2005.

the level of information about employment opportunities in the UK, available in the country of origin. The 'Not All Roads Lead to Britain' campaign, which also distributed information leaflets and ran workshops for potential migrants, may have highlighted this requirement to some and, arguably, may have increased the numbers of people who did seek employment before arrival, most likely with the help of an employment agency (Spitzer 2004).

This requirement to register is not imposed upon national workers or other EU migrant workers in the UK. Therefore, it is clear that EU8 migrant workers are treated differently by being required to register. However, in the light of the transitional arrangements, it is unlikely that the requirement to register would be considered as unlawful discrimination under EU law; after all, the UK is entitled to regulate the conditions under which nationals from the EU8 access employment,[21] and the registration scheme is regarded as a condition of access. Moreover, in the light of the ability of the EU15 to invoke the safeguard clause,[22] it appears that the UK is justified in introducing such a scheme for the purpose of monitoring the numbers of EU8 migrants in the labour market.[23]

What is not so clear-cut is whether the UK is entitled to confer the status of 'unlawfully resident', which carries the implicit threat of deportation, upon a person who does not register. An analogy can be drawn with the Article 39 EC case law relating to registration requirements. It is settled Community law that expulsion cannot be an automatic consequence of a failure to comply with administrative formalities on entering a Member State.[24] Arguably a lesser sanction, such as a small fine, would be a more appropriate and proportionate consequence of non-registration.[25] The legitimate consequences of non-registration of Member State nationals under Community law is clearly limited in scope and, as the UK has purportedly extended free movement rights to EU8 workers, it seems that such principles are relevant despite the existence of transitional restrictions. Under Article 39 EC, expulsion by a Member State of a migrant worker can only be justified in very limited circumstances.[26] During the operation of the transitional period, of course, the safeguard clause can be relied upon to justify the imposition of labour market restrictions in relation to EU8 workers. What is not clear, however, is if it would justify the expulsion of any EU8 workers previously admitted to employment. Arguably, if a Member State did invoke the safeguard provision in the wake of significant labour market disruption it would apply only prospectively. In any event, a Member State is unlikely to deport an

21 Para. 2, Annexes.

22 Para. 7, Annexes.

23 Para. 6, Annexes.

24 See Case 48/75 *Royer* [1976] ECR 497, para. 38.

25 See Case 118/75 *Watson and Belmann* [1976] ECR 1185.

26 Article 39(3) EC states that Member States may restrict free movement on grounds of public policy, public security or public health. These provisions will be reproduced in Article 45 TFEU providing the Lisbon Treaty enters into force. Article 27, Directive 2004/38 [2004] OJ L158/77 now gives further details replacing Directive 64/221 [1964] OJ 850/64.

EU8 national in employment, but the transitional arrangements do suggest that those *voluntarily* unemployed forfeit their rights in that Member State.[27]

It is clear that the UK rules place obligations on both the workers and employers in relation to the registration requirement, but the balance of power is tipped in favour of the employers. While for some EU8 workers non-registration is a positive choice, for others their employer's tendency to favour irregular workers can disadvantage them in terms of the working conditions they experience. Additionally, in the longer term, non-registration may harm the worker's ability to access certain social advantages and benefits in the UK, should they fall on hard times at a later date, because the UK rules purport to restrict full applicability of worker's rights (under EU law) to those who have worked (and been registered) continuously for 12 months.

The 12 Month Rule

The registration requirement applies for the first 12 months of an EU8 national's employment in the UK. Once such a worker has accumulated 12 months of uninterrupted legal employment, the requirement to register ceases and residence is no longer contingent upon employment. The worker will then be eligible for an EEA residence permit.[28] An EU8 worker who ceases to work during the first year of employment can retain the months already accumulated by finding alternative work and re-registering within 30 days from the date the worker's right of residence terminates.[29] The Accession Monitoring Reporting (Home Office Border and Immigration Agency 2007, 16) shows that 52 per cent of the workers who registered between September 2006 and September 2007 were in temporary employment, so it seems that this 30-day deadline is likely to be an issue for these temporary workers. On expiry of a temporary contract, if new employment is not found within 30 days, the worker's residence terminates and, formally at least, they are obliged to return home.

These requirements also rule out casual, cash-in-hand posts that are often more readily accessible to migrants through informal migrant networks (Waldinger and Lichter 2003). Ironically, formal advertised posts often take longer than 30 days to arrange, with the result that the deadline for registration may not be met. Again, employers' input can be crucial here. An employer who does not supply the necessary confirmation letter pending the official start date of the job consigns the worker to a status of 'illegality'; an employer who delays providing the necessary confirmation until after the 30-day deadline may cause the worker to forfeit the all-important months of uninterrupted employment already

---

27 Para. 2, Annexes.

28 Regulation 5, WRR. As a consequence of transposition of Article 8, Directive 2004/38 into UK law, the correct terminology is actually now EEA 'registration certificate' (pursuant to Regulation 16, the Immigration (European Economic Area) Regulations 2006 SI 2006/1003).

29 Regulation 2(4), WRR.

accumulated.[30] The following respondent had changed jobs after six months of work with one employer and, although she was aware of the need to re-register on the WRS, her new employer had not acted quickly enough and had exceeded the 30-day deadline:

> I gave the letter to my employer at the time and I am still waiting for it so I haven't got a clue what will happen because I was told 30 days is the deadline and I have passed the deadline. (Interview 011.MW)

Technically this respondent was working unlawfully and had no right to reside under UK law. In addition, she had lost six months of uninterrupted employment that could have counted towards the required 12, even though she had no actual break between the two contracts of employment. It is questionable, however, whether the position of UK law is compatible with the terms of the Accession Treaty. Indeed, a distinction can be drawn between what the UK *purports* to do, in this instance deny a right of residence after the expiry of a deadline, and the restrictions that EU law may impose on the UK. Surely it would be difficult for the UK to claim that the situation in which the above respondent found herself was simply 'one of those things' or a necessary inconvenience. After all, following cases such as *Baumbast*[31] the Member States are required to take into account the principle of proportionality when seeking to place limits on the right to reside of a migrant Union citizen. It would certainly seem that the denial of residence following the passing of a registration deadline would be a disproportionate response on the UK's part.[32]

Implications of the Link between Registration and Residence: Entitlement to Social Welfare Benefits

Earlier in this chapter the point was made that the UK has sought to prevent EU8 migrants who find themselves without work from accessing benefits in its territory by changing the test which governs benefit entitlement. While the compatibility of this component of the UK regime with aspects of EU law is discussed later in Chapter 6, it is useful here, given that an aim is to describe the detail of the UK system, to note the connections between registration of employment, lawful residency and the consequent ability to access benefits on the basis of non-discrimination. In this respect, the Social Security Regulations work alongside the Worker Registration Regulations by changing the eligibility criteria in social security legislation to the effect that claimants need to satisfy

---

30 Regulation 8(4), WRR.

31 Case C-413/99 *Baumbast* [2002] ECR I-7091, discussed further in Chapter 6.

32 The cases of *Zalewska v Department for Social Development* [2007] NICA 17 and *Putans v Tower Hamlets BC* [2006] EWHC 1634 (Ch), discussed in the next section involved EU8 migrants who had failed to comply with an element of the UK rules. The UK authorities were not explicitly seeking to revoke the individuals' residence, rather they were seeking to deny them entitlement to some form of social benefit.

a 'legally resident' residence test, in addition to the standard habitual residence test, in order to access certain social benefits.[33] Habitual residence is designed to establish which individuals are sufficiently connected to the territory to qualify for means-tested benefits. Previously, habitual residence was the sole threshold an applicant, whether a UK national or EU migrant, need overcome before gaining access to social benefits. The concept is not defined in any legislation, and, while it is beyond the scope of this discussion to provide a comprehensive overview of the relevant case law,[34] it is worth noting the following comment by White (2005a, 22) on the operation of the habitual residence test:

> Decision makers are required to determine whether, taking account of all the circumstances of the case and having regard to the length, continuity and general nature of the actual residence together with the person's intentions, there is evidence of a settled and viable pattern of living in the United Kingdom as a resident.

Additionally, however, applicants must now satisfy the requirement of being 'lawfully resident'. In order to fulfil this limb of the test, an EU8 applicant must show they have a right to reside in the UK by virtue of their registration certificate, or that they have already completed 12 months of continuous, registered work.[35] The benefits triggered by this additional residence condition include: income support, income-based jobseekers' allowance, housing benefit, council tax benefit, pension credit, child tax credit, child benefit[36] and housing and homelessness assistance.[37] This further residence requirement serves to exclude EU8 new arrival work seekers, and workers who cease employment during the first year of employment, from entitlement to the social benefits mentioned above, by virtue of the fact that EU8 migrants have no right to reside under UK law unless they are in work or have accumulated one year of continuous lawful employment. The compatibility of this approach under EU law, in light of developments in the Court's citizenship case law, is dubious at best.[38]

---

[33] Although the intention was to prevent EU8 nationals from abusing the benefits system the changes to the habitual residence test apply to all potential claimants. The Social Security (Persons from Abroad) Amendment Regulations 2006 SI 2006/1026 have formally revoked the SRR but the changes to the habitual residence test remain in force.

[34] Habitual residence has never been given a decisive definition by the UK courts, this is likely to be a deliberate position to allow for some flexibility on the courts' part. See *Nessa v Chief Adjudication Officer* [1999] 4 All ER 677. The main ECJ decision on this point is Case C-90/97 *Swaddling v Adjudication Officer* [1999] ECR I-1075.

[35] Regulation 3(c), SSR.

[36] Tax Credit (Residence) (Amendment) Regulations 2004 SI 2004/1243; Child Benefit (General) (Amendment) Regulations 2004 SI 2004/1244.

[37] The Allocation of Housing and Homelessness (Amendment) England Regulations 2004 SI 2004/1235.

[38] EU8 workers who cease to work during first year of employment are only lawfully resident for the remainder of month in which they worked (reg. 5(4)(b) WRR). The incompatibility of the UK system is discussed in detail in Chapter 6. For example, Case C-85/96 *Martinez Sala* [1998] ECR I-2691, Case C-138/02 *Collins,* [2004] ECR I-2703 (new

EU8 workers who do comply fully with the WRS satisfy the new legal residence requirement. As a consequence, registered EU8 workers are treated no differently from general EU15 migrant workers as regards access to 'social advantages' on the basis of the principle of non-discrimination on the ground of nationality, in compliance with Article 7(2) of Regulation 1612/68, so long as they continue to fulfil the conditions of the WRS. UK social security legislation treats EU (including EU8) migrants working in the territory as automatically satisfying the habitual residence test.[39] Registered EU8 workers are therefore eligible to receive in-work benefits, such as tax credits for example. If, however, an EU8 worker leaves work before accumulating 12 months of uninterrupted employment and does not undertake alternative employment within 30 days, as they no longer fulfil the condition of lawful residence, he or she is not entitled to receive social benefits on the basis of the equal treatment principle.

As a result of these rules, it seems that individual EU8 nationals have been denied the opportunity to claim certain benefits, despite being in work, as a consequence of non-compliance with the registration requirement. In the small number of cases which have come before them, the UK courts have applied the rules relating to the WRS strictly and have not been persuaded to deviate from the black letter provisions of the law to grant benefit entitlement to migrant workers who have been registered for only part of the 12 month period. *Putans v Tower Hamlets*[40] involved a Latvian man who had ceased work after nine months due to ill health. On release from hospital his application for homelessness assistance was rejected on the basis that, as he had not acquired the full 12 months of registered employment, he did not fulfil the residence requirement. The High Court upheld this decision. In *Zalewska v Department for Social Development*,[41] a Polish woman had worked continuously for a 12 month period in Northern Ireland but, due to a change of employment, had only been registered on the WRS for part of this period (six months). She left work after one year and applied for income support. It is not clear exactly why Ms Zalewska left her employment, but it is clear that she was living in a Woman's Aid hostel with her daughter at the time of her application, after allegedly being subjected to domestic violence by her partner. Again, the application was refused on the basis that the applicant did not have a right to reside in the UK: Ms Zalewska only had six months of registered employment. This decision was upheld by the Court of Appeal in Northern Ireland.[42]

The rather strict approach of the courts towards the migrants in these cases stands in contrast to the UK authorities' treatment of defaulting employers which, as has already been pointed out, seems to be rather lenient. In addition,

---

arrival work seekers) and Case 39/86 *Lair* [1988] ECR 3161 (former workers who are now unemployed). Also Directive 2004/38 [2004] OJ L158/77.

39 For example, The State Pension Credit Regulations 2002, Regulation 2(a), SI 2002/1792.

40 *Putans v Tower Hamlets BC* [2006] EWHC 1634 (Ch).

41 *Zalewska v Department for Social Development* [2007] NICA 17.

42 Both of these cases are discussed further in Chapter 6.

there is evidence of increasing levels of hardship amongst those EU8 migrants who have been unsuccessful in their search for work and, crucially, those who initially found work but have since found themselves unexpectedly unemployed or unable to work before accumulating 12 months of employment. This latter group would clearly have no right to reside (and consequently no access to social benefits) under the WRS, regardless of how many months of employment they have accumulated or how unfortunate their individual circumstances. Research carried out with EU8 workers in both London and Dublin has found a number of migrants from these Member States experiencing a high level of poverty and, increasingly, homelessness (Staniewicz 2007). Mr Putans was himself homeless following the decision of the High Court that the denial of assistance was lawful. Such occurrences have also been highlighted by a Polish-based charity, the Barka Foundation, which was approached by British charity workers concerned about the number of homeless Polish nationals they were encountering (McLaughlin 2006; Connolly and Pook 2006).

In reality, the benefits to which correctly registered EU8 workers are entitled on paper have so far not been used to any great extent. That said, it is paradoxical to grant people in work the right to claim, for example, income-based jobseekers' allowance. As the whole basis of their legal right to claim rests on being in work, it is unlikely that EU8 nationals will be entitled to receive jobseekers' allowance, even during the 30 day period of grace 'in-between' jobs. In any event, from a practical perspective, it is unlikely that the process of obtaining such an allowance could be completed, from application through to obtaining the benefit, within a time period as short as 30 days (although, the allowance can be backdated). Between May 2004 and September 2007 there were 12,212 applications made by EU8 nationals for jobseekers' allowance (Home Office Border and Immigration Agency 2007, 25); unsurprisingly, 78.2 per cent of these were rejected on the basis of the new residence test.

The profile of registered workers corroborates the view that benefits have not initially played a meaningful role in the majority of EU8 migrants' experiences in the UK. A predominant characteristic of EU8 nationals working in the UK is youth: 83 percent of the EU8 nationals who registered on the WRS between May 2004 and September 2007 were below the age of 34 (Home Office Border and Immigration Agency 2007, 10). Furthermore, only six percent of those who registered during this time had dependents living with them in the UK (ibid., 11).[43] Hence there would appear to have been no immediate demand for old age or family-related benefits.[44] Of course, this may alter over time if greater numbers of family members join the 'pioneering' migrant worker in the UK and there are some indications that this has started to occur (Pemberton and Stevens 2007).[45]

---

[43] Though, there is no way of knowing how many family members joined the worker after the date of registration.

[44] In 2006, there were 32,803 EU8 claimants of child benefit (Home Office Border and Immigration Agency 2007, 27).

[45] The issues of family reunification, welfare and sustaining families post-migration are discussed in Chapter 5.

The qualitative work carried out with Polish migrants would support the argument that claiming social welfare has been neither a primary migration motivation nor an expectation. The following statement from a respondent represents a common viewpoint articulated in the interviews:

> We are not allowed to claim lots of benefits, but, actually it is useless for us anyway. Mostly, people from the new countries come here just for a short period to earn some money. The idea of claiming benefits has never entered my mind. (Interview 002.PZ)

Now that the regulatory system put in place in the UK to address EU8 migrants' labour market access, and the various rules relating to it, have been set out, attention can turn to the manner in which migrants have negotiated the evident complexity in the system.

EU8 Migrants' Navigation of the Regulatory Regime in the UK

The WRS appears to have created a maze of bureaucracy that both workers and employers must navigate. The details of this system are complex and information regarding the scheme has not been easily accessible. The WRS application forms and the accompanying guidance notes are provided in English only. Moreover, the documents relating to the WRS are not readily available in hard copy and must be downloaded from the government's 'Working in the UK' website (presuming the EU8 worker has access to the internet and a printer).[46] The last-minute nature of the UK's response to the accession 'problem' complicated this information-shortage, as there was very little time prior to accession for any widespread publicising of the scheme.[47]

This layer of bureaucracy has generated widespread uncertainty among EU8 workers and UK employers alike. Many of the Polish respondents interviewed in 2004 and 2005 were aware that the UK had opened its borders, often because of what they had read in Polish newspapers or been told by friends, but many were unaware of the specific details of the WRS. The following interview was carried out in August 2004 and the respondent had been working in the UK since May 2004. As he had not registered, his employment and residence in the UK were technically illegal according to national law.[48] The respondent had lost the opportunity to accumulate three months of continuous legal employment, 12 of which would

46 Available at <http://www.bia.homeoffice.gov.uk/workingintheuk/wrs/> (last accessed 25 February 2008).

47 The government's decision on the position regarding transitional measures was taken comparatively late. Announcements of the broad policy were made in February 2004 but it was not until March/April that the specific nature of the legal provisions began to emerge. See Hansard, HC, vol. 48, col. 23 (23 February 2004).

48 His employer was also committing an offence by employing an unregistered EU8 national under regulation 9(1), WRR.

enable him to enjoy security of residence and full access to social benefits should he subsequently become unemployed:

> I was trying to get to know what is my position here but they [the Home Office] didn't respond ... They didn't answer my emails. What am I supposed to do? Am I supposed to register myself? (Interview 016.D)

The atmosphere of uncertainty surrounding the scheme was referred to on several occasions by respondents. Additionally, the IOM representative interviewed stated that the scheme was frequently the reason why people resorted to their telephone helpline. She confirmed that in the beginning, from May 2004 until August 2004, they received approximately 350 calls per day. Queries regarding the WRS were a common cause for concern and the following respondent's experience supports the view that the information was not readily available:

> After some weeks of the campaign people got to know about this registration scheme and some questions started about registration. For example, where can I get the WRS forms? Why is it only on the internet? This was a prohibitive restriction for people. If you are poor and have no Internet access and want to go to London to work as a cleaner, or you are already there, getting access to the Internet and filling in four or five pages of questions in English is not an easy task. This was kind of a restriction to the market. (Interview 102.INFO)

The Home Office itself seemed to have experienced some teething problems, particularly in the initial stages of the operation of the WRS. The following extract provides an example of an employer who was very aware of the need to find out about the status of EU8 nationals working for him after 1 May 2004. The Home Office, unfortunately, was unable to offer any clear response:

> My employer chose me for the position before 1st May and he did absolutely everything to find out. He phoned the Home Office every day and they kept saying 'we don't know yet, we don't know yet. You have to be patient'. But it was a week until 1st May and they still said they didn't know. (Interview 007.LR)

The employer in this case had taken active steps to educate himself about the status of EU8 workers after 1 May 2004. However, when there is uncertainty as to the law, legitimate employers are more likely to err on the side of caution. This is especially true of smaller businesses without human resources departments, which are often the very places where EU8 nationals have sought work, as the following respondent pointed out:

> For registration we need a letter from an employer but when you go to a coffee shop looking for work sometimes people don't know about it and they think if you don't have certificate already then you don't have permission to work so they don't want to speak with you ... You can't start work because you're not registered but you can't register because you're not in work. (Interview 012.GP)

It seems, therefore, that the general lack of awareness on the part of employers, migrants and even Home Office officials alike in the immediate time-frame following the 2004 enlargement regarding the rights of EU8 nationals left some people in a 'catch 22' situation when seeking employment.[49]

A further consequence of the confusion that has surrounded the system is that it provides the potential for exploitative actors involved in the migration process to take advantage of a migrant's uncertainty of the national framework. The perpetrator may be an employer, or it may be an agency which a migrant has approached to seek out job information.[50] It also seems, however, that opportunistic, 'unofficial' third parties have used the complexity of the system to their own benefit. For example, a particularly unsavoury aspect of the uncertainty created by the introduction of the WRS relates to the online guidance notes and application forms. The representative from the IOM confirmed that the telephone helpline had received a number of calls from people who said that the forms, which can be downloaded free of charge, were being sold unlawfully in London for £50. When this sum is considered alongside the actual registration fee, which at the time was also £50,[51] it is clear that some people had to part with quite a considerable amount of money unnecessarily when they first arrived in the UK.

The crucial point for the focus of this chapter is that this level of uncertainty, most prevalent in the initial post-accession months, has had an impact on the services accessed by EU8 citizens and the actors to whom they have turned when seeking to migrate to the UK or to access information. Those who are unsure of their rights to reside or work in a state may be particularly reluctant to seek advice from the authorities for fear of exposing themselves to the threat of deportation and, instead, may rely on third parties for advice and 'security'. Such third parties may include agencies, employers or other migrants who have been established in the host state for a longer period. Employment agencies, both in the EU8 prior to migration and the UK after arrival, appear to play a particularly central role in facilitating migration from the EU8 to the UK. The concept of 'agency' covers a variety of different businesses, each with distinct consequences for the type of employment relationship in which workers find themselves (Forde 2001). The sections below focus on two types of employment agency. First, there are those based in the state of origin that act as a link between the employer in the state of destination and the worker seeking to migrate to that state. These agencies can place single applicants in employment abroad but many also have partnered employers with whom they have an ongoing relationship. It is via these agency-employer partnerships that organized schemes operate whereby a single business in the UK will recruit a group of EU8 workers. Secondly, after migrants have made the move to the UK, many look to domestic agencies that specialize in finding workers temporary work placements. Such host state-based agencies

49 More recent initiatives, such as the ECAS hotline mentioned earlier, may have had a more positive impact on levels of awareness more latterly.

50 Agencies are discussed further below.

51 As already mentioned, it later rose to £70 and then £90.

are also considered. Finally in this chapter, EU8 migrants' reliance on migrant networks as a means to find work is discussed.

Reliance on Agencies Based in the Home State to Facilitate Mobility

Ward et al. (2005) have drawn attention to the role of home-based agencies in facilitating mobility from central and eastern Europe in the post-accession climate (see also Coe et al. 2007a; 2007b, 503–20). The CEE region has been described as a key 'globalization arena' (Beaverstock et al. 1999) and large multinational employment agencies have established offices in these so-called 'emerging' markets in recent years. Furthermore, the research carried out by the author in Poland evidenced examples of a number of opportunistic agencies which had set up with the primary aim of providing potential migrants with information about jobs across the EU in the wake of accession. There is clearly a greater need for such intermediary businesses when individuals are uncertain about their legal rights to work in another country and evidence suggests that these agencies themselves are a growing and profitable market within Poland (Ward et al. 2005, 27). As regards the nature of the legal relationship which emerges with an agency based in the home state, there are two distinct possibilities. First, there is the situation whereby an agency simply arranges employment in the host state for the worker. Here, the agency is merely providing a service to the worker and any employment contract that comes into existence will be with the UK-based employer. Secondly, in contrast, on other occasions the agency itself constitutes the employer and the worker is posted temporarily to an undertaking in the host state.

Agency as employment 'arranger' As the UK only grants a right to reside to those EU8 nationals in work, there is increased pressure to arrange employment before arrival. Even without this legal incentive to find work quickly, migrants are inclined to start the job search prior to the move in order to reduce the anxiety that often goes hand-in-hand with moving away from home. The empirical findings certainly support the view that migrants are increasingly relying on agencies to arrange work pre-migration. Specifically, 23 out of 44 migrant workers confirmed they had approached an agency in Poland to help them find work in the UK. There are potential problems when migrants rely on such agencies to provide information about the host state. As agencies are not often subject to stringent quality assurance assessments, some are not appropriate bodies to provide ongoing information. The respondent below experienced a number of problems with the employer to whom she was sent by an agency in June 2004. In particular she was paid below the national minimum wage and was required to work excessive hours in a hotel. She contacted the agency based in Poland for advice but they were not forthcoming. This was quite a common experience described by the respondents:

> The agency gave me the address of my employer but later on if you had any problems they never were on your side. They were protecting themselves. This is a business I understand. (Interview 013.EW)

Prior to accession, in April 2004, an Act regarding the promotion of employment and labour market institutions was passed by the Polish parliament (EIRO 2004). This law included rules governing the registration of employment agencies. Employment agencies in Poland are obliged to have a state-issued certificate in order to act as a middleman between the Polish jobseeker and foreign employer. Additionally, the Polish law provides that employment agencies are forbidden to charge the job seeking person for their services. The potential employer is the party supposedly responsible for paying the agency. While this is the legal position in Poland, given the increasing number of employment agencies being established[52] it is likely that these rules are infringed on occasion. In reality, it is likely that many 'agencies' operate unofficially and are not subject to regulation. This is certainly a view supported by the migrant workers interviewed, as three had been charged unlawfully by a Polish-based agency. For example:

> I paid a lot of money, it was around £800 to organize a job here. (Interview 016.D)

The respondent who had worked on the IOM telephone helpline also confirmed this:

> In Poland we have the same law as in Britain that employment agencies cannot take money from the job seeking person, instead it gets its money from the employer. There were some people who mentioned on the phone that they were charged by an employment agency. I remember the price mentioned was 4000 zloty[53] and this is quite a lot because it is double the average wage in Poland. There were examples of people who were cheated by employment agencies and left with nothing in London at Victoria station. (Interview 102.INFO)

The following respondent had paid money in Poland to an apparently informal and clandestine agent only to be asked for more when he arrived in the UK in May 2004. He eventually secured employment independently by meeting with other Polish workers:

> I just looked for an agency advertisement in Polish newspaper and found this number that said 'Go to the United Kingdom' or something like this and I phoned and spoke about getting a job … I paid money and someone gave me an address, name and phone number for someone … and then, when I arrived here, I paid again to find

52 There are no comprehensive statistics on the number of employment agencies in Poland. However it seems that the number is rising. Ward et al. (2005, 18) state that in 2002 there were 25 officially registered and that in 2004 the number had increased to 70. In contrast, the International Confederation of Private Employment Agencies (CIETT) contends that in 2004 Poland had a total of 138 employment agencies (CIETT 2004, 2).

53 Approximately £715 based on the exchange rate as it stood in January 2008.

accommodation, to find work for first time but after two weeks I left this place. I didn't have a very bad experience but I heard about people who take passport and take lots of money from you and make you work in a factory like it was 100 years ago. (Interview 001.JK)

The representative from the IOM who had worked on the telephone helpline suggested that, in her experience, people were prepared to pay to have a degree of security once they arrived in the country of destination, despite knowing the agency was acting unlawfully:

> It was a common attitude that they would prefer to pay, even though it is illegal to charge them, they would rather pay and have a job than not pay and not have a job. People are very pragmatic, especially in small villages or towns, where they have no prospects and there is no industry in town; they are willing to do what it takes to get a job. (Interview 102.INFO)

That is not to say that all agencies operate in such an illicit manner; many of the migrants who took part in the research were happy with the service they received and clearly the majority are reputable. Certainly the five agencies that took part in the study claimed to place the best interests of the migrant workers as a high priority. However, many agencies are ill-equipped to provide workers placed abroad with the required degree of assistance and this can leave some people in a potentially vulnerable situation if the employers to whom they are sent are not entirely legitimate. Indeed, one of the employment agency representatives interviewed expressed regret that they were unable to guarantee the respectability of employers they dealt with in the UK:

> Of course we try to check but you know you can't always be sure. In January we started to cooperate with a company who needed drivers. They even came for two days so we had twenty drivers here in our office and they recruited some of them. They gave tests, talked with them and did some driving. They chose five or six to go so, they went to the UK, but then there were no jobs for them! The employer kept saying they would find something in a few days. After a week or so, they started to work in the warehouse but it was only two days a week and still not driving. I know that two of the drivers came back to Poland because they couldn't stand it and, I think, eventually only two stayed. The most terrifying thing is that the boss of this whole company was so rude. When he came here he seemed very nice and we thought he was alright but then when my boss started to call him when the candidates were in England and ask him why they didn't have a job he started to be very rude, he used really horrible language about the candidates. We were shocked and then we were afraid about the other employers that we don't even meet in person, only over the phone; we can't even think how they will act. (Interview 404.P)

On some occasions it was apparent that the agency relied on the employer to provide information to the workers, for example regarding the WRS, when it could itself have done so:

> It is for the employer to tell them things like [registering under the WRS and setting up bank accounts]. We count on them to do that. We could do it but it is more expensive for us. (Interview 403.I)

Often employers and agencies form a partnership to operate an organized migration scheme. It has already been noted that the decision of the UK government to open up its labour market to EU8 nationals was very much based on the notion of plugging labour market gaps. Accordingly, it has become increasingly popular for employers with significant staff shortages to look towards the CEE accession countries for recruits. This process of internationalization is becoming a common strategy adopted by employers who experience trouble recruiting at national level (Salt 1992, 485). Such schemes involve an employer making contact with a partner of some kind, usually an agency, in Poland (or other EU8 Member State) and the subsequent recruitment of a group of migrants.

The empirical work included a case study on a transport firm which recruited over 100 Polish workers. The interviews conducted with employment agency representatives in Poland also confirm that such schemes have been carried out in a number of sectors. The five agencies involved in the study had helped to arrange schemes for employers requiring the following: factory workers, doctors, drivers (including bus and delivery), engineers and IT professionals. A manager at the transport company confirmed that the motivation behind setting up such a scheme was to counteract the low level recruitment of national workers they had been experiencing for some time. Indeed, the company had enjoyed the support of the Local Authority Council and local newspaper because the shortage of drivers had previously disrupted bus services in the area.

Schemes across sectors have certain shared characteristics. For example, it is extremely common for the employer and agency to arrange intensive language training prior to the move and once the migrants are in employment. It is often part of the agreement that employers arrange and cover the costs of travel and provide accommodation for the workers (at least in the initial post-migration period). It is clear that such schemes can be of considerable benefit to migrants as they can help to overcome some of the practical hurdles associated with moving to a new country (language and housing in particular).[54] This is not to suggest that, once in the UK, such workers will never experience any problems with their employer or their conditions of work. Rather, the crucial point here is that the migrants involved in the schemes often receive valuable assistance in 'setting up'. The manager of the transport company described part of the process:

> We usually rent a coach and put all of the people, about 20–40, to one coach and drive them directly to the place where they work. Then we've got the person who arranges their accommodation so someone takes them from the coach and gives them keys to their accommodation. (Interview 101.RBC)

---

54 The gender and family related implications of such schemes are discussed in Chapters 4 and 5 respectively.

Furthermore, as groups of Polish workers had moved out at different stages, a 'buddy' system had been set up so that new arrivals were assigned to longer established workers who could help them settle into the job.

In some instances these schemes may foster a degree of dependency on the employer and agency involved as, effectively, 'everything is taken care of' and there is little impetus for the migrants to research their rights in the host society unless a specific problem arises. When a worker moves individually they themselves often have the task of finding out about issues such as accommodation, and the greater control they have over the process helps to increase the degree of autonomy and self-assurance felt in the host society. There is greater scope for the migrants' rights awareness to be dictated, and for them to be deliberately misled, when they move as part of a scheme. There was a limited example of this amongst the respondents who took part in the study. For example, one man had moved to Liverpool with a group of workers, with the support of such a scheme, to take up employment in a care home for the elderly. Although he enjoyed the work, he was unhappy due to the poor relationship he had with one of his co-workers. When asked if he had considered looking for an alternative job he reported that he was waiting until he had worked for a year as his employer had informed him that, should he leave within the first year, he was required to pay a fine of £1000.[55] Essentially, the dependent status of such workers places them in a less autonomous situation and renders them more vulnerable to exploitation.

There is an interesting dichotomy here in relation to the role of such agencies based in Poland and the connection they have to the culture of uncertainty described earlier. Sometimes securing employment before moving is an effective way in itself of negotiating the complexities of the UK system, as the agency and employer between them can help to navigate the workers around the various requirements and other practicalities relating to the WRS. This would account for the popularity of such agencies amongst migrants. This is dependent, however, on both the employer and agency being well-informed, legitimate and law-abiding. On the occasions where one, or both, of the parties is rather ambivalent in its attitude to the migrants, or has insufficient knowledge of the system, it may well be that the uncertainty of the migrants in the host state is compounded.

From a legal perspective, the role of private-sector recruitment agencies in acting as a cross-national intermediary has received the recent attention of the European Court of Justice. This perhaps demonstrates the increasing relevance of such bodies in labour relations in the EU as a whole. In its judgment in *ITC Innovative Technology Center GmbH v Bundesagentur für Arbeit*,[56] the Court confirmed that private-sector recruitment agencies which act as an intermediary between an applicant and an employer can rely directly on Article 39 EC.[57] The reasoning being that, in order for the free movement of workers to be truly effective, intermediaries must be allowed to assist them in their transnational

55 Interview 010.JF.

56 Case C-208/05, judgment of 11 January 2007.

57 In Case C-350/96 *Clean Car Autoservice* [1998] ECR I-2521 the ECJ made clear that employers can benefit from Article 39 EC.

search for work. The case concerned a German national who, with the help of the ITC agency, had found employment in the Netherlands. German legislation provided that the Member State would pay a fee owed to a private-sector recruitment agency only where the work found by the agency was subject to compulsory social security contributions in that state. Consequently, when an applicant found work in another Member State (not subject to compulsory social security contributions in the home state) as a result of an agency's assistance, the fee was not paid to the agency by the authorities. The inevitable result was that the fee was passed on to the applicant for whom the employment had been found. The Court found the national legislation to be, in principle, prohibited by Article 39 EC as it created an obstacle capable of discouraging individuals from seeking employment in a Member State other than their own (para. 36).

The German authorities had put forward reasons of public interest in an attempt to justify the rules;[58] for example, it was submitted that they represented an attempt to reduce the national unemployment rate and to protect the social security system. The Court was not convinced that Germany had demonstrated the effectiveness of the national legislation in achieving either of these policy objectives (paras 38–42). Interestingly, the Court also rejected the third argument of justification put forward – that the national legislation sought to protect the German national labour market against the loss of qualified workers:

> Such a measure is tantamount to an outright negation of the freedom of movement for Community workers laid down by Article 39 EC, which aims to guarantee to workers and persons seeking employment the right to gain access to employment of their choice and to exercise that activity in the territory of another Member State. (Para. 44)

The interest in this final attempt of justification by the German authorities stems not only from the particular issue of agencies but also from the broader focus of this book; essentially, migration in the context of EU enlargement. The argument of protecting a Member State from 'brain drain' or loss of skilled workers to other Member States is one of particular pertinence to the new CEE Member States. Concerns have been expressed about the impact of post-accession migration (to the UK and Ireland in particular) on the national labour markets on a number of the new Member States (Kaczmarczyk 2007). The Court's response to Germany in *ITC* seems to suggest that it is unlikely to accept such arguments as justification for national policies which have the effect of discouraging nationals, or indeed agencies, from moving abroad. Therefore, should one of the CEE Member States put in place legislation that could be interpreted as punishing a move abroad, in an attempt to retain national workers, it could be open to legal challenge. Furthermore, justification may prove difficult.

The discussion here has focussed on placement agencies which specialize in finding an employer in the host Member State – or working in partnership with

---

[58] As it is entitled to do in the case of obstacles to free movement which do not directly discriminate on grounds of nationality. See *inter alia* Case C 379/87 *Groener* [1989] ECR 3967; Case C-281/98 *Angonese* [2000] ECR I-4139; Case 15/69 *Ugliola* [1969] ECR 363.

such an employer – to facilitate the worker's move. Under such arrangements, which were evident in the empirical investigations, the agency based in the home state does not ordinarily have an employment relationship with the placed workers. In other words, the agency is not the employer of the workers; rather, it is the undertaking in the host state. Under these arrangements, the migrant workers exercise a personal right of free movement under Article 39 EC. As the free movement of workers operates primarily on the basis of extending 'national treatment' to migrants, or non-discrimination on the ground of nationality, the level of employment protection extended to the workers is then largely a matter of national regulation.[59]

Agency as employer: posting of workers abroad In contrast to those agencies that merely arrange work abroad on behalf of migrants, some employment agencies based in the CEE region may provide workers to undertakings based in a host state, such as the UK, as part of a cross-border provision of services pursuant to Article 49 EC.[60] This type of arrangement is likely to be of particular significance during the transitional periods owing to the continuing relevance of Article 49 EC and the freedom to provide services under the terms of the transitional arrangements.[61] In those Member States with more restricted access for workers, a temporary posting by an agency (or other employer) may constitute an alternative means of 'working' abroad for CEE accession nationals. This is not equivalent to exercising a personal right to move as a worker as posted workers have no access to the labour market of the host state and are obliged to return once the contract has expired. In the UK, for example, the distinction between 'posted workers' and 'migrant workers' is demonstrated by the non-applicability of the WRS to those who move as part of a transnational provision of services.[62] Under these arrangements, the agency constitutes a service provider and will enter into a contract with the undertaking based in the host Member State to provide a workforce for a temporary period (Bercusson 2007).[63]

---

59 Although non-discrimatory hindrances to mobility are also prohibited by Article 39 EC; therefore, if national regulation creates a potential barrier to movement, a Member State may be required to justify such rules on the basis of imperative requirements. See, *inter alia,* Case C-415/93 *Bosman* [1995] ECR I-4921 and Case C-18/95 *Terhoeve* [1999] ECR I-345.

60 To become Article 56 TFEU should the Treaty of Lisbon enter into force.

61 It will be recalled that the transitional arrangements do allow Germany and Austria to place restrictions on the posting of workers from the CEE accession states in some sensitive sectors, such as construction and industrial cleaning (para. 13, Annexes). Case C-113/89 *Rush Portuguesa* [1990] ECR I-1417 is a case which involved the posting of Portuguese workers to France during the time that transitional arrangements on the free movement of workers applied to Portugal.

62 Regulation 2(6)(a), WRR. Thus, posted workers avoid the registration fee.

63 Frequently, workers are posted by companies (as opposed to agencies) following the award of a contract to carry out some work in another Member State. Contracting-out in this way, which for the host state undertaking usually represents a more cost-effective mode of operation, brings to the fore the idea of 'social dumping'. This is a particular

In cases such as this, where the home state-based agency does have an employment relationship with a worker, who is then posted to an undertaking based in a host state, the provisions of Directive 96/71, the Posted Workers Directive,[64] will be relevant (see Davies 1997). Essentially, the Directive lays down minimum standards which must be guaranteed to posted workers in respect of their work within the host state. Therefore, Article 3(1) provides that, whichever system of law applies to the employment contract (on the basis of the choice-of-law rules considered below), undertakings must ensure to posted workers the host state's terms and conditions of employment in respect of: health and safety at work; minimum rates of pay (importantly); minimum paid holidays; maximum work periods; equality of treatment between men and women and other non-discrimination provisions.[65] The Directive, though, does include an exception for *de minimis* work as Article 3(5) allows Member States to derogate from the provisions of Article 3(1) on the basis that the amount of work to be carried out is 'not significant'. Under Article 3(9) of the Directive, Member States are entitled to stipulate that posted workers employed by agencies must be guaranteed the same terms and conditions which apply to temporary workers in the Member State where the work is carried out.

Also of significance to the legal status of posted workers is the Rome Convention of 1980 on the law applicable to contractual obligations.[66] This Convention sets out choice-of-law rules for application in contractual disputes and links with the Posted Workers Directive. The Convention can help to determine which system of law governs the employment contract between a posted worker and a home state-based agency. Article 3 of the Convention allows the parties to choose which law governs the contract. If no choice has been made, the contract of employment will be governed by 'the law of the country in which the employee habitually carries out his work in performance of the contract'.[67] Furthermore, Article 6(1) provides that if a choice has been made it should not have the result of depriving the employee of the protection which would be afforded to them under the latter obligatory rule. Article 7(1) of the Convention stipulates that, in certain circumstances, when applying the law of one country, effect may be given

concern for trade unions that fear employment and labour standards in the host state will suffer as a result of service providers taking advantage of cheaper labour standards in their home states in order to win contracts elsewhere. Given the relevant economic and wage differentials between the new and old Member States, the recent enlargements pose specific difficulties in this regard which are beyond the scope of this book. Cases C-438/05 *Viking* (judgment of 11 December 2007) and C-341/05 *Laval un Partneri Ltd* (judgment of 18 December 2007) demonstrate the tensions between the Single Market free movement provisions (establishment and services, respectively) and social rights / concerns of trade unions at the national level to protect the national workforce and maintain labour standards.

64 [1996] OJ L18/1.

65 These rules can be set out by law, regulation or administrative provision (Article 3(1)).

66 [1980] OJ L266/1.

67 Article 6(2)(a).

to the 'mandatory rules' of the law of another country, in particular those of a Member State within the territory in which the worker is temporarily posted. The Convention does not does not define 'mandatory rules' but Directive 96/71 assigns Community level mandatory rules within the meaning of the Convention in cross-national posting arrangements. From this perspective, the Directive lays down certain minimum standards to be complied with during the posting period without attempting to amend the law applicable to the employment contract.

Like other Community private law instruments, following the insertion of Title IV into the EC Treaty by Treaty of Amsterdam[68] steps have been taken to re-enact the Rome Convention in the form of a Regulation.[69] In 2005 the Commission put forward a proposal for a Regulation of the European Parliament and Council on the law applicable to contractual obligations (Rome I) (see European Commission 2005d). In addition to the change in legal form, the Commission's proposal contains certain modifications to the provisions of the 1980 Convention. For example, added to Article 3 (which allows the parties to choice the applicable law) would be a statement to the effect that 'the choice must be expressed or demonstrated with reasonable certainty'. Courts would be able to take the conduct of the parties into account in order to ascertain their 'true tacit will'. At the time of writing, the Council's first reading of the proposal is pending (scheduled for April 2008). Thus, it is not clear whether the Commission's proposed amendments to the Convention will survive to the final act. Furthermore, as it is a Title IV measure, the Regulation will not automatically apply to Denmark, Ireland or the UK. As a result of the opt-outs these Member States have in relation to Title IV legislation, they would need to make a decision opt-in in order for the measure to apply in their territories. Therefore, the 1980 Convention may yet remain significant even post the adoption of the Regulation on the law applicable to contractual obligations.

Despite being a minimum standards Directive, the provisions of Directive 96/71, in conjunction with the choice of law rules in the Rome Convention (and the likely future Regulation), do grant valuable protection to those workers placed temporarily in a host Member State by an agency with which they have an employment relationship. Indeed, some argue that it hinders the provision of services and that the requirement that the home state-based service provider afford their workers the host state's minimum standards of pay and protection is too burdensome an obligation, particularly for those based in the CEE Member States (Davies 1997).[70] It is certainly the case that a worker posted to an EU15

---

68 The Treaty of Amsterdam gave the EC competence to adopt private law measures in the field of judicial cooperation in civil matters (Articles 61(c) and 65 EC). If the Lisbon Treaty enters into force, these provisions will be detailed in Articles 67 and 81 TFEU respectively.

69 This follows the approach taken with instruments such as, *inter alia,* the Rome Convention on the law applicable to non-contractual obligations which has been replaced by Regulation 864/2007 [2007] OJ L199/40 (Rome II).

70 On posted workers and the Court's approach to claims that Member States standards of labour protection constitute obstacles to the provision of services see Joined

Member State by an agency, such as the UK, as part of a cross-border provision of services, could benefit considerably from the application of Directive 96/71. Of particular significance, given the current differences between rates of pay in the EU15 and EU8 (and EU2), is the stipulation that they receive the minimum rate of pay guaranteed in the host Member State.

Finding Employment with the Assistance of Temporary Work Agencies in the UK

For a significant number of EU8 migrants, agencies also have an impact on their access to and experience of the UK labour market after they have moved into the territory. These domestic level employment agencies, which produce employment relations often referred to as temporary agency work (TAW) (Arrowsmith 2006), differ from those based abroad that were discussed above. The defining feature of employment arising out of contact with these domestic agencies is its triangular nature:

> Although the agency is the normal legal employer of temporary agency (TA) workers … the work that they do and the workplaces to which they are assigned are the responsibility of other organizations. (Ibid., 5)

Unlike the agencies in the state of origin, which simply arrange work, these agencies have contractual relationships with the workers. The Employment Agencies Act 1973[71] defines agencies that directly recruit temporary workers who, in turn, work under the control of others as 'employment businesses'.[72] This type of employment is becoming increasingly prevalent in the UK, one of the biggest users of TAW in the EU (Arrowsmith 2006, 5–7). For example, Forde (2001, 631) points out that between 1984 and 1999, the number of temporary agency workers increased from 50,000 to 250,000. The rise in prominence of TAW is linked to the so-called flexible labour market in the UK. Due to the temporary nature of the work, such agency workers can be easily dispatched should their presence no longer be required, or should they become too expensive to employ (so that cost outweighs value). Research has noted how such short-term employment relations have enabled employers to avoid risks flowing from longer-term employment, such as sick pay, maternity pay and holiday pay (Allen and Henry 1996, 65).

The precarious nature of agency workers' legal status in the UK is further exacerbated by the system of qualification for statutory employment rights. Only those who qualify as employees under the Employment Rights Act 1996 are entitled to the full protection of statutory provisions on, for example, unfair dismissal, redundancy, holiday and sick pay. The legislation defines employees as

Cases C-49, 50, 52, 54, 68, & 71/98 *Finalarte* [2001] ECR I-7831; Case C-164/99 *Portugaia* [2002] ECR I-787.

71 C.35.

72 Employment businesses (s.13(3)) are distinguished from 'employment agencies' which seek to find people permanent employment (s.13(2)). See also Conduct of Employment Agencies and Employment Business Regulations 2003 SI 2003/3319.

those workers who work under a 'contract of service'[73] as opposed to a 'contract for service'[74] but it is necessary to look to the case law in order to explore further the types of worker likely to satisfy the test. As far back as 1952 Lord Denning gave some guidance on the relevant distinction:

> ... under a contract of service, a man is employed as part of the business and his work is done as an integral part of the business; whereas under a contract for services, his work, although done for the business, is not integrated into it but is only accessory to it.[75]

Cases such as *Ready Mixed Concrete (South East) Ltd v Minister of Pension*[76] illustrate that a worker will constitute an employee, and thus be extended more extensive employment rights, if: the employer provides payment in return for the service provided; the employer exercises some degree of control; and there are no other elements of the contract which are inconsistent with a contract of service. It is frequently difficult for agency workers to demonstrate they are employees. Such workers work under the control of the end-user client but have a contractual relationship with the agency. Consequently, it is not clear that either constitutes an 'employer' under English law, moreover, the case law on this issue is unpredictable.[77] In *Wickens v Champion Employment,*[78] the Employment Appeal Tribunal (EAT) held that an agency worker was not an employee even though there was a written statement which described the workers as having a contract of service with the agency. The lack of control exercised by the agency over the workers was cited as a crucial factor.

Traditionally, the possibility of the end-user client amounting to an agency worker's employer has not been granted much credence given the lack of express contract. Recently, however, there has been some stress placed on the idea of an implied contract of service being in existence between these two parties.[79] This was finally found to be the case in *Cable & Wireless plc v Muscat.*[80] Here, the Court of Appeal stated that an implied contract could only be inferred if the particular circumstances so demanded it and if that reflected the business reality of the situation. Thus, it is by no means an automatic finding and agency workers remain in a vulnerable position. This is exemplified by the recent case

73 S.230(2) Employment Rights Act 1996.

74 Self-employed workers, or independent contractors, work under a contract for services.

75 *Stevenson, Jordan and Harrison Ltd v Macdonald and Evans* [1952] 1 TLR 101.

76 [1968] 2 QB 497. See also *O'Kelly v THF plc* [1983] IRLR 369.

77 See, *inter alia, Ironmonger v Movefield Ltd* [1998] IRLR 461; *McMeechan v Secretary of State for Employment* [1997] IRLR 353; *Bruce v Postworth* Ltd [2005] IRLR 557; *Motorola Ltd v Davidson* [2001] IRLR 4; *Montgomery v Johnson Underwood* Ltd [2001] IRLR 269.

78 [1984] ICR 365.

79 Mummery LJ mentioned this possibility in *Franks v Reuters Ltd* [2003] IRLR 423 and *Decas v Brook Street Bureau (UK) Ltd* [2006] IRLR 354.

80 [2006] IRLR 354.

of *James v Greenwich London Borough Council* which involved a woman who had worked for a local council, crucially through an employment agency, from 2001 until 2003.[81] She had previously been employed directly by the council for a number of years but had left in 1997. Her contract with the agency purported to be a contract *for* services and also stated that no contract of employment was in existence either with the agency or council. In contrast to those employed directly by the council, the worker was not entitled to holiday or sick pay. She was absent from work due to sickness for a two month period of time and, on her return, discovered that the agency had replaced her with another worker. She brought a claim for unfair dismissal against the council but, according to both the employment tribunal and the EAT, the factual evidence did not suggest an implied contract was in existence with the council. The EAT emphasized that the mere fact an agency was involved did not render it necessary for a contract to be implied with the council. In addition, the fact that the worker had been at the council for a significant period of time was not sufficient to imply a contract was in existence. As she was not an employee, her claim was dismissed and she was left without any protection.

Interestingly, both the Working Time Regulations 1998[82] and the National Minimum Wage Act 1998[83] make special provision for agency workers by specifying that the rights set out in the legislation apply equally to them even in the absence of an employer. This approach is useful and it has the potential to be applied in other areas in order to enhance the legal protection afforded to agency workers (see Pitt 2007, 84). There is no doubt, however, that agency workers in the UK remain in an extremely vulnerable legal position and it is unlikely that many of them will satisfy the 'employee' test; clearly, this means that valuable employment protection rights are beyond their reach. Anderson and Rogaly (2005, 7) link the uncertain employment status of agency workers with the position of migrants:

> Migrants are often engaged through a bewildering array of subcontracting chains and agents, all of which can make it difficult to claim and safeguard their basic human and labour rights.

Moreover, the UK has no licensing scheme to register or control the activities of these agencies; rather, the industry is self-regulating under the management of the Recruitment and Employment Confederation (REC). While this representative body undoubtedly works to improve the standards of employment for those

[81] [2007] ICR 577.
[82] SI 1998/1833.
[83] C.39.

engaged by such temporary work agencies by, for example, establishing a Code of Good Practice,[84] it falls short of a rigorous, legal licensing authority.[85]

At European level, there have been efforts to further secure the legal status of agency workers. In 2002, the European Commission proposed a Directive on agency work (European Commission 2002d). This would have ensured that temporary workers were entitled to equal treatment with comparable workers in the end user client as regards a variety of working and employment conditions (such as pay, paid holidays, seniority in the job and so forth). There were certain exceptions to the operation of the principle of equal treatment. For example, if a contract of employment did exist between the worker and the agency, the end user client could decide to derogate from the equality principle.[86] Furthermore, the end user client would always have the opportunity to attempt to justify a difference in treatment between the agency worker and comparable worker. In any event, the proposal is currently held up, with little sign that it will resurface in the near future, following objections by business leaders and protracted negotiations in Council. The UK was one of the Member States opposed to the Directive. Presently it seems that the balance is tipped in favour of maintaining the flexibility of the labour market as opposed to enhancing (agency) worker protection (see Lorber 1999).[87]

Temporary agencies are common in the (low-skilled) sectors in which migrants are concentrated (such as agriculture, hospitality and the wider service sector). Furthermore, due to its flexible nature, this type of work is often readily available upon arrival to a host state; it is not surprising then that a number of EU8 migrants have resorted to temporary agency employment. The Accession Monitoring Report (Home Office Border and Immigration Agency 2007, 12) lists 'administration, business and management' – the category which covers TAW – as the sector within which the greatest number of EU8 nationals have registered (38 per cent of registrations between May 2004 and September 2007). Further, as has already been acknowledged, 52 per cent of the workers who registered between September 2006 and September 2007 were in temporary employment (ibid., 17).[88] Many of the respondents interviewed for this study had at some point been engaged in TAW (seemingly, without being aware of the restricted nature of their employment rights as a result of working under such a contract).

In addition to the issue of restricted labour rights, the qualitative data demonstrates how such agencies have, both purposely and inadvertently, misled migrants in respect of their obligations flowing from the WRS. For example,

---

84 REC Code of Professional Practice, available at <http://www.rec.uk.com/rec/about-the-rec/code-of-practice-2006.pdf> (last accessed 8 January 2008).

85 According to Arrowsmith (2006, 29), the REC represents 67 per cent of the temporary agency industry and all members are obliged to abide by the Code of Practice.

86 Article 5(2). This applies also if the posting is less than six weeks (Article 5(3)).

87 Similar concerns were voiced in relation to the Fixed-Term Work Directive 1999/70 OJ L175/43 which did enter into force.

88 It is however not clear how many registered with a TAW.

there were three instances of agencies mistakenly telling migrants they did not have to register.[89] As a result, the workers had lost the opportunity to start accumulating months of legal employment. It seems that many agencies find the UK system a complicated regime to comprehend (Anderson et al. 2006, 101). Yet many of the migrants interviewed assumed that they could rely on these bodies to safeguard their legal position. For example, the following extract portrays a common outlook:

> To be honest I don't worry about it ... If I worked for a normal employer – not the agency – then maybe I should've known about it [the WRS] but the agency is responsible for that. It is their job to know. (Interview 019.KS)

Such levels of faith placed in the actions and knowledge of the agencies could have potential negative effects in the long term. For example, a migrant may seek to enforce the full rights of residence that flow to those who have worked lawfully in the UK for one year (having been registered on the WRS continuously for this period) only to be denied the opportunity as a result of an agency's (or employer's) failure to comply with the WRS. Again, relying on a body such as a temporary work agency may be perceived as a way to negotiate the UK's regulatory regime. UK law, by requiring EU8 migrants to find work quickly, and as a result of the uncertainty which has surrounded the detail of the system, has undoubtedly contributed to the factors encouraging people to make use of services offered by recruitment agencies.

There is a further interesting dimension to this discussion which stems from the intersection of broader provisions of Community law with both the transitional arrangements and the UK national regulation. Should the worker qualify as an employee under national law, by virtue of an employment contract with either the agency or end-user, the employer (whichever entity that should be) should no doubt assist the migrant with WRS registration. Once registered, the migrant worker will fulfil the requirements of the UK system: they will qualify as being lawfully resident and, in turn, will be entitled to access benefits on the basis of the equal treatment principle (as per the nationals provisions considered above). In the event that no employment contract is in existence, however, the worker, despite not falling within the scope of the favoured 'employee' status under national law, may actually hold a self-employed status under Article 43 EC. According to the ECJ, self-employed workers operate independently outside of any relationship of subordination, under their own responsibility and in return for remuneration paid to them directly.[90] This is a definition that indeed appears relevant to the situation of a number of agency workers. Holding such a status could have significant implications. Importantly, the migrant would fall outside the scope of the Accession Treaty's transitional arrangements on the free movement of *workers*. Consequently, there would be no obligation to register on the WRS and the UK's restrictions in respect of lawful residence and benefit

89 Interviews 019.KS, 304.P, 015.RO.

90 Case C-268/99 *Aldona Malgorzata Jany* [2001] ECR I-8615.

entitlement would be inapplicable. Under this analysis, it is possible for an agency worker without an employment contract to make a 'trade-off': they may forego the valuable 'employee' status under national law (and the related employment rights), but have a stronger claim to residence and benefit rights by virtue of their self-employed status.[91]

Networks as Information Disseminators

In addition to the formal channels of information provision, such as the various types of agencies, migrants have also turned to more informal sources of information to find out about employment opportunities, and life generally, in the UK. Networks constitute the most significant informal providers of information (Faist 2000; Waldinger and Lichter 2003; Rees 1966; Choldin 1973). A classic definition of networks in action, or 'chain migration', is provided by MacDonald and MacDonald (1964, 82):

> That movement in which prospective migrants learn of opportunities, are provided with transportation, and have initial accommodation and employment arranged by means of primary social relationships with previous migrants.

It would appear that there are two types of network that new arrival Polish migrants have activated in order to help find work in the UK: there is the long-established, 'traditional' community, many of whom moved in the aftermath of the Second World War; but, already it seems that there is a younger, post-accession community developing and providing fresh potential for networks to thrive.

The vast majority of the migrants interviewed had family, friends or 'friends of the family' in the UK prior to moving and had received some form of assistance upon their arrival. In turn, many of these migrants subsequently acted as facilitators in the migration chain, helping new arrivals in much the same way. The most common sort of help is that which involves finding new arrivals work. In addition, migrant networks can also help new arrivals financially, or by introducing them to new social connections or providing them with a place to stay (Choldin 1973, 167).[92] One family that took part in the study,[93] for example, had joined friends in Edinburgh. Not only did the more established migrants provide accommodation for the new arrivals, but the man had also secured a job for his friend as a kitchen porter in the same hotel in which he himself worked.

---

[91] Although the right to receive the same social advantages as nationals set out in Article 7(2) of Regulation 1612/68 [1968] OJ L257/2 does not expressly apply to the self-employed, the ECJ has extended the group social rights largely equivalent to that of migrant workers. See, *inter alia,* Case C-111/91 *Commission v Luxembourg* [1993] ECR I-817. Now, Article 24(1) of Directive 2004/38 [2004] OJ L158/77 extends the self-employed (as Union citizens lawfully resident in another Member State) an explicit right to equal treatment on the ground of nationality.

[92] See the discussion in Chapter 5 which stresses the importance of extended family in this regard.

[93] A married couple and their baby son, interviews 307.P and 308.O.

The qualitative data provides numerous examples of migrants utilizing social connections to secure labour market access. This involved very close family relations in some cases but also more distant and general Polish connections in others:

> When I arrived my uncle told his friends that I was here and he asked around saying that anyone who had work should let him know … and they did. (Interview 012.GP)

> Basically, Polish people are everywhere around. There are plenty of people so I just kept asking, asking, asking and I found a job in central London no problem. I worked on the building site but the problem was the language. They couldn't explain to me exactly what they wanted so I had the Polish supervisor on top of my head all the time at first. (Interview 016.D)

It was also apparent from the interview data that many of the migrants had relied upon networks of friends and, to a lesser extent, family to access information about the WRS. For example, many had been told about the need to register and the practicalities of registering, such as where to get the form and how to complete it.

It is not just migrants who rely on networks to find jobs, employers also benefit from networks. Migrant workers are often able to recommend new migrant arrivals to employers and this type of informal recruitment practice is often more cost-effective and efficient than formal recruitment procedures (Waldinger and Lichter 2003, 89). Though it is hardly an example of good practice from an equal opportunities perspective, the following view was expressed on a number of occasions during the interviews:

> My manager says he likes Polish people because we are very hard workers so whenever we are short staffed he asks me if I've got any friends who need a job. Soon I think all my friends will be working here which may be a problem as I want to improve my English! (Interview 012.GP)

Interestingly, the organized schemes that employers have set up with the help of partner-agencies may have laid the foundations for the development of migrant networks. By recruiting large groups of migrants in a short period, it would appear that the workers' transnational links to kin back in Poland may have been activated on quite a significant scale. The flow of information from the early arrivals about available job opportunities appears to have had an almost immediate impact on the number of new migrant work seekers, who are not involved in any formal employment scheme themselves. For example, one of the respondents who was herself working for a company that had recruited a large number of Polish drivers explained how, in the aftermath of the formal scheme they had operated, word had apparently spread about the potential availability of jobs:

> Half of them came through an agency and half of them came here by themselves ... they just turned up. I remember the first day I got the phone call because seven just appeared here. Later on another 14 came so suddenly everything crashed because they needed training and everything had to be organized quickly. Now we have about 60 Polish drivers. (Interview 013.EM)

Finally, it should also be noted that only two migrants interviewed recounted negative experiences as a result of relying on networks.[94] In both instances the individuals moving to the UK had been put in touch with a 'friend of a friend' who had pledged to help them meet other Polish nationals and to find work upon arrival. In both cases the individuals had been disappointed with the actions of the supposed aide. The following respondent recounts quite a stressful experience although, from another perspective, it also provides a positive example of how a transnational network[95] was able to share information quickly and provide assistance to the new arrival:

> I got a phone call from my friend in Poland asking me 'can you help me because the cousin of my wife has arrived at Victoria station, and someone was supposed to come and pick her up, but he didn't. She's desperate and she's crying. Can you put her up for one or two nights?' I said 'okay, it's going to be difficult because we don't have spare bed but give her my telephone number and we can arrange it'. So she arrived and it turned out that her cousin had put her in touch with someone who was supposed to come to Victoria station and pick her up and he didn't, he just didn't show up. (Interview 014.KW)

On the whole, therefore, migrant networks seem to have been playing quite a positive and crucial part in assisting migrants in negotiating the complexities of the system. Not only do they inform people of employment opportunities and available accommodation, the traditional functions of a network, they also help to disseminate information to EU8 workers about the WRS and other peculiarities of the UK system.

Conclusion

This chapter has built on the discussion in Chapter 2 by taking a closer look at the UK's system of regulation towards EU8 migrants. It is apparent that the complexity of the system, by adding a layer of bureaucracy, has compounded the difficulties faced by migrants (particularly those who moved in the immediate aftermath of enlargement). As a result migrants have looked to agencies, employers and networks of fellow migrants in order to find work and make sense of the regulatory framework. Such actors, which exist outside of the formal framework, also shape the ability of individuals to find employment in a host state. Of course, turning to such third parties does not guarantee the appropriateness or indeed

---

94 Interviews 007.LR and 014.KW.

95 Transnational family networks are discussed in Chapter 5.

accuracy of the advice given. In actual fact, relying on others, agencies and employers in particular, has resulted on some occasions in EU8 migrant workers inadvertently failing to comply with the legal requirements of the WRS. In turn, this may have negative effects for their future status under UK law. This may occur as a result of genuine confusion on the part of a legitimate third party, as it would appear that uncertainty about the operation of the WRS has been a common feature of formal actors' understanding of the post-accession regime. On the other hand, the lack of clarity surrounding the WRS does seem to have enabled, or encouraged, the development of exploitative working relationships. Enforcement actions against employers (or agencies) continuing to restrict EU8 migrants' employment activity to the black labour market have been practically nonexistent. Moreover, the lack of any widespread understanding has increased the likelihood of the migrants' rights awareness being hampered by a party in a stronger bargaining position than them.

An understanding of how EU8 migrants gain access to the UK labour market is extremely important for the discussion of the migrants' status and experience whilst in employment, the focus of the next chapter.

Chapter 4

De-Skilled and Devalued: Labour Market Status and Experience in the UK[1]

Introduction

In this chapter the discussion moves away from the factors which determine accession nationals' entitlement to access employment in the UK and, instead, seeks to examine the status accorded to such migrants within the UK labour market once access has been secured. Drawing upon both the personal experiences of Polish respondents interviewed and the wider inter-disciplinary literature on the recognition of migrant workers' skills and experience in host countries, the chapter explores the notion of de-skilling in relation to EU8 migrants who took up work in the UK in the aftermath of the 2004 EU enlargement.

Amidst the discussions of the eastern enlargement(s) of the EU, concerns have been evident about the potential for 'brain drain' from the accession countries to occur. Such fears inevitably intensify when opportunities for highly-qualified personnel to move in order to take advantage of higher salaries, prestige and more comfortable working conditions increase.[2] Primarily, the focus has been upon medical professionals such as doctors, dentists and, to a lesser extent, nurses (Vlad 2004; McLaughin 2005). Scientists have also been researched within the context of the CEE 'brain drain' (Dickson 2003; Ackers 2005, 99). This image of the highly-qualified migrant leaving their home country in order to increase their earnings abroad stands in contrast to the image of the hard-working but low-waged migrant, working in the lower-skilled (or at least lower-status) sectors of the labour market. In the UK media there has been some emphasis on the benefits EU8 migrants have brought to the economy by performing work that nationals are not willing to do (Shennan 2005; Grice and Brown 2006). The discrepancy between the accession states' concerns about the loss of their highly-qualified and the host societies' celebration of low-skilled workers raises the question of whether the accession states' brain drain leads to any notable brain gain for the receiving state or whether, in actual fact, there is a significant degree of 'brain

1 An earlier version of part of this chapter has been published in Currie 2007.

2 While the notion of east-west 'brain drain' became popularly associated with the 2004 EU enlargement it is an issue which has been researched and commented on over a longer period, especially since the collapse of Soviet regime in the CEE region. See Ardittis 1992; Vizi 1993.

waste' (Morokvasic and de Tinguy 1993) as the migrants' expertise and skills are devalued and downgraded in the UK.[3]

The discussion begins by sketching the employment profile of CEE accession migrants in the UK. The notion of de-skilling is then explored in relation to EU8 migrants who took up work in the UK in the initial period following enlargement. In particular, the legal factors contributing to the devaluation of the migrants' skills are highlighted and examined: the UK's regulatory system (the Workers' Registration Scheme) and the EU's mutual recognition of qualifications regime. Attention will then turn to the gender-dimension of skill-degradation and the particular consequences for female migrants. Again, this is examined from the discrete perspective of recent EU8 migration and the chapter considers the differential gender-impact of formalized employer-driven migration schemes. Finally, the chapter concludes by questioning whether the devalued position occupied by migrants in the UK may have any long-term consequences for the migrants' labour market activity and professional progression should they return to their home state.

CEE Workers in the UK Labour Market

As the discussion in the previous chapter demonstrated, the nature of the political debate in the UK prior to enlargement on the granting of labour market access for EU8 migrants focussed very much on 'what they can do for us'.[4] From the outset the suggestion was that migrants from the EU8 would 'fill the gaps' in the labour market and, consequently, their rights to access employment have been shaped by this proposition.

Between May 2004 and September 2007 there were 715,000 registrations on the WRS and Polish migrants accounted for the majority (66 per cent) of registrations during the time period. The ten occupations in which registered EU8 workers are most frequently employed are categorized in the Accession Monitoring Report as follows: process operative (factory worker): 27 per cent; warehouse operative: 8 per cent; packer: 6 per cent; kitchen and catering assistants: 6 per cent; cleaner/domestic staff: five per cent; farm worker/farm hand: 4 per cent; waiter/waitress: four per cent; maid/room attendant (hotel): 3 per cent; care assistant and home carers: 3 per cent; and labourer (building): 3 per cent (Home Office Border and Immigration Agency 2007, 13–15). When these occupations are considered alongside the finding that 72 per cent of the registered workers earn £4.50–£5.99 per hour (ibid., 16),[5] it is clear that the majority of post-accession EU8 workers are currently situated within the lower echelons of the UK labour market.

Taking the health sector as an example, it is interesting to note that, despite the attention often placed on staff shortages within the UK health service (Buchan

3 Some writers prefer to use the term 'brain abuse', for example Bauder 2003.

4 Hansard, HC, vol. 48, col. 23 (23 February 2004).

5 Since 1 October 2007 the minimum wage in the UK for workers over the age of 22 is £5.52 per hour; for those aged 18–21 the figure is £4.60.

and O'May 1999), only a very small minority of EU8 workers have registered on the WRS as health professionals. For example, of the 715,000 registrations in the first three years following accession, only 215 fell within the category of hospital consultant. Furthermore, 700 registered as hospital doctors, 115 as GPs, 350 as nurses and 310 as dental practitioners (Home Office Border and Immigration Agency 2007, 32–8). Considering that there were 19,025 registrations under the care assistant category (ibid.), it would seem that EU8 migrants are (currently) concentrated in the lower-status and lower-paid occupations within the health service.

Of the 44 Polish respondents interviewed by the author who were either employed in the UK labour market, or who had been employed in the UK but had since returned to Poland,[6] a majority were employed in the hospitality and catering industry (15 respondents).[7] Bus drivers were the second most represented occupational group in the sample (13 respondents). A further six were employed in administrative or clerical roles. The sample also included two care assistants, two domestic workers, a cleaner, a human resources manager, a construction worker, a nursery assistant, a shop worker and an agency worker who gave advice to other Polish migrants.[8]

Traditionally, the positioning and experiences of migrants within the labour markets of EU Member States differed depending on their status as either privileged, internal EU-nationals or non privileged, third country nationals. There has been a general acceptance that third-country nationals have been undertaking the 'degrading, dangerous and dirty' work in the Member states that EU nationals 'are no longer prepared to do' (Kofman et al. 2000, 119). Kofman et al. (ibid., 122) have acknowledged the existence of a dual labour market, 'one for EU nationals and one for nationals of third countries who provide cheap and flexible labour power'. Although, clearly, third-country nationals within the EU are not a homogenous group. There is a hierarchy of entitlement in existence here also and it would be inappropriate to equate the experience of US or Australian migrants with that of, for example, migrants from African countries. Nevertheless, the dual labour market notion is useful as a general indicator of migrants' status and entitlement within the EU. The most recent EU enlargements have altered this established order on a scale unlike any accession that has gone before it as it involved the accession of a large number of countries with significantly poorer-performing economies. The evidence emerging post-accession would suggest that the newest EU citizens continue to occupy the lower rungs of the labour market, thus their current employment status is more akin to that of third-country

---

6 Forty-five migrants were interviewed but only 44 had worked in the UK. The remaining one was the spouse of an EU8 migrant worker.

7 Either in hotels or restaurants.

8 Note that the occupations referred to here relate to either the migrant's job at the time of interview or, in the case of return migrants, the last job they had before leaving the UK.

nationals than that of nationals from the older EU Member States.[9] There is no longer a simple labour market split between third-country nationals on the one hand and EU nationals on the other. Following the eastern accessions it would appear that divisions also exist within the traditionally 'privileged' group of EU nationals with regards to the work they undertake as migrant workers. Indeed, a discussion paper prepared on behalf of the 2005 UK Presidency by Patrick Weil used this trend as an argument to support the lifting of labour market restrictions on EU8 migrants by the rest of the EU15:

> The countries who continue to close their labour markets find themselves in a counter-productive situation; with new European citizens immigrating anyway and working illegally. In the EU states that have opened their labour market, the new European citizens fill the jobs that are fulfilled in the rest of Europe by illegal migrants, either from the new Member States or non EU countries. (Weil 2005)

Effectively, a new layer of disadvantaged migrants has been added to the hierarchy. The position of EU8 migrants in the UK's secondary labour market mirrors the secondary status granted to them at EU level under the transitional arrangements on the free movement of persons. Seemingly, the position of third-country nationals has been further exacerbated as, in the UK at least, they are competing against EU8 migrants for certain jobs.[10]

The 2007 enlargement adds an additional interesting facet to this discussion. The decision of the UK government to impose transitional mobility restrictions on the nationals of Bulgaria and Romania was accompanied by the promise that all of the places on the low-skilled migration schemes would be reserved for this group:

> From 1 January 2007 we will be phasing out all low-skilled migration schemes from outside the EU. Places on the two low-skilled migration schemes (the seasonal agricultural workers scheme and the sectors based scheme which between them

[9] It would be misguided, however, to suggest the status and labour market experience of third-country nationals and CEE nationals are analogous. For example, the experience of third-country nationals in the labour market may be shaped by other variables, such as the existence of racism (although forms of racism may also be experienced by CEE nationals).

[10] Particularly as the transitional arrangements oblige employers to give preference to EU8 and EU2 nationals over third-country nationals in access to jobs: para. 14, Annexes. The issue may not be quite so straightforward, however, due to the recent Directive on the position of third-country national long-term residents (Directive 2003/109/EC [2004] OJ L16/44). This Directive grants the right of equal treatment as regards access to employment to third-country nationals who have resided in an EU Member State for five years or more. Thus, in the older Member States fully applying the transitional restrictions on free movement, EU8 and EU2 nationals will occupy an inferior status to third-country nationals who fulfil the conditions in the Directive for securing long-term resident status (see Rettman 2006). The date for implementation was 23 January 2006. Note that the UK, Ireland and Denmark have opted-out and hence are not bound by the Directive. See more generally on the Directive Halleskov 2005.

currently have 19,750 places) will now be restricted to nationals from Romania and Bulgaria.[11]

This decision, which reflects the preference clause in the Treaty of Accession's transitional provisions (see Chapter 3), undoubtedly further demonstrates the potential negative impact of EU enlargement on the position of third-country nationals in the Member States as they must compete even more directly against EU2 nationals. Moreover, it again highlights the expectation held by the UK about the role the newest EU citizens will fulfil; essentially, they too are expected to carry out the low-skilled, low-status and low-paid work.[12]

The Phenomenon of De-Skilling

Despite this concentration in the lower rungs of the employment market there is evidence to indicate that a significant proportion of the post-accession migrants are highly qualified and work in occupations not commensurate with their skills and levels of education. Research across the disciplines has acknowledged the widespread phenomenon of de-skilling that can accompany cross-border mobility (Erel 2003; Raghuram and Kofman 2004). Bauder (2003, 699) expresses this by stating '[migrants] are highly educated, yet accept work for low wages in occupations outside of their formal training'.

Morokvasic and de Tinguy's work (1993, 245) has highlighted the incidence of 'brain waste' from the CEE region as professional migrants find themselves concentrated in lower sectors of the labour market than they previously occupied. The concept of 'occupational skidding' has been coined to describe the fall experienced by some migrants in terms of their occupational status (Morawska and Spohn 1997, 36). These researchers point out that during the 1980s, only approximately 30 per cent of highly-skilled Polish migrants were in an occupation which corresponded to their level of education (ibid., 38). There are indications that this trend prevails amongst EU8 nationals in the post-accession climate. The WRS data illustrates that 83 per cent of workers who registered between May 2004 and September 2007 were under the age of 34 (Home Office Border and Immigration Agency 2007, 10) and it is reasonable to suggest that many of the recent migrants are educated to a high standard.[13] A report by the European Foundation for the Improvement of Living and Working Conditions pointed to the occurrence of both youth and brain drain in the enlarged EU and defines a

[11] (Former) Home Secretary John Reid's written ministerial statement, Hansard, HC, vol. 450, col. 83 (24 October 2006). See Home Office Border and Immigration Agency 2007c.

[12] Although, as was acknowledged in Chapter 2, there is also scope for very highly skilled individuals to enter.

[13] Commission research confirms that post-accession migrants from the EU8 resident in the EU15 have high levels of educational attainment, see European Commission 2006c.

'typical' EU8 migrant as 'young, well-educated or studying in third-level education and living as a single, non-cohabiting person' (Krieger 2004, 3).

Certainly, of the 44 migrant workers interviewed, 28 had graduated from university in Poland and were overqualified for the jobs they occupied in the UK. To illustrate the point with just two specific examples: one male respondent was a qualified medical doctor in Poland but worked as a care assistant in a private care home in Manchester; furthermore, a female respondent who worked as a chambermaid in Glasgow was a qualified special needs teacher in Poland. These findings also corroborate those of a research project conducted by Anderson et al. (2006) on CEE migrants working in low-skilled sectors in the UK. The research report acknowledged the 'significant mismatch' between migrants' qualifications and skills and the skills required to competently carry out their primary job (ibid., 36). Qualitative examples, similar to those given above from the research which informs this book, are also given of migrants with a de-skilled status; such as an accountant working as a waitress and a philosopher working as a labourer (ibid., 37). The post-accession move to the UK (thus far), therefore, appears to have incorporated an element of de-skilling for many migrants. The policy in the UK of allowing regularization of previously unlawful labour market activity may partly account for the low-status position of some EU8 migrants in the job market as, once a worker has been integrated into the black labour market, it is likely to be difficult to escape from that particular type of work. However, although this may account for the de-skilled position of those migrants who arrived prior to May 2004 it does not help to explain the position of those who moved legally post EU enlargement.

A majority of the respondents who took part in the study recognized their diminished social status and expressed disappointment with their social ranking in the UK. The following respondent had been a teacher in Poland:

> I am working as an office assistant which is a real downfall for me from what I was doing before… it's a bit of a shock for me because it's just like you cross a couple of borders and then your social status falls like a lead balloon. (Interview 011.MW)

It seems correct to classify the change in social status connected to this initial de-skilling as 'contradictory class mobility' (Parreñas 2001, 1129). This stems from the fact that whilst there is a fall in social status in the UK, on the other hand, there is also an increase in financial status since wages are often higher than those obtained in Poland. This was also recognized by some of those who were interviewed. The following respondent had worked as a waitress in a hotel and housekeeper for a wealthy family and when she returned to Poland she took up a position in the civil service:

> It is difficult in London to get a proper job. After two years the only jobs we could get were like waiters or something like this. There is no way of getting a job in a good company, so we decided to just come back. The funny thing is that we had more money from being waiters than we do here for doing proper jobs. (Interview 312.G)

Effectively, during their time in the UK, many of the migrants appear willing to make a trade-off between professional investment and economic gain.

Due to the dramatically different free movement policies adopted by the UK towards the EU8 and EU2, and the obviously more stringent rules applicable to the EU2, it is impossible to compare the de-skilling experience of the different groups. It is generally assumed that levels of education in Romania and Bulgaria are lower than that in many of the EU8, although it is certainly the case that qualification levels have increased and continue to do so (Traser and Venables 2008; Gospodinova 2006). Nevertheless, of course, de-skilling is relevant to the experience of some Bulgarians and Romanians in the UK (Markova and Reilly 2006; Anderson et al. 2006). Interestingly, as was pointed out in Chapter 2, there is a specific route of entry for highly skilled EU2 nationals under the Accession (Immigration and Worker Authorization) Regulations 2006. The fact that this appears to be under-utilized perhaps highlights the different dynamics at work in the two newest Member States;[14] nevertheless, it is noteworthy that UK law formally recognizes a right of labour market access for highly skilled EU2 nationals, especially as the right is not conditional upon holding a specific job offer.

The remaining provisions of the UK's system of regulation on the mobility rights of EU2 nationals blatantly works to ensure that only those deemed as useful, either by an employer who sponsors a work permit application or in the sense that they are reserved places on the low-skilled migration schemes, gain access to the labour market. These routes of entry clearly channel EU2 nationals into certain types of employment, particularly where the Sectors Based Scheme and Seasonal Agricultural Workers' Scheme are concerned, and may directly result in a form of de-skilling for those that take them. Interestingly, though, those that do secure a work permit will (more than likely) do so in relation to a highly skilled position. In these circumstances, de-skilling seems less likely to occur.

Before moving on to the legal factors contributing to the de-skilling of EU8 migrants, it is interesting to speculate on the extent to which this particular type of de-skilled migration fits with the EU's model of mobility. Given that 2006 was designated the title of 'European Year of Workers' Mobility' this is a particularly apt time to consider whether the EU is concerned about the 'quality' of free movement it promotes or whether its aim is simply to secure higher levels of intra-Community mobility at any cost (European Commission 2005c). On the one hand, the occurrence of de-skilling appears to conflict with the long-term EU policies to encourage the mobility of students (through SOCRATES and ERASMUS initiatives)[15] and researchers, through the development of the European Research Area (European Commission 2002c). Indeed, the recent concern of the EU, tied in to the Lisbon Agenda aim of making the EU 'the most competitive and dynamic

[14] For example, between July and September 2007 there were only 45 EU2 nationals who made use of this route of entry (Home Office Border and Immigration Agency 2007b, 6).

[15] Council Decision of 15 August 1987 [1987] OJ L166/20. See also European Commission 2002b.

knowledge-driven economy by 2010',[16] appears to have focused on the movement of highly skilled persons between Member States:

> Promoting transnational mobility is a simple, particularly effective and powerful means of boosting European excellence ... It creates opportunities for significantly improving the circulation and exploitation of knowledge, and helps to establish world class centres of excellence. (European Commission 2002c, 20)

Curiously, in the context of post-accession mobility there seems to almost be some tacit approval of the de-skilling which is occurring. For example, in its report published in February 2006 the Commission cites evidence of the highly-qualified nature of migrants from the EU8 (European Commission 2006c, 12). In the same report, however, the point is made that these very migrants are helping relieve labour shortages in 'construction and in the domestic and catering services sectors that would risk not being filled otherwise in some countries' (ibid.,13).

This acceptance of the usefulness of CEE migrants for filling shortages, particularly in lower-skilled sectors, contradicts somewhat the established objective of encouraging knowledge circulation throughout the EU. Indeed, the initial post-accession employment trends involving EU8 migrants appear very far detached from another of the Lisbon Agenda's aims, that of creating 'more and better' jobs for Union citizens (European Commission 2005b). It seems that many EU8 workers in the UK have, at least in the early stages of the transitional period, exercised mobility rights within the context of 'more and worse' jobs.

Legal Factors Contributing to the Skill-Devaluation of EU8 Migrants

The focus in this section is primarily on the legal and regulatory 'mechanisms of de-skilling' (Erel 2003, 265) which have contributed to the experience of downward social and professional mobility for many EU8 migrants in the aftermath of enlargement.[17] That is not to deny, however, the existence of other social contributory factors, or 'mechanisms of de-skilling', which may be as or more important in shaping experiences of de-skilling, of which constraints of space prevent any in-depth consideration. To summarize these briefly; forms of social and institutional discrimination can play a part in the de-skilling or degradation of a migrant's labour market position, as can the migrant's knowledge of the host society's language.[18] Kofman et al. (2000, 19) submit that migrants from the CEE region are racialized despite the lack of any colour differences between themselves and nationals of the host country. Public and employer perceptions

---

16 European Council Presidency Conclusions, Lisbon, 23–24 March 2000.

17 The importance of legal obstacles has been acknowledged by other scholars. For example, Erel (2003, 265), in her study of migrant women in Britain and Germany, found that immigration legislation constituted a barrier to satisfactory labour market positioning.

18 Linguistic competence is discussed further below.

about the group's alleged dependence on benefits and lack of ambition stigmatize the migrants and can contribute to the attainment of an inferior employment position. Such stereotypical perceptions may well still shape the migration experience of EU8 nationals.[19] However, as lawful EU migrant workers in the UK, they are now *legally* entitled to equal treatment with nationals as regards access to employment and conditions of work under Community law.[20]

The Post-Accession Regulatory Regime in the UK

The practicalities of the WRS have been discussed in Chapter 3 in relation to how EU8 migrants access employment in the UK.[21] The concern here is to draw out how those conditions of access may contribute to the occurrence of de-skilling. It will be recalled that the registration rules limit the right of residence for EU8 migrant workers to the effect that an EU8 national is only considered to be legally resident when in work and registered on the scheme. There is only a 30 day period of grace within which a migrant can search for employment before UK law classifies him or her as being unlawfully resident.[22] Similarly, an EU8 worker who becomes unemployed during the first year can retain the months of work already accumulated by finding alternative work and re-registering within 30 days from the date the original employment relationship ceased.[23]

This 30 day deadline has consequences for the type of work EU8 migrants are initially able to access. As was acknowledged in Chapter 3, migrants may seek employment in the UK before leaving the home state, usually via an employment agency (Ward et al. 2005). However, those that fail to do so and arrive without a pre-arranged job are faced with the pressure of finding work quickly to avoid being categorized as an irregular migrant. It is sometimes difficult to access professional occupations in the formal economy within 30 days since the recruitment process for such posts often extends over a longer time-frame. Human resources have become increasingly formalized and many employers have detailed recruitment procedures which comprise a number of stages, utilize a number of different advertisement channels, and rely upon lengthy selection procedures (McKenna and Beech 2002,

---

19 Pemberton (2007, 91) has argued that discrimination based on surname has been directed at EU8 national jobseekers by employers.

20 Pursuant to Article 39 EC on the free movement of workers and Article 7 of Regulation 1612/68 [1968] OJ L257/2. Article 12 EC embodies a general non-discrimination on the grounds of nationality provision (to be reproduced in Article 18 TFEU if the Treaty of Lisbon enters into force).

21 Under the Accession (Immigration and Worker Registration) Regulations 2004, SI 2004/121, referred to here as 'Worker Registration Regulations' (WRR).

22 Regulation 7(2)(b)(i), WRR. See Chapter 6 for discussion of the unlawfulness of this categorization under Community law.

23 Regulation 2(4), WRR. This is important because after an EU8 migrant has complied with the registration process continuously for a year, the worker will be eligible for an EEA residence permit (registration certificate following the transposition of Directive 2004/38 into UK law), under regulation 5 WRR, and the restrictions on social benefit access will no longer apply.

140–51). By contrast, informal work in the lower-skilled sectors of the labour market is often accessible more rapidly (Düvell 2004). For EU8 migrants, taking up work in a low-skilled position may simply be the most pragmatic decision. For example, the following respondent had been hoping to secure work in marketing for which she held a degree from Poland. However her priorities changed after moving to the UK; after searching for work for over a month she eventually found employment as a cleaner with the help of a London-based agency:

> I started to look for a job in July and it was very difficult. For almost one month and a half I couldn't find anything [in marketing] so I tried looking for other work. I left my CV in shops, in cafés and in bars. I was so depressed. (Interview 304.P)

Research supports the view that migrants can more easily gain entry into the informal economy than they can into the more regulated and formal sector (Anderson 2000). Migrants make use of certain employment strategies which are open to them in the host society, such as: placing advertisements in newspapers; tapping into kin networks; making contacts in churches and NGOs; and, of course, relying on agencies (ibid., 34–9). The effect of taking these particular avenues into employment, however, is to restrict the employment opportunities available and consign the migrants to holding a particular type of occupation. The pressure on even highly qualified migrants to make use of these strategies is arguably more pronounced when faced with a deadline of just 30 days.

The registration rules may also have a hindering effect on the migrant's ability to change occupation. The requirement to re-register,[24] again within 30 days, each time new employment is taken up was mentioned by a number of the EU8 migrants interviewed, for example:

> We have the necessity of registering every time we change job within 30 days ... But what happens if I change job and I don't like the job and I leave after a week or two, I need to register every time, I mean it's absolutely stupid. That's actually what's keeping Polish people in jobs that they don't like and where they don't get treated well. They think: "we better stay now we've registered. If I change I have to re-register and what if the other job is worse and I need to change again?" It's just so much hassle ... personally I don't see the point. (Interview 011.MW)

It seems this additional bureaucratic requirement may constitute a psychological, as much as a legal, barrier to the frequent changing of occupation, thus preventing migrants from climbing up the social, professional and economic ladder. Of course, the WRS and the requirements that attach to it are time-limited and apply only until the EU8 migrant has accumulated one year of continuous employment. Therefore, although the system initially steers EU8 nationals towards low-paid jobs in the lower echelons of the employment market, this initial occurrence of de-skilling may not prevent them from later progressing to jobs

24 Regulation 2(4), WRR.

which better reflect their levels of skills and qualifications.[25] Again, this raises the issue of the comparability of the status of EU8 nationals with that of third-country nationals. Despite the apparent similarities in the type of work carried out by both groups at present it may well be that in the future when transitional arrangements are lifted and the EU8 become more integrated into the EU, that the status and experience of the two categories of migrant will become more disparate.

Securing Recognition of Qualifications under EU law

A further factor contributing to the de-skilling of EU8 migrants relates to the problem of securing recognition of their foreign qualifications. The problem of non-recognition of qualifications and the subsequent exclusion of highly educated migrants from the upper sections of the labour market has been researched in a Canadian context. Bauder (2003, 699) has argued that professional organizations adopt a protectionist stance which serves to exclude migrants from specialized occupations. On the whole, this is unlikely to be the result of any overt racism. Rather, it seems that there is an inherent scepticism regarding foreign qualifications that operates covertly. Such organizations adopt a much harsher assessment of the credentials of migrants than they do when examining those of nationals. Man (2004, 135) sees the lack of recognition given to international qualifications as originating from the very nature of capitalism so that:

> Regardless of education and experience, immigrants are treated as a source of cheap labour and relegated to low paid, menial positions.

Clearly we should not stress too much the Canadian experience in this context because the EU, with its emphasis on ensuring free movement as a fundamental component of the Common Market, has developed a system of mutual recognition of qualifications and non-discrimination (at least formally). This system is of immediate application to EU8 (and EU2) migrants as the Treaty of Accession contained no transitional arrangements on the operation of EU mutual recognition rules. The EU recognition system and its particular features, however, may still help to explain how CEE migrants find their skills devalued when in a different Member State. The establishment of a system of mutual recognition of qualifications has been an obligation imposed on the Member States by the EC Treaty under the provisions designed to ensure free movement of workers, the self-employed and those providing services in other Member States.[26] Thus, the system works primarily to ensure that professional qualifications are

[25] Although this does not necessarily mean that de-skilling will not occur as a result of other factors. Indeed, subsequent ascendance may be hampered by the fact that they have had a break in their career.

[26] Articles 39, 43 and 49 EC respectively. The Treaty on the Functioning of the European Union will retain these provisions in Articles 45, 49 and 56 (according to the table of equivalence annexed to the Lisbon Treaty [2007] OJ C306/01).

recognized, rather than general educational or academic qualifications (Stalford 2000c; Peixoto 2001). While the Member States have been comfortable with the exercise of Community competence under Article 47 EC, the legal basis that enables measures to be adopted in order to make it easier for persons to take up and pursue activities as self-employed persons, there has been much less desire to relinquish sovereignty in the more general area of education. Thus Article 149 EC, which provides the basis for Community action in the education field, grants the Community only complementary competence and very much enshrines the subsidiarity principle.[27] Thus, the role of the Community is limited to encouraging Member State cooperation. The continuing prominence of national autonomy in the general sphere of education policy reflects the desire of the Member States to retain control over an area closely informed by cultural and political heritage.

Community policy early on adopted a vertical approach to the mutual recognition of professional education and a number of sectoral Directives were enacted, on the basis of Article 47 EC, which covered mainly the medical professions and architects.[28] These Directives enabled EU migrants to take up activity in the professional sectors under the same conditions as nationals who had qualified in that state. However, the long drawn out process of negotiating such Directives led to a change of approach by the Community and, rather than attempting to achieve a level of harmonization via the vertical method, a horizontal system of mutual recognition was seen as a more suitable goal (White 2004, 61–77). The Community later sought to implement a general system for the recognition of professional qualifications via the adoption of three 'general system' Directives.[29] These Directives, rather than focussing on the qualifications required to take up a particular occupation, instead concentrated on the characteristics of the qualifications which can grant entitlement to take up a wide range of professional activities. For example, the basic design of Directive 89/48 was that, if a national of a Member State wanted to pursue a regulated profession in another, the competent authorities in the host state could not deny

27 Article 5 EC. Should the Lisbon Treaty come into force, the subsidiary provisions will largely be enshrined in Article 5 TEU.

28 Directive 75/363 [1975] OJ L16714 (Doctors); Directive 77/453 [1977] OJ L176/8 (Nurses); Directive 78/687 [1978] OJ 233/10 (Dentists); Directive 78/1027 [1978] OJ L362/7 (Veterinary surgeons); Directive 80/155 [1980] OJ L33/8 (Midwives); Directive 85/432 [1985] OJ L253/37 (Pharmacists); Directive 85/384 [1985] OJ L223/15 (Architects); and Directive 96/26 [1996] OJ L223/15 (Road haulage and passenger transport operators). Note that these Directives were repealed by consolidating Directive 2005/36 [2005] OJ L255/22.

29 Directive 89/48 [1989] OJ L19/16 on a general system for the recognition of higher education diplomas awarded on completion of professional education and training of at least three years' duration; Directive 92/51 [1992] OJ L209/25, as amended by Directive 2001/19 [2001] OJ L206/1 on a second general system for the recognition of professional education and training to supplement Directive 89/48; and Directive 1999/ 42 [1999] OJ L201/77 establishing a mechanism for the recognition of qualifications in respect of the professional activities covered by the Directives on liberalization and transitional measures and supplementing the general system for the recognition of qualifications. Note that these Directives were also repealed by consolidating Directive 2005/36 [2005] OJ L255/22.

authorization on the basis of inadequate qualifications if that person satisfied the conditions of having pursued a three year higher education course in the Community and had completed the necessary professional training in order to be qualified to take up the regulated profession.[30]

Clearly, the key distinction between the two systems is that whereas recognition follows automatically from the sectoral Directives, under the general system recognition is contingent upon the individual's training being considered equivalent by the host Member State and thus there is a lesser degree of legal certainty (White 2004, 77). Where there are discrepancies in training, compared to the training undertaken by the state's own nationals, the state can require the migrant to undertake a period of adaptation or an aptitude test.[31] More recently, a Directive on the recognition of professional qualifications has been adopted which consolidates the law on mutual recognition and repeals 15 sectoral Directives and the three general system Directives.[32] Although this Directive merges the law on the two systems into a single legal document the distinction between them remains very much intact.

The role of professional organizations A defining feature of the Community's system of mutual recognition is that it allows the professional bodies which regulate professions in the Member States to exercise a considerable degree of control over the process. The competent authorities in the Member States are able to supervise the process of recognition and the system is, therefore, 'heavily reliant on mutual trust and on the adoption of a non-protectionist attitude by national competent authorities' (Craig and de Búrca 2003, 780). Thus, the above mentioned analysis of the Canadian context may hold significance after all. In particular, Bauder's research (2003, 703) demonstrates that the tendency of such professional bodies, when carrying out this function of 'professional gate-keeping', is to devalue foreign qualifications. Essentially, distinctions are made on the basis of where the qualification was obtained such that the 'foreign' skills of migrants are judged to be of less value (ibid., 702). While it may often be in the interest of an organization to employ foreign labour, such practises can masque deep-seated discrimination.

It could be argued that the national professional bodies in the EU Member States will be less inclined to adopt such a differential assessment of qualifications from other EU states; after all, they have been socialized by the process of EU integration over a period of many years and should, in theory, have adapted to the system of mutual recognition. Furthermore, it has long been held by the ECJ that such bodies which are neither public nor private but, rather, are involved

30 Note that if a profession is unregulated in a Member State, and thus the general system does not apply, the Court has stressed that there must be a prompt, good faith assessment of the equivalence of qualifications followed by a reasoned decision which could be challenged in the national courts: Case C-164/94 *Aranitis* [1996] ECR I-135.

31 Article 4, Directive 89/48 [1989] OJ L1916.

32 Directive 2005/36 [2005] OJ L255/22 (the deadline for implementation into national law was 20 October 2007).

with regulating employment in a collective manner are duty bound to respect obligations of Community law, including the principle of non-discrimination on the ground of nationality,[33] contained in the Treaty.[34] Consequently, such bodies should be well aware of their duties under EU law.

It is questionable, however, whether professional bodies will readily accept the mutual recognition of EU8 (and EU2) qualifications in the wake of accession. Indeed, Kofman (2000, 55) has pointed to the general devaluation of CEE education which occurs in western countries. As this 'mindset' is unlikely to have altered in the short time since EU accession it seems that CEE migrants may be at particular risk of facing difficulties ensuring their professional qualifications are recognized. This is not to say that such devaluation is specific to CEE educational qualifications as it appears that an undervaluing of foreign education occurs even between the EU15 owing to the closely related nature of education to the Member States' cultural heritage. White (2004, 77), for example, refers to the *Dreessen* case as a 'remarkable' example of professional gate-keeping by a national competent body.[35] Dreessen was a Belgian national who held engineering qualifications from Germany and had later worked in architects' practices for a period of 25 years in Belgium. Despite clear evidence of his competence the Belgian authorities refused his application to practice as a self-employed architect on the basis of his German qualification which was not covered by the relevant sectoral Directive. The Court stressed the importance of the principle of equivalence which must be taken into account when dealing with a qualification not covered by the secondary legislation. The case law clearly states that such qualifications should be subject to a good faith assessment of their equivalence to national standards.[36] Despite this principle now being well-established, it would seem that some competent authorities continue to question the legitimacy of qualifications obtained in other Member States.[37]

Furthermore, it is well documented that the mutual recognition of qualifications is already a very poorly implemented area of EU law (White 2004, 72; Pertek 1992, 293; Peixoto 2001, 33):

> The number of preliminary rulings and infringement proceedings in this area is testimony to the continuing reluctance of Member States, and professional bodies within them, to recognise qualifications obtained in other Member States. (White 2004, 77)

---

33 Article 12 EC (to become Article 18 TFEU if the Lisbon Treaty enters into force).

34 Case 36/74 *Walrave* [1974] ECR 1405; Case C-415/93 *Bosman* [1995] EC R I-4921.

35 Case C-447/93 *Dreessen* [1994] ECR I-4087.

36 See Case 222/86 *Heylens* [1987] ECR 4097; Case C-164/94 *Aranitis* [1996] ECR. I-135; Case C 340/89 *Vlassopoulou* [1991] ECR 2357; Case C-238/98 *Hocsman* [2000] ECR I-6623 (this case extended the obligation to consider the equivalence of qualifications to those obtained even in third-countries).

37 In practice, a refusal of recognition may not prevent a migrant from working under a regulated profession's title (unlawfully) in the host Member State.

Bringing infringement proceedings against Member States for non-implementation, or incorrect implementation, of mutual recognition legislation has been a recurring task for the Commission (White 2004, 77). Furthermore, it seems that such actions have not had any significant deterrent effect on the Member States. For example, infringement proceedings against seven Member States were brought for failing to fully implement the third general system Directive.[38] This reluctance to engage in a true system of mutual trust and to leave protectionism behind will only be compounded by professional CEE migrants seeking to gain access to certain professional occupations. It seems, therefore, that the failures of the mutual recognition system may well be another contributory factor to the de-skilling of migrants from the EU8 in the UK.

Of the five Polish employment agency representatives interviewed as part of the study, four of them admitted that their organization had found it difficult to understand the law on the recognition of professional qualifications. This suggests that the advice given to migrants is not always reliable or comprehensive. The following extract from a Warsaw-based agency representative demonstrates the difficulties experienced when trying to grapple with the mutual recognition law, as well as the potential for conveying misleading information to professionals seeking to migrate:

> Nurses have to be registered with the College of Nurses and some of these women graduated this year and start work [in the UK] straight away but sometimes there is a problem and we are told they need two years experience. At first it seemed that experience in Poland was not good enough but now we are not having a problem with this being counted. We've also started to recommend that pharmacists should work in Poland first after graduation and then apply for positions in the UK. To be honest with you we are not exactly sure that is correct. (Interview 403.I)

Despite the confusion in some cases, it should also be pointed out that one of the Polish agencies (based in Krakow) that took part in the study had developed a very comprehensive workshop which provided practical information for doctors wanting to register with the General Medical Council.[39]

A further repercussion of the endemic 'professional gate-keeping' and the reluctance to recognize migrants' qualifications and skills is that, whilst migrants may gain access to their chosen profession, they also experience a downgrading *within* that profession. For example, research has suggested that foreign doctors in the UK often work in less-specialized areas of health care than they did in their home state (Kofman 2000, 49). Migrant nurses may also experience a devaluing of their skills and experience, often being asked to undertake routine tasks and 'not being trusted' to perform certain medical procedures (Matiti and

[38] Directive 99/42 [1999] OJ L201/77. The Member States concerned were Germany, Spain, Ireland, Italy, the Netherlands, Austria and the UK. See, for example, Case C-388/02 *Commission v Ireland* [2003] ECR I-2173.

[39] Interview 402.B.

Taylor 2005, 7).[40] The implication is, then, that migrants are not only de-skilled between professions but also within a profession. A further finding is that, due to the difficulty of trying to access professional occupations, migrants sometimes volunteer their services in the hope that it may lead to a permanent, paid position later on (Bauder 2003, 712-13). This may either be for a reduced wage, or for no wage at all, consequently undermining the earning power and professional worth of the migrant worker.

The role of employers The way in which employers assess skills and qualifications gained in the home state also has an impact on the migrant's labour market position. Under Community law EU migrant workers are entitled to equal treatment with national workers and, thus, should not experience discrimination on the grounds of nationality in the course of employment.[41] Indeed, Article 6 of Regulation 1612/68 provides that nationality-based discrimination should not be perpetrated against migrants in the form of 'vocational or other criteria' which are not applied to nationals who wish to pursue the same activity.[42] Therefore, from a legal perspective, in assessing qualifications discrimination is strictly prohibited. Research by Erel (2003, 270) on the migration of skilled women to the UK and Germany has, however, uncovered the tendency of employers to underestimate and undervalue migrants' qualifications and, instead, to recognize only their linguistic abilities. A migrant's ability to communicate in the language of the host state is clearly an important consideration for employers.

Linguistic competence is a factor that can stifle a migrant worker's performance in the host labour market (Erel 2003, 268). For example, the doctor in the sample who was working as a care assistant in a private care home for the elderly did express an intention to register as a doctor in the future.[43] However, at the time of the interview he did not feel his proficiency in English was at a standard adequate to enable him to fulfil his duties. Similarly, the following extract is taken from an interview with a Polish employment agency representative who had experience of assisting people arrange a move to the UK:

> It's weird because a lot of people who we send are really well educated. Sometimes they've got medical degrees but they work in factories on the line because they need to learn English first. (Interview 405)

---

40 If access to the nursing profession proves difficult the women may instead transfer their skills to the precarious sector of domestic work (Kofman 1999, 283). Domestic work is also discussed later on in this chapter.

41 Article 39 EC; Articles 1–6 Regulation 1612/68. As already stated, nationality discrimination is also prohibited by Article 12 EC, and Union citizens have a right to equal treatment under Directive 2004/38 [2004] OJ L158/77.

42 Although this is tempered somewhat by the inclusion of an employer's right to request the migrant undergo a vocational test, if such a request is made when making the offer of employment.

43 Interview 009.BS.

Linguistic competence is an interesting issue because a migrant's lack of language proficiency can provide employers with the opportunity to legitimate, otherwise prohibited, discrimination on the grounds of nationality as regards access to employment. Article 3(1) of Regulation 1612/68 allows 'conditions relating to linguistic knowledge required by reason of the post to be filled' to be imposed on migrant workers employed by public bodies. This was successfully relied on, in the case of *Groener*,[44] by the Irish government. Here, a Dutch woman had been teaching at an Irish design college but was refused a permanent position as a result of her lack of proficiency at speaking Gaelic. The language requirement was upheld, despite the fact that Gaelic was not needed to actually perform the duties of the post, because there was a government policy to promote the use of the Irish language as a means of expressing national culture and identity (paragraphs 18-19). Education, and teachers in particular, were to play an important part in the implementation of this policy and, therefore, the language requirement was lawful.[45] The relevant point for the discussion here is that employers are entitled to impose language conditions if the post so requires linguistic knowledge. *Groener* suggests that, even if the post does not require actual linguistic knowledge, then there may still be circumstances where linguistic competence is a prerequisite of employment. Although Article 3(1) itself applies only to 'provisions laid down by the laws, regulations or administrative action or administrative practices of Member States', private employers, who are also bound by the principle of non-discrimination under Article 39 EC,[46] will have the opportunity to justify any language requirements on the basis of the objective justification test which applies to indirect discrimination.[47]

In any event, as this chapter seeks to demonstrate, language is not the only factor that contributes to the de-skilling of migrant labour. The following extract from an EU8 worker demonstrates this point:

> My experience is that Polish people coming over here do jobs that other people are not interested in and actually a lot of Polish people are really well educated and they work below their qualifications. I speak fluent English so theoretically I should have the same opportunities as British people but I don't. (Interview 011.MW)

Employers, in addition to having concerns about a migrant's proficiency in English, may also express doubt about the suitability of foreign qualifications. Two of the five agencies interviewed as part of the study put forward the view that the British employers they dealt with had a particular preoccupation with

---

44 Case 379/87 *Groener v Minister for Education* [1989] ECR 3967.

45 Provided that the level of knowledge was not disproportionate to the objective pursued (para. 21). For discussion on the impact of this judgment on migrant workers in Ireland see Ackers 1998, 204-08

46 See Case C-281/98 *Angonese* [2000] ECR I-4139.

47 That the requirement is justified by objective factors unrelated to the nationality of the persons concerned and in proportion to the aim legitimately pursued. Note that an employer cannot require the linguistic capabilities to be obtained within the host Member State, see *Angonese* judgment.

National Vocational Qualifications (NVQs).[48] The suggestion was that many employers had been unconvinced of the suitability of some Polish candidates who did not have such a qualification:

> Polish school isn't seen as being as valid as NVQs. When someone finishes school in Poland it is a problem because we can't describe what he can do. It would be easier for us to say he has an NVQ in something but we haven't got this system. So we need to check these people are qualified and their qualifications are ok and then try to persuade the employer of this. (Interview 405.N)

As a form of vocational qualification NVQs may also come under the mutual recognition regime. Previously, the third general system Directive applied to a wide array of occupations, ranging from hairdressing to mining, whether pursued in an employed or self-employed capacity.[49] Now, the relevant provisions are enshrined in consolidating Directive 2005/36. Thus, it would be open to a migrant with some Polish vocational qualifications relevant to a particular profession to attempt to gain recognition of them as equivalent to NVQs under this Directive. Moreover, in the absence of such a regulated profession falling within the scope of the Directive, there is still the possibility of reliance on the principle of equivalence which has been discussed above in relation to the role of professional organizations.

The problem with relying upon the obligation to undertake a good faith assessment of the equivalence of foreign qualifications is that this principle has developed out of the case law on the right of establishment, not the free movement of workers.[50] In *Vlassopoulou*,[51] for example, the Court made clear that Article 43 EC (concerning the freedom of establishment) imposed an obligation on the national authorities responsible for granting access to professions, in this case the legal profession, in that they were required:

> ... to take into consideration the diplomas, certificates and other evidence of qualifications which the person concerned has acquired in order to exercise the same profession in another Member State by making a comparison between the specialized knowledge and abilities certified by those diplomas and the knowledge and qualifications required by the national rules. (Para. 16)

Thus, although the duty is imposed on the competent authorities in a Member State when an EU national is seeking to gain access to a profession it is not entirely clear whether the principle can apply in a horizontal fashion

---

48 A vocational qualification accredited by the National Council for Vocational Qualifications (NCVQ) in the UK and based on the assessment of specific competencies in the workplace in accordance with a prescribed national standard.

49 Directive 1999/42 [1999] OJ L201/77.

50 As discussed above in relation to professional organizations. See Case C-164/94 *Aranitis* [1996] ECR I-135; Case C 340/89 *Vlassopoulou* [1991] ECR 2357; Case C-238/98 *Hocsman* [2000] ECR I-6623; Case C-447/93 *Dreessen* [1994] ECR I-4087; Case 222/86 *Heylens* [1987] ECR 4097.

51 Case C-340/89 *Vlassopoulou* [1991] ECR 2357.

against private employers. Arguably, however, it is not outside the realms of possibility to suggest that the positive obligation to assess the equivalence of foreign qualifications can also apply to such employers. The Court, in the case of *Angonese*, has already established that the prohibition of discrimination on grounds of nationality in Article 39 EC applies to private employers.[52] Therefore, if the principle of horizontal application of the free movement provisions, from *Angonese*, is combined with the duty to consider the equivalence of foreign professional qualifications, from *Vlassopoulou*, it would appear that, when it comes to professional qualifications at least, in principle employers do have an obligation to consider in good faith the equivalence of qualifications obtained abroad. Effectively, the duty to consider the equivalence of qualifications amounts to an extension of the obligation not to impose indirectly discriminatory restrictions on access to employment,[53] as the failure to take into account foreign qualifications will obviously affect migrants in a disproportionate manner. From this perspective, the additional responsibility on the private employer can be absorbed into the duties they are already required to comply with under the Treaty. This principle, however, is problematic in a number of respects.

First, it can be criticized on the basis that it imposes an unfair obligation on the private employer who may well be unaware of a Community obligation to compare the equivalence of qualifications from other Member States with that of domestic diplomas.[54] Perhaps more importantly, one may also wonder how an employer would actually set about establishing whether or not the qualifications were equivalent. It is not clear what steps an employer would have to take or how far they would 'reasonably' be required to go. These considerations, which relate to the fairness of the obligation, would no doubt be relevant to an objective justification assessment. Thus, although in principle employers may be bound by a *Vlassopoulou*-type obligation, they would have the opportunity to justify their failure to undertake such a comparison. A second problem relates to the workability of the horizontal application of the mutual recognition of qualifications. It is not clear how an individual would prove that an employer had failed to consider the equivalence of qualifications obtained in a home state and, moreover, it appears unlikely that an EU8 migrant would mount a legal challenge on this basis.[55] Thus it does appear that there is scope legally, for a migrant to challenge an employer's devaluation of a foreign qualification but, in practice, this

52 Case C-281/98 *Angonese* [2000] ECR I-4139

53 The prohibition of nationality-based discrimination in the area of employment, enshrined in Article 39(2) EC and the provisions of Regulation 1612/68 [1968] OJ L257/2, covers measures and practices that either directly or indirectly discriminate against non-nationals. See, *inter alia*, Case C-15/69 *Ugliola* [1969] ECR 363.

54 Although, of course, certain directly effective Community law can be horizontally binding against private parties, an example being Article 141 EC on the principle of equal pay, see Case 43/75 *Defrenne v Sabena* [1978] ECR 1365. Article 141 EC will be renumbered as Article 157 TFEU if the Lisbon Treaty comes into force.

55 For a number of reasons including resources, access to legal representation and, again, actual awareness that such discrimination has occurred.

route poses significant difficulties. The confusion surrounding mutual recognition law demonstrated by the employment agencies rather seems to illustrate this.

The implication of this is clearly that employers do have a part to play in the devaluing of EU8 migrants' qualifications and hence lowering of their labour market position. Even if it is accepted they have an obligation not to discriminate on the basis of qualifications, it is not a well-enforced one. The following extract from an interview with a male return migrant in Poland (a history graduate) provides an example of how he perceived his relationship with his employer in London:

> When I was working in the hotel as a waiter I applied for a better job in the office as a secretary. Actually I applied a few times for different jobs in the hotel and they always said no. I feel like I could go to only one level. It was like I could be a waiter or a housekeeper but I couldn't go to a higher level. They were not interested in what I had done in Poland. I know about my rights but there is something that stops you getting higher. (Interview 311.D)

Similarly, the following respondent (a psychology graduate who worked as a shop assistant in London) describes his perception of how employers place a higher premium on British qualifications:

> I met lots of educated Polish people including lawyers and psychologists and all of these people are working in the jobs at the level of, for example, retail or restaurants. I couldn't do it for long time. I knew I wouldn't get a better job. I think if you want to get proper job in London you need an English degree. I only worked in a shop and they asked about English qualifications! (Interview 301.B)

These two extracts bear testimony to the existence of a form of 'glass ceiling' (Li 2001, 23) which prevents some migrants from experiencing any significant upward professional mobility in the workplace. Although the attitude of employers is likely to be only one of many contributory factors to this phenomenon, it would certainly appear that their views of migrants' qualifications, skills and experience are significant.

Gaining access to further educational studies The professional focus of the EU mutual recognition regime also has ramifications for those migrants who seek to take up additional studies once they are working in the UK. The ability to access educational courses whilst working in the host state may be particularly important as a mechanism for improving one's labour market position and essentially achieving a form of 're-skilling' (Erel 2003, 269; Raghuram and Kofman 2004, 95); after all, it is clear from the discussion above that employers do value national qualifications. However, it may be difficult for migrants to access certain educational courses in the host state on the basis of their previously-obtained Polish qualifications, as Stalford (2000c, 246) points out:

> Current provision … does not address the situation in which nationals are required to possess specific qualifications to gain access to certain systems of education, and how qualifications obtained from other Member States will be regarded'.

It is important to recognize the distinction between academic recognition and professional recognition. EU law, as it currently stands, provides no binding mechanisms for the recognition of academic qualifications outside of the 'professional occupation' context and thus it can be extremely difficult to transfer purely academic qualifications from one country to another (Stalford 2000c). This may prevent the migrants from building on qualifications obtained in the home state by gaining access to a higher-level educational course which requires prior completion of particular qualifications. Seven of the 45 migrants interviewed expressed a desire to gain a qualification during their time in the UK. The following extract is taken from an interview with one woman who had actually taken steps towards this and provides an example of how lack of recognition can be a barrier to re-skilling. She had graduated with a Masters degree in English Literature and had previously been a teacher in Poland; at the time of the interview she was working as an administrative assistant in London and was hoping to be able to complete a PhD part-time:

> I was thinking of doing my PhD here part time but it turns out that my Masters [degree] will not be recognized as a Masters here. I spoke to a university and they told me my Masters will only count as a Bachelor's degree which was really surprising to me, so it depends whether I will be accepted on the basis of that. The people who warned me that my diploma would not be recognized were right. (Interview 011.MW)

Despite the absence of binding Community rules on the recognition of academic qualifications, the National Academic Recognition Information Centres (NARIC Network) was established to provide higher educational institutions and individuals with information concerning the validity of qualifications in other Member States.[56] In relation to gaining access to university courses on the basis of Polish (or other Member State qualifications), therefore, there is a system in place to provide assistance and advice; although, higher education institutions have significant discretion as to how they apply and interpret guidelines on equivalence. A contrast can be drawn here with the position of employers (discussed in the above section) who are less likely to be as familiar with systems and policies governing recognition. In addition, universities will often have a set policy on the recognition of foreign qualifications which enhances the transparency of the decisions. There is a greater degree of ambiguity when employers make judgments about the value of qualifications.

Importantly, the Court has indicated that it is willing to *encourage* the recognition of academic qualifications. In a number of cases involving discrimination as regards access to higher education the ECJ has made clear that indirectly discriminatory measures which require university applicants to have

---

[56] Council of Ministers of Education Resolution [1976] OJ C38/1.

completed their secondary education within the host Member State fall foul of Article 12 EC.[57] Therefore, Member States should take the necessary measures to ensure that holders of secondary education diplomas awarded in other Member States can gain access to higher education under the same conditions as those who have obtained their previous education in the host state.[58] Arguably then, academic recognition is binding so far as it falls within the scope of application of the principle of indirect discrimination. This principle is still in the relatively early stages of development but it does appear that it can potentially be far-reaching, especially when considered within the context of the case law on equal treatment of Union citizens. In *D'Hoop*,[59] for example, it was held that Belgian rules which denied an individual access to a tideover allowance on the ground that she had not completed her secondary education in Belgium were unlawful. Therefore, not only are individuals entitled to have their secondary education in their home Member State taken into account when seeking to access university courses in the host Member State, but they are also entitled to expect that their home education will not be used as a condition to deny them access to related benefits within that host state.[60]

The focus here on universities may blur the distinction between the status of migrant worker and migrant student.[61] However, it has been included to illustrate the current lack of formal Community regulation in the area of academic recognition and how this may be challenged by judicial developments in the area of discrimination as regards access to higher education in a citizenship context. Furthermore it has demonstrated that, despite the lack of binding Community input, services offered by initiatives such as the NARIC network, perhaps in

---

57 Read in conjunction with Articles 149 and 150 EC which provide the legal basis for Community action in the area of education (later to be Articles 165 and 166 TFEU if the Lisbon Treaty comes into force). Case 65/03 *Commission v Belgium* [2004] ECR I-6427; Case C-147/03 *Commission v Austria* [2005] ECR I-5969.

58 Case C-147/03 *Commission v Austria* [2005] ECR I-5969, para. 75.

59 Case C-224/98 *D'Hoop* [2002] ECR I-6191.

60 The status of migrant students generally has been fortified as a result of the Court's interpretation of Union citizenship. See Case C-209/03 *Bidar* [2005] ECR I-2119 on equal treatment as regards subsidized student loans. This is also discussed in Chapter 6. For a detailed discussion of the status of students see Dougan 2005, 943. Recently, in Cases C-11/06 and C-12/06 *Morgan* (judgment of 23 October 2007), the ECJ held that a home Member State (Germany) could not render access to an educational grant for studies in another Member State conditional on the studies being a continuation of education pursued in the home state for at least one year. As, in the Court's view, this would constitute an 'unjustified restriction' on the right to free movement (para.28). This suggests a move away from the 'discrimination model' in the realm of non-economic free movement. As regards workers, non-discriminatory obstacles have long been held to fall foul of the free movement provisions. For example, in relation to Article 39 EC see Case C-18/95 *Terhoeve* [1999] ECR I-345.

61 A migrant may continue to be a migrant worker whilst studying, provided that the work constitutes an effective and genuine economic activity and is not marginal or ancillary, see for example Case C-357/89 *Raulin* [1992] ECR I-1027.

combination with other aspects of the developing European Education Area,[62] may help de-skilled EU8 migrant workers to re-skill by providing information about accessing higher education in the UK on the basis of their Polish (or other EU8/EU2) qualifications.

Moving away from the focus on higher education and shifting attention back to workers, it should be acknowledged that migrant workers are able to access 'training in vocational schools and retraining centres' under the same conditions as national workers.[63] This may provide an opportunity to re-skill for some de-skilled workers. However, this is restricted to training linked to occupational activity and will not normally extend to studies at university:

> It should be noted that in order for an educational institution to be regarded as a vocational school for the purposes of that provision, the fact that some vocational training is provided is not sufficient. The concept of a vocational school is a more limited one and refers exclusively to institutions which provide only instruction either alternating with or closely linked to an occupational activity, particularly during apprenticeship.[64]

This quite limited approach to Article 7(3) has been circumvented by the panacea of Article 7(2) of the same regulation. This may help workers to achieve a level of re-skilling. The Court has held that this provision enables migrant workers to access 'all advantages available to [national] workers for improving their professional qualifications and promoting their social advancement'.[65] In *Matteucci* the Court held that the social advantages provision granted a migrant worker entitlement to a maintenance grant in an institution not falling within the Article 7(3) definition.[66] Van Der Mei (2003a, 349) argues that:

> It may be assumed that all forms of education not covered by Article 7(3) can be regarded as social advantages in the sense of Article 7(2) of the Regulation.

62 As a result of the Bologna Process, the Member States have made a commitment to reform their higher education systems in order to create convergence at the European level. The aim of the Process is to establish a European Higher Education Area by 2010 in which academic staff and students could move with ease and have quick fair recognition of their qualifications. See the Bologna Declaration of 19 June 1999.

63 Article 7(3), Regulation 1612/68 [1968] OJ L257/2. Children of migrant workers have broad rights to education in the host state under Article 12 of this regulation. See Stalford 2000a; 2000b; 2000c.

64 Case 39/86 *Lair* [1988] ECR 3161, para. 26. Note that university study is not excluded from the definition of vocational training *per se* but in order to qualify the course must aim to prepare people for occupation rather than simply improving their general knowledge, see Cases 24/86 *Blaizot* [1988] ECR 379 and 197/86 *Brown* [1988] ECR 3205.

65 Case 39/86 *Lair* [1988] ECR 3161, para. 22.

66 Case 235/87 *Matteucci* [1988] ECR 5589; See also Case C-337/97 *Meeusen* [1999] ECR I-3289.

Thus a migrant worker still in employment could make use of his or her right to equal treatment as regards social advantages in order to help gain access to a wider variety of institutions and obtain assistance that would facilitate a degree of re-skilling.[67]

With regard to those EU8 migrants who seek to access educational courses after a relationship of employment has terminated, a distinction must be drawn between those who are voluntarily unemployed and those who are involuntarily out of work. CEE accession migrant workers are not entitled to voluntarily leave the employment market in order to access such social advantages that enable take up of an educational course.[68] This is in contrast to the position of EU15 nationals following *Lair*.[69] Here the Court held that voluntarily unemployed migrants could retain their worker status so long as there was an element of continuity between the previous occupation and the course of study. Conversely, EU8 migrants who become involuntarily unemployed are entitled, under Community law, to rely on the continuing worker-status and make use of the equal treatment provision in Article 7(2) in order to take up studies to help them re-train[70] or, using the terminology of this chapter, re-skill. This does, though, need to be read in the context of the UK national dynamic as the post-accession domestic regulatory regime works to deny EU8 workers this opportunity. As a consequence of the WRS rules, once an EU8 worker is unemployed the residence and non-discrimination rights under national law expire whether the unemployment is voluntary or involuntary.[71]

The Gender Dimension of De-Skilling among EU8 Migrants

The decision to explore the gender dimension of de-skilling is justified by the findings of research which suggest that the phenomenon of skill devaluation can manifest itself in distinctly gender-specific ways (Kofman 2000; Kofman et al. 2000; Campini 1993; Phizacklea 1983; Raghuram and Kofman 2004). It has been suggested that there is a greater tendency for female migrants to be de-skilled and this has been exacerbated by the global shift towards a service economy (Campini

67 The ability to impose transitional restrictions on the movement of EU8 workers only allows derogation from Articles 1–6 of Regulation 1612/68. Once access is granted there can be no derogation from the social rights contained in the remainder of Regulation 1612/68. For details of the transitional restrictions see the annexes referred to in Article 24 of the Act of Accession [2003] OJ L236/33 (discussed in Chapter 3).

68 A provision in the Accession Treaties allows EU15 Member States to withdraw the rights of CEE nationals who become voluntarily unemployed during the transitional period: para. 2, Annexes.

69 Case 39/86 *Lair* [1988] ECR 3161.

70 This has been embodied in Article 7(3)(d), Directive 2004/38 [2004] OJ L158/77.

71 See Chapter 3 for details on this restriction and Chapter 6 for a critique of the UK law's compatibility with Community law. Such a worker could seek to rely on the Community law rights directly (assuming they can access legal advice and have the practical resources to do so).

1993, 192). This, in turn, has led to an increased demand for 'female' labour in some of the more precarious sectors of the labour market (such as domestic work). This demand increases the likelihood of female migrants being de-skilled and, hence, being subject to poorer conditions of employment. This is despite evidence to suggest that female migrants are now often more highly educated than their male partners (Kofman 2000, 54). Other researchers have confirmed that de-skilling is not gender-neutral and add that gender stereotyping about 'appropriate' women's work contributes to the occurrence of female migrants' 'brain waste' (Raghuram and Kofman 2004, 95).

Of particular relevance to the discussion here is the assertion that de-skilling can have specific consequences for CEE women migrants (Friese 1995, 194). Morokvasic (2004, 7) has emphasized the historical context which has increased the tendency of women from the CEE region to migrate westwards and thus also increase their chances of experiencing some degree of de-skilling. Under the socialist regimes paid employment was a norm for women. Thus when the Soviet economic and political system in the CEE region collapsed and unemployment levels rose, women looked elsewhere (often to the then EU12) for work in order that they could continue to fulfil their role as family carers by generating income.[72] This is a trend which has continued. The majority of such women, however, were unable to access regular employment as readily as men in the host societies and instead turned to the informal economy. Such informal 'female' employment includes, *inter alia*, work as domestic helpers, carers or prostitutes, occupations within which women typically experience some form of status demotion.

De-skilling is, of course, not specific to the experiences of CEE women. Ackers, in her research on the experiences of EU15 national migrant women within the EU Member States (1998, 183), found that women with established professional careers in the state of origin often suffered a 'significant loss in status'. To be more specific, Ackers draws a distinction between those women whose motivation to migrate was based on their own career and those who migrated for the purpose of their partner's career. Whilst the former group often achieved a degree of career-progression, the latter were more likely to suffer skill devaluation and downward occupational mobility. This distinction between employment experience, based on migration motivation, may well be relevant to migrant women *in general* and, therefore, also hold significance for women from the CEE region.

Before the discussion moves on, it is useful to reflect briefly on the decision of the ECJ in *Rinke*.[73] This case is of relevance as it knits together two of the issues this discussion has set out to explore; gaining access to a profession and the greater likelihood of women to be de-skilled. Ms Rinke challenged the legality of Community secondary legislation, governing the mutual recognition of training and qualifications relating to the profession of doctor,[74] on the ground that the legislation itself was contrary to the principle of equal treatment on the

72 Indeed in the 1980s, Polish women migrants outnumbered men: Kofman 2000, 282.

73 Case C-25/02 *Rinke* [2003] ECR 8349.

74 Directive 86/457 [1986] OJ L267/26; Directive 93/16 [1993] OJ L165/1.

grounds of sex. The argument centred on the requirement that, in order to be recognized in another Member State, part-time medical training must include a certain number of full-time training periods.[75] The Court accepted that the requirement impacted negatively on a greater number of women than men as men clearly have greater opportunities to undertake such full-time training due to the 'unequal division of domestic tasks' and, hence, the condition could be considered indirectly discriminatory (para. 35). However, it verified the validity of the legislation on the basis that the full-time training requirement could be objectively justified. Essentially, the Court found that it was reasonable for the legislature to require doctors to have fulfilled periods of full-time training as a means of demonstrating they had sufficient levels of medical experience (para. 40). This case demonstrates that migrant women who seek to gain access to the medical profession in another Member State may find it more difficult than men to fall within the application of EU law and, consequently, are more likely to be excluded from accessing the occupation they held in their home state.

The remainder of this section explores the phenomenon of de-skilling further in relation to the experiences of migrant women from the EU8 in the post-accession environment.[76] In particular it seeks to demonstrate that women from the accession countries may still face greater difficulties than men in accessing regular employment and hence remain at greater risk of entering the informal and private economy. This, in turn, can have serious implications for the degree of de-skilling they experience and the conditions of employment they face.

Employer-Organized Migration Schemes

Chapter 3 has already pointed out that in the light of EU enlargement and the subsequent decision of the UK government to open up its labour market to EU8 nationals, it has become increasingly popular for employers with significant staff shortages to look towards the CEE accession countries for recruits. This process of internationalization is becoming a common strategy adopted by employers who experience trouble recruiting at national level (Salt 1992, 485). Such schemes involve an employer making contact with a partner of some kind, usually an employment agency, in Poland (or other EU8 Member State) and the subsequent recruitment of a group of migrants. The majority of schemes set up so far appear to be based on male-dominated industries and, as will be demonstrated below, this has consequences for the migration opportunities available to women in the EU8.

As was stated above, the research included a case study on a transport firm which recruited over 100 Polish drivers. Furthermore, employment agency representatives in Poland confirmed that such schemes had been carried out in a number of sectors (such as factory workers, doctors, bus and delivery drivers,

75 Article 5, Directive 86/457; Article 34(1), Directive 93/16.

76 The ratio of male:female migrants who registered on the WRS between May 2004 and June 2006 was 58:42. Thus a sizeable proportion of those EU8 migrants working in the UK are female: Home Office et al. 2006, 13.

engineers and IT professionals).[77] It is clear that such schemes can be of real benefit to migrants as they can help to overcome some of the hurdles associated with moving to a new country: language and housing in particular.[78] In addition, they often involve no 'occupational skidding' (Morawska and Spohn 1997, 36) because the migrant is employed in the UK in the same profession they occupied in Poland. It seems, however, that these schemes may be operating in a gender-specific way that excludes many migrant women from such beneficial assistance.[79] The employment agency representatives interviewed confirmed that the majority of migrants they sent to the UK as part of such employer-organized 'group' schemes were male.[80] This is undoubtedly related to the fact that many of the sectors in need of labour are associated with 'men's work'. Arguably then, these schemes favour male migrants and do not offer women the same opportunity to work in the occupation they already occupy.[81] When confronted with such obstacles women are more likely to turn to casualized work in the informal sector carrying out cleaning and domestic work and, as a result, can experience a greater degree of de-skilling:

> Demand for migrant women seems to concern the lowest levels of the employment hierarchy in sex-segregated labour markets (Campini 1993, 191).

In addition, the lack of regulation by a formal agency or official employer and the absence of any official employment contract can leave migrant women in a particularly vulnerable situation. Women who take up casualized employment find themselves in a more isolated set-up with few formal support networks to turn to should problems arise in the host society.

Particularly precarious employment situated in the informal economy is that which operates largely in the private sphere and is, consequently, hidden from any

---

77 Based on Interview 401.S; Interview 402.B; Interview 403.I; Interview 404.P and Interview 405.N.

78 This is not to deny that some agencies can be exploitative migration intermediaries, see Currie 2006. The employment agencies interviewed in Poland were all included on a national register and thus subject to, at least some, regulation. The same obviously would not apply to 'rogue' agencies in Poland and the UK.

79 This mirrors the way in which IT shortages in the 1990s favoured male migrants, see Kofman 2004, 654.

80 As part of the empirical work the author visited a transport depot in the UK which had 60 Polish drivers working for them, only one of whom was female. There is insufficient scope here to consider the issue but one may wonder whether the gender-specific employment schemes can be linked to a weak enforcement of the gender equality *acquis* in Poland (or the CEE Member States in general). On the gender *acquis* see Velluti 2005, 213. See also the Enlargement, Gender and Governance project, based at Queen's University Belfast, which has country reports on the EU8 available to download. <http://www.qub.ac.uk/egg/> (last accessed 20 February 2008).

81 Research also confirms that women have less access to training schemes adapted to labour market demand (see Morokvasic 2004, 13) and also to overseas company transfers (see Kofman 2000, 50).

rigorous public scrutiny. Such employment includes domestic and sex work, two areas where women, and migrant women in particular, dominate (Anderson 2000). One of the employment agency representatives remarked that they frequently encouraged women who wished to move to the UK to consider moving as an au pair when they had no other suitable work to offer them.[82]

The following subsection specifically examines domestic work and explores its continuing relevance to EU8 migrant women in the UK.[83] Furthermore, it examines how the migration process results in highly qualified migrant women being de-skilled to such a degree that they undertake work within the informal sphere.

Women in the Informal Sphere: Domestic Workers

'Domestic' work[84] encompasses a variety of tasks connected to the 'home', including housework and childcare (Anderson 2000, 15). It is widely documented that a considerable number of these workers face poor living and exploitative working conditions and exist outside of any legal regulation (Schwenken 2005). There has been increased demand for female domestic workers in western industrialized countries, such as the UK, due to various demographic and social changes, the most notable of which are an ageing population and increased levels of female employment:

> The demand of 'unprotected' female workers for employment in private households grows in the same measure as the trend of western middle-class women towards employment continues with increasing levels of education. (Friese 1995, 194)

The sample of migrants who took part in the study includes two female domestic workers employed by private households (one lived-in) and one female employed as a cleaner in a private household. In addition, three other women had previously worked as live-in domestic workers.[85] None of this work, located in the domestic sphere, had been registered under the WRS.[86] This appears to confirm

---

82 Interview 404.P.

83 Space prohibits a review of the issue of sex trafficking but note that there is evidence that women from the EU8 and EU2 appear to be victims of such practices in some instances, see BBC News Report 2005; Kofman 2000b, 282–3; Morokvasic 2004, 18.

84 For the purposes of this discussion the label of 'domestic work' is used in a broad sense to refer to both 'domestic workers' and 'au pairs' as categories of migrant who primarily exist within the informal sphere and in private homes. This is not to deny that significant distinctions exist between the two categories. In addition it should be noted that in the UK a very limited definition is given to the term 'domestic worker' as it applies only to those workers given permission to enter the territory with their employer. The term is used in a wider sense here. On the experience of au pairs see, Williams and Baláž 2004.

85 Each subsequently took up the posts of nursery assistant, administrative assistant and waitress respectively.

86 The women technically held an illegal status.

Schwenken's (2005, 2) argument that, even when methods of regularization are open to domestic workers, the majority hold an irregular status and are thus located firmly in the informal sphere with an absence of any tax or social security contributions. As a result of the hidden nature of this work it is difficult to estimate accurately the number of EU8 national women engaged in such employment. The WRS statistics tell us that 36,645 EU8 nationals registered under the occupation category of 'cleaner/domestic staff in the first three years of the scheme's operation (Home Office Border and Immigration Agency 2007, 16).[87] Furthermore, it was estimated that there were 14,300 foreign (including third-country national) domestic workers in the UK in 2000 (Crawley 2001). This, coupled with the view that the number of domestic workers registered is probably an under-representation of the true figure,[88] suggests that the number is likely to be sizeable. It may also be correct to say that there is an element of cultural heritage at work here. For example, statistics on the au pair scheme in the UK[89] show that 3,490 of the 15,300 au pairs in the UK in 2003 were from Poland (Home Office et al. 2003, 30). Given that a further 4,560 were from the Czech Republic and 2,690 were Slovakian it would appear that the trend for EU8 women to work in a domestic capacity has continued post-accession and, additionally, this cultural heritage of domestic work may have shaped the expectations of what constitute 'appropriate' jobs for EU8 women.

Due to the informal nature of this type of work it would seem that the WRS plays a less valuable role here with regard to the monitoring of EU8 migrants. More importantly, from the perspective of the (predominantly female) migrants who undertake such work, they are excluded from the *benefits* associated with registering in the UK. Once registered, EU8 workers are entitled to equality of treatment as regards access to certain social welfare entitlement under UK law.[90]

Domestic work is a sphere in which a significant degree of de-skilling occurs. Certainly the six respondents mentioned above who had experienced this type of work were all Polish graduates. Studies confirm that the women carrying out

---

87 There is no gender or occupation breakdown given of this figure.

88 It is generally accepted that this is a sector where the estimates are likely to be inaccurate, see Kofman et al. 2005.

89 The UK scheme, established by the Immigration Rules made under section 3(2) of the Immigration Act 1971, C.77 enables single people between 17–27, with no dependents, come to the UK 'to study English' for up to two years while living with a family. The au pairs can help in the home for up to five hours per day and, although they do not receive a salary, they should be given an 'allowance' (£55 per week is recommended). They must not require any assistance from public funds and must not stay in the UK when the au pair period comes to an end. The EU8 countries were covered by the scheme prior to 2004 and, even though the scheme no longer formally apples to them, EU8 nationals can still enter the UK as au pairs (as can all EU nationals). For information on the working of the scheme see <http://www.bia.homeoffice.gov.uk/workingintheuk/aupairs/> (last accessed 20 February 2008).

90 The Social Security (Habitual Residence) Amendment Regulations SI 2004/1232. For discussion of the UK law's compatibility with Community law see Chapter 6.

domestic work are often just as highly educated, if not more so, than the women they relieve from domestic tasks so that they can gain better access to the labour market (Sassen 2000, 510). It would appear that 'whilst domestic labour is classified as unskilled, many of those who do it are not' (Kofman 2000, 55).[91] In private households with a domestic worker the housework and childcare, or 'reproductive labour' (Newcombe 2004), remain 'women's work' but it is transferred to a female migrant worker (Ehrenreich and Hochschild 2003).

Anderson's research on domestic workers (2000, 28-39) has identified certain 'routes' into domestic work which are usually relied upon if avenues into more regular employment are closed off. This would seem to apply to the case of EU8 migrant women who have more restricted access to organized schemes, such as those mentioned above. Indeed when we consider the male-focussed migration schemes alongside the obstacles discussed earlier (such as qualification recognition) in relation to de-skilling generally, it is not difficult to see that, currently, taking up a form of domestic labour may appear to be the only available option. Despite the degree of de-skilling it may represent 'getting a foot in the door' to the UK labour market (Anderson 2000, 28). The routes into domestic work open to EU8 (and EU2) women include: placing (or reading) a personal advertisement in a newspaper in the host country; accessing informal networks (such as friends working as 'domestics' whose employer has contact with other people requiring a worker); or relying on an agency that places workers in private households. The migrant women involved with the author's study had found domestic employment via all of these methods.[92] Given that more stringent transitional rules of access are directed towards nationals of Romania and Bulgaria, it seems reasonable to suggest that domestic work may similarly be a migration route of relevance to women from the EU2. Indeed, domestic work and au pairing, along with nursing, are 'occupations' categorized as an otherwise 'authorized category of employment' under the UK's transitional rules.[93]

This is an area of employment where the consequences of de-skilling can be particularly negative, exploitative or even dangerous, precisely because the migrant worker is situated in the informal sphere. Of the six respondent domestic workers who took part in the study, one had found it to be a wholly negative experience. This woman worked as a domestic worker for one year in London and had since returned to Poland to work as a librarian. In the extract below she describes the

---

[91] The case of *Morgan* concerned a young German woman who had spent time in the UK as an au pair before taking up university studies there (Cases C-11/06 and C-12/06, judgment of 23 October 2007). This also stands as a reminder that it is not only CEE accession nationals that may utilize the au pair scheme.

[92] One had found her job by reading the advertisements posted on the so-called 'wailing wall' in Hammersmith, London (a window situated by the Polish Social and Cultural Association). This has become a popular place for Polish migrants to exchange information about employment. Another two women had accessed their employment in the private sphere through an informal friendship network and three had made use of London-based employment agencies.

[93] Schedule 1, Accession (Immigration and Worker Authorization) Regulations 2006 SI 2006/3317.

manner in which the close proximity with her employer, which goes hand in hand with 'living in', led to her working excessive hours and essentially never being able to 'escape':

> They wanted someone to be a housekeeper and to take care of an old woman who was ill. She was from Poland and so that's why they wanted a Polish worker. She couldn't speak very well so it was very hard work … maybe not physical hard work but mental hard work. This woman had MS and she was also very depressed. I had only one free day, Sunday, and even then I was asked to do things for them. I had no time to myself. (Interview 316.M)

The remaining domestic workers in the sample spoke in a more positive way about their time living in private households. Three expressed their relationship in the terms of being 'part of the family' although the literature suggests that this common perception may, in reality, work against domestic workers. For example, Hess and Puckhaber (2004, 65) have demonstrated that the more integrated a worker is into the family, the more difficult it becomes for them to take issue with poor working conditions. Furthermore:

> As 'one of the family,' employers could ask the au pairs to work more than the hours agreed upon, their argument being, 'we are one family, you cannot leave us alone with the childcare'. In so doing, they disguised the working relationship by using the discourse of the moral economy emphasizing cooperation and mutual responsibility. (Ibid., 73)

There is plenty of scope for exploitation, whether intentional or inadvertent, when the private household becomes a place of work. Kofman et al. (2000, 123) cite a particular example of how domestic workers' dependency on their employers can result in hidden mistreatment. In the 1980s the UK government enabled migrating foreign employers and repatriated British professionals to bring their domestic workers with them to the UK. However, these workers had no independent legal status in their own right and thus, in what was effectively a form of modern slavery, they were completely tied to their employers. The authors point out:

> The system was widely abused with one agency alone handling over 4000 reported cases of imprisonment, physical and sexual abuse, as well as widespread under and non payment of workers by their employers. (Ibid.)

This example, in some respects, is specific to the scheme operating at the time but it does provide an illustration of the vulnerable and potentially dangerous situation some domestic workers can find themselves in as a result of the domestic sphere's isolation from the mainstream. Employers are largely able to determine the worker's rights on their own terms and hence the workers are dependent on the good nature of their employers.

Domestic Workers as Community 'Workers'

It is not entirely clear whether or not CEE women occupying domestic positions would be entitled to access certain rights in the UK, perhaps as a means of alleviating hardship caused as a result of their de-skilled status, by means of reliance upon the provisions of EU law applicable to workers. The definition of worker under Community law is well established, the Court has defined features of an employment relationship as follows:

> The essential feature of an employment relationship ... is that for a certain period of time a person performs services for and under the direction of another person in return for which he receives remuneration.[94]

The Court has also stressed the importance of activities being 'effective and genuine' rather than 'on such a small scale as to be regarded as marginal and ancillary'.[95]

The problem with domestic work is that it is commonly considered to fall outside the scope of so-called 'real work'. If one considers the position of au pairs in the UK, for example, the immigration rules stress that they are not to receive a salary. Rather, they are to be granted a 'reasonable allowance' of around £55 per week.[96] If such work does fall outside the definition of migrant worker established by the Court of Justice then, consequently, migrants undertaking such work fall outside the scope of the equal treatment principle enshrined in Article 39 EC (and Article 12 EC). In practice, this means they would have no entitlement to claim the panoply of social rights accorded to those migrants who do qualify as workers.[97] Perhaps even more significantly, domestic workers face the possibility of falling outside the scope of protection offered by employment equality legislation.[98] For example, they may be denied access to work-related rights, such as parental leave and pension rights, or work in conditions that do not meet adequate health and safety standards. Importantly for the particular situation of EU8 migrants, if an EU8 migrant does not qualify as a 'worker' under EU law, those working in the informal, domestic sphere may be denied the opportunity to rely on EU law to

---

[94] Case 66/85 *Lawrie Blum* [1986] ECR 2121, para. 17.

[95] Case C-357/89 *Raulin* [1992] ECR I-1027.

[96] See <http://www.bia.homeoffice.gov.uk/workingintheuk/aupairs/> (last accessed 20 February 2008).

[97] Pursuant to Article 7(2), Regulation 1612/68 which entitles migrant workers to the same 'social and tax advantages' as national workers (now supplemented by Article 24(1), Directive 2004/38). Article 7(2) has been interpreted broadly, see Case 207/78 *Even* [1979] ECR 2019; Case 32/75 *Fiorini v SNCF* [1975] ECR 1085; Case 65/81 *Reina* [1982] ECR I-33; Case 59/85 *Netherlands v Reed* [1986] ECR 1283.

[98] Extended to those qualifying as EU migrant workers on the basis of Article 7(1), Regulation 1612/68 which provides that the principle of non-discrimination covers conditions of employment.

rebut the UK's attempt to deny them rights of residence and social entitlement should they find themselves involuntarily unemployed.[99]

EU8 migrants denied access to the security of the worker status, however, would have the opportunity to enforce rights of residence and equal treatment in the UK, despite the UK's transitional rules, by virtue of their status as Union citizens under Articles 18 and 12 EC.[100] Although very valuable, citizens' rights in a host Member State are not as secure as workers' rights. In particular, the right of residence is subject to the requirements of possessing sufficient resources and medical insurance and, in turn, the right to equal treatment is contingent upon such lawful residence.[101] Those carrying out domestic work could benefit from the worker classification as it applies in a very absolute fashion without any scope for the Member State to rescind the right to reside if they consider the migrant has become an 'unreasonable burden' on the public purse. The important point here is that, given that the majority of domestic workers are women and that EU8 men have had greater opportunities to migrate under schemes connected to their area of employment, those affected mostly by this (possible) exclusion from EU worker status would be women.

Although it is important to recognize this potential scope for denying migrants in the domestic sphere the rights granted to workers, or perhaps more correctly, the potential for the UK authorities to argue that such migrants are not workers, it is also vital to stress that the Court has been keen to apply the definition broadly.[102] One case of particular relevance is *Steymann*.[103] Here, a German national in the Netherlands was contributing to the life of a religious community by carrying out general housework and plumbing. Although Steymann did not receive a salary he did receive an element of 'pocket money' from the community which also provided for his keep. It was held by the Court that his activities could be considered as economic in nature by virtue of the value the community gained from them. Furthermore, and potentially of particular relevance to au pairs in the UK, a wide reading of the 'remuneration' concept was adopted:

> ... the services which the [community] provides to its members may be regarded as being an indirect quid pro quo for their work. (Para. 12)

This suggests that being paid 'in kind', something those in the domestic sphere often experience (Hess and Puckhaber 2004, 65) may not prevent a migrant

---

[99] Discussed in Chapters 3 and 6.

[100] See for example, Case C-85/96 *María Martínez Sala* [1998] ECR I-2691; Case 274/96 *Bickel and Franz* [1998] ECR I-7637; C-184/99 *Grzelczyk* [2001] ECR I-6193. Citizenship is discussed in more detail in Chapter 6.

[101] Previously, Directive 90/364 OJ [1990] L180/26; now Directive 2004/38 OJ [2004] L158/77.

[102] Holding that part-time work, work falling below the host state's minimum subsistence level, and work carried out in conjunction with benefit claiming can still constitute 'work' under Article 39 EC. See Case 53/81 *Levin* [1982] ECR 1035; Case 139/85 *Kempf* [1986] ECR 1741; Case C-357/89 *Raulin* [1992] ECR I-1027.

[103] Case 196/87 *Steymann* [1988] ECR 6159.

from falling within that all-important worker definition. Ackers (1998, 115) has acknowledged the potential importance of *Steymann* for those workers, mostly women, engaged in more marginal forms of employment. However, she also makes the point that it is not clear how significant the fact that Steymann carried out plumbing work was in the Court's eyes:

> The significance of the plumbing work is unclear, and the extent to which it may be interpreted as distinctively different to other forms of domestic or caring work may simply reflect yet another example of the ways in which women's unpaid work is accorded low status.

Thus, it is possible that domestic, 'female' tasks would be considered less like 'real work' and, therefore, be more likely to fail the 'effective and genuine' test than would 'male' activities such as plumbing.

De-Skilling: A Permanent Feature of EU8 Migrants' Labour Market Experience?

Clearly, it is important to consider whether de-skilling of highly qualified migrants is a permanent feature of the migration experience or whether migrants, once established in the labour market, are able to re-skill and subsequently obtain employment commensurate with their education. There are obvious drawbacks of using the data collected for the purposes of this study to consider this issue as the data was collected around the time of enlargement (2004 and 2005). Thus, there is no longitudinal analysis of consequent occupational mobility. Many of the respondents who did not plan to return to Poland in the short term did express a desire to reach a higher level of employment in the UK. Often they stressed the temporary nature of their current work and, in particular, emphasized that they anticipated progressing once their grasp of written and spoken English had improved. So that the issue of re-skilling may be addressed in some capacity, the first part of this section examines the evidence (limited though it currently is) relating to the potential for migrants to re-skill in the UK. The second part of the section then analyses the labour market position of return migrants in Poland, in an effort to consider whether the de-skilled status in the UK had any implications once the migration experience had ended.

Upward Occupational Mobility in the UK

There were a small number of instances amongst the sample of occupational mobility *within* a sector. For example, one female respondent who had been a chambermaid was working in a restaurant at the time of interview and, in addition to earning a higher wage, felt her social status had improved.[104] Similarly, the

[104] Interview 012.GP.

following male respondent had experienced internal occupational mobility, albeit to a modest extent:

> For three months I was a kitchen porter and then I became a waiter in the same hotel, it was kind of a promotion! (Interview 307.P)

This mirrors Düvell's (2004, 11) findings of Polish migrants' occupational mobility in the 1990s. He points out that (limited) upward mobility was a common feature of migrants' experiences and that they could increase their earnings by being promoted or changing jobs.[105] He gives the following examples:

> A woman who started on £1.50 an hour in a fish factory in 1994 was by 1998 earning £3.50 an hour working for a fish wholesaler. A man who started sewing in a factory for £2.50 an hour was earning £6 an hour in another factory less than two years later. (Ibid., 11)

The key point here is that the internal occupational mobility witnessed in the above author's research did not result in a full re-skilling which led to an occupational position that corresponded to their levels of qualification. The migrants' experiences described by Düvell to illustrate the supposed phenomenon of upward mobility do not display any significant degree of re-skilling. The conditions of employment, although an improvement on the original position, continued to be poor.

There were three instances of upward professional mobility within the sample that did represent a more genuine form of re-skilling. Interestingly, the circumstances of all three such respondents share a common characteristic in that their 're-skilled' work was connected in some way to the Polish migrant community.[106] First, one female respondent had started work in the UK as a chambermaid and, in this job, was paid below the national minimum wage and subject to longer hours. She later found employment as a Human Resources manager for a company which operated an organized scheme to recruit a large number of Polish drivers and her role here predominantly centred around these drivers.[107] Secondly, a woman who had started working as an administrative assistant later found work as the manager of an office, set up by the Polish Social and Cultural Association in London, to advise Polish migrants about their rights in the UK and to give information about the WRS.[108] Finally, a man who had worked as a labourer on a construction site was able to find work as the manager

---

105 Of course, Düvell's research was conducted within a different context because the Polish migrants he studied were irregular and it is not clear how EU enlargement and the regularization of migration from the EU8 has impacted on the dynamics of occupational mobility. However, given that this discussion has suggested that the current trend is for pre-accession conditions to prevail for Polish migrants in the UK, the comparison holds some value.

106 They were also all Polish graduates.

107 Interview 013.EM.

108 Interview 014.KW.

of a bar in a Polish social club in Scotland. Thus the migrant community provided an opportunity for some skilled, bilingual migrants to provide services and fulfil an occupational role more commensurate with their qualifications. This phenomenon has been acknowledged by Kofman (2004, 652), who also suggests that this avenue to re-skilling may be particularly accessible to women due to the perception of them having better inter-personal, social and caring skills. Despite the positive impact that the Polish community had on the migrants' ability to re-skill, the fact that the upward occupational mobility only occurred at the instigation of other migrants illustrates the quite limited nature of these examples. They are clearly very isolated cases and such opportunities will not be extended to the vast majority of migrants working below their level of educational attainment.

Re-Skilling upon Return to Poland

One of the predominant trends in migration from the CEE region is that of temporary migration patterns as opposed to long-term or permanent movement (Okólski 2000, 329). The 16 return migrants interviewed as part of the study all corroborate this viewpoint as all had returned to Poland after spending between six months to two years in the UK. All of the return migrants were graduates; in the UK eleven had been employed in various occupations within the hospitality and catering industry (hotels and restaurants), three had been employed privately by households as either a cleaner or domestic worker, and one worked as a shop assistant. Upon return to Poland,[109] two of the migrants were unemployed, although the majority (11) were in employment commensurate with their level of education and,[110] on the whole, were satisfied with their work. To provide two examples: a man who had worked as a kitchen porter was working for an advertising agency;[111] and a woman who had worked as a domestic worker was a teacher of English.[112]

A migrant's decision to return to Poland was often a frustrated response to a lack of labour market progress in the UK, for example:

> I decided I didn't want to be a waiter for ten or more years because I have more ambition than that. I have studied here in Poland and I don't want to abandon that. I wanted to do something more interesting, more creative than be a waiter. (Interview 307.P)

It would seem that the de-skilled status held in the UK did not impact negatively on the respondents' subsequent employment upon return to Poland. A link can be drawn with the work of Williams and Baláž (2004), who researched the experiences of return migrants from Slovakia who had worked as au pairs in the UK. This research found that during their time as au pairs, an occupation generally considered to be of a low status, the migrants gained a variety of skills

109 At the date of interview (July/August 2005).

110 Note that two of the return migrants had taken up further study in Poland.

111 Interview 302.P.

112 Interview 313.K.

which could be utilized to later increase their occupational standing in the state of origin:

> Migrant workers acquire financial capital, human capital, social capital, and cultural capital from working abroad, but these have different values in the spaces of destination and origin. (Ibid., 1814)

Such skills, which have a higher degree of marketability in the home state,[113] include English language skills, interpersonal skills and a greater degree of self confidence (Williams ibid., 1823–4). The experiences of return migrants in the author's study corroborate these findings. For example, one woman who had worked as a kitchen assistant in the UK had been able to secure employment within the marketing department of an international company in Warsaw, precisely because of her strong grasp of English. Thus she was able to secure employment in the field in which she had graduated from university:

> The reason they took me was because I speak English so well … so my plan worked! I actually applied for a job on the reception desk but they said 'your qualifications are better than you think' so it worked out well for me. (Interview 309.I)

This illustrates the potential value of international experience, regardless of what that actually entails. Furthermore, many of the return migrants framed the general benefits of the migration experience as being good 'life experience'. This would seem to confirm the argument that the migration experience can provide an opportunity to gain a greater degree of self confidence and enhance interpersonal skills. The following extracts are representative of the majority view:

> I think moving for a while is good for everyone because it's very important to get good experience. It will stay with you forever. I think everybody should do it! (Interview 302.P)

> When I was there [in London] I needed to survive somehow but I think that getting a job and all of the things you have to do to find a job is a good experience to go through. (Interview 313.K)

Therefore, the de-skilled position occupied in the host society may actually itself constitute a form of re-skilling, which builds upon the qualifications they already have, and helps to increase the opportunities available upon return to the home state (Raghuram and Kofman 2004, 97). It seems that migrants are able to make the trade off between professional investment and economic gain (mentioned earlier) without harming their labour market status at home. In fact, despite the skill-degradation they experience in the host state, their labour market potential in the home state may be enhanced after the migration experience, it appears that the migration experience provides the return migrants

[113] In the home state the migrant does not face the mechanisms of de skilling described above which work in the host state to devalue their qualifications.

with an advantage over those who have not exercised mobility rights. When this international experience is included on a return migrant's CV it is likely to hold particular weight in countries, such as Poland, with a high unemployment rate and greater competition for jobs (Keune 1998).[114]

Conclusion

By exploring the status and experiences of Polish migrants working in the UK this chapter has attempted to demonstrate how the documented brain drain from the EU8 countries has, in many instances, become de-skilled labour in the UK. The concepts of brain drain and brain gain relate to macro-level arguments about who the 'winners and losers' of migration are (sending countries or receiving countries) (Man 2004). By considering the de-skilling experiences of migrants, this chapter has sought to examine how such notions resonate at an individual (micro) level.

The legal regime adopted by the UK has facilitated the apparent brain waste, as has the ineffective enforcement of mutual recognition of qualifications at Community level. In addition to these legal obstacles, certain ideological barriers have also been preventing migrants from the EU8 realizing their occupational potential. These obstacles flow from a tendency by employers to continue to categorize EU8 migration in a similar way to third-country national migration. This inclination is, arguably, influenced by the current imposition of transitional movement restrictions by many of the EU15 Member States. This EU-level legal restriction appears to have reinforced the hierarchy between different groups of migrants by espousing the notion that CEE accession nationals are not (yet) 'full' citizens of the EU. Therefore, CEE accession nationals are not accorded an equal status with EU15 nationals. This 'second class' status has implications even in the UK, a Member State which did open up its labour market following the first eastern enlargement.[115] The differential treatment of migrants by the law clearly has implications for the labour market status they are accorded.[116] However, even formal equality of legal status would only go so far in remedying the disadvantaged labour market position of EU8 migrants; in order to overcome the deeply embedded discrimination against foreign labour it would be necessary

---

[114] In 2003 the unemployment rate amongst under-24s in Poland was 34 per cent. See Vaughan-Whitehead 2003, 31.

[115] The second of the eastern enlargements raises slightly distinct issues in relation to de-skilling due to the difference in approach taken by the UK. By simultaneously reserving places on the low-skilled migration schemes and requiring work permits for other forms of employment, there is still an expectation that EU2 nationals will continue to be useful and 'fill the gaps'. In contrast to the 'open' policy towards the EU8, however, the 'gaps' are more precisely defined.

[116] The extent of the differential treatment, or downgraded citizenship status, promulgated by the formal provisions (the transitional arrangements) is discussed in Chapter 6.

also to pursue a long-term strategy of cultural reconditioning to complement legal rights to equal treatment. Currently, for example, the discretion granted to employers in the area of mutual recognition of qualifications masques the propensity to discriminate on the basis of nationality.

Furthermore, de-skilling does not appear to be a gender-neutral phenomenon. Shortages in specific employment sectors, and the subsequent propensity of employers to arrange migration schemes, seem to offer more favourable migration conditions to men than to women. With less opportunity to access these formal schemes it appears that women from the EU8 (and, indeed, the EU2) may be drawn to domestic work in the UK and, hence, often experience a significant degree of de-skilling in the private sphere. Despite the quite negative emphasis on de-skilling, however, there is also evidence to suggest that migrants can benefit from their (short-term) experiences in the lower echelons of the employment market, on return to Poland. One question that remains is whether, given time, EU8 migrants currently in low-skilled work will be able to re-skill and access work commensurate with their skills and qualifications *in the UK*. Not only does this have implications for the UK, but it is also of importance for the wider European Union because it has ramifications for the issue of whether the inferior status granted to CEE accession migrant workers (and by extension future accession-national migrants) is a temporary or more permanent feature within the Member states.

Finally, the discussion has raised the issue of whether the EU is concerned about the type of mobility it wishes to encourage in the light of Lisbon Agenda and the development of the European Research Area. The 'brain waste' from the CEE region, and the acceptance of this phenomenon on the part of the Commission, contrasts markedly with recent initiatives to increase intra-Community 'brain circulation' by promoting highly-skilled mobility.

Chapter 5

Facilitating Family Life in the Aftermath of Post-Accession Migration to the UK

Introduction

The emphasis of the discussion in this chapter moves away from the employment experiences of CEE accession nationals to look at how moving to the UK for the purposes of work impacts upon the migrants' experiences of family life. The very reason people often make the decision to migrate as a worker is to try and enhance the living standards and life chances available to themselves and their family members. Thus, migration may be a household/family strategy for increasing available income (Boyd 1989, 645). The aim here is to explore the implications of such migration decisions on the family units and family life of post-accession CEE migrant workers.[1] Particular attention will be given to the implications of cross-national mobility for relationships between family members, the provision of care within families and, importantly, to methods of sustaining families following migration.

First, the chapter details the entitlement of CEE migrant workers' family members to join the worker in the UK. The EU free movement provisions are the primary point of reference but, in the case of EU8 and EU2 migrants, this formal entitlement is juxtaposed with certain aspects of the transitional restrictions on the free movement of persons. Despite the existence of formal family reunification rights, the early empirical evidence generated for the study that informs this book suggests that EU8 migrants in the UK have not initially utilized such entitlements to a significant extent. Secondly, the wider social entitlement of the family unit is considered. The ability to access certain welfare benefits and services in the host state may be important for sustaining family units. The engagement of EU8 workers and their families with such benefits, however, must be placed within the specific legal and social domestic context of the UK. The discussion, therefore, examines some constraints on the exercise of family reunification (and related) rights by EU8 workers that flow from the UK's post-enlargement regulatory regime which may have delayed the migration of family members.

1 As they have elsewhere in the book, the experiences of Polish migrant workers provide a case study of the broader EU8 group and, where appropriate, reference is also made to the EU2.

The final part of the chapter explores the applicability of the notion of the transnational family, evident in the research literature on transnational kinship (Boyle 2002; Bryceson and Vuorela 2002; Silver 2006), to post-accession EU8 migrant workers in the UK. Patterns of migration from the CEE region in the post-Soviet era have largely reflected a transnational family model: the predominant image has been that of workers travelling independently to spend temporary periods of time abroad while maintaining active cross-border links with family remaining in the home state (Kofman 2004, 250). This type of migration has been evident post-accession amongst EU8 workers in the UK: certainly, an apparent culture of family separation has characterized the early experience of many Polish migrants. It is not yet clear whether patterns of migration from the region will alter, and begin to reflect more of a family unity model, now that enhanced rights of family reunification have been extended to the group in the light of EU accession, or whether the transnational family model will continue to fit better with patterns of CEE migration for some time to come.

The Relevance of Family Reunification Rights

This section considers the law that governs the ability of family members of CEE accession migrants to move with the worker to a host state, the UK in particular, during the transitional period(s). In practice, family members will join a worker at different stages of the migration process and stay in the host state for differing lengths of time. For example, entire family migration may occur from the outset, where the family and worker migrate as a unit; alternatively, it may be that the worker migrates initially and the family members subsequently join them in the host society (for either a short-term or longer-term/permanent period). Attention turns first to the legal provisions which establish the parameters of the migrants' rights to family reunification and then, secondly, to the rights of those who do qualify as family members to work in the host Member State. Evidence relating to the extent to which such family reunification entitlement is being utilized is then examined.

The Right to Reunification: Which Family Members are Covered?

It is necessary to consider both the rights available at EU and domestic (UK) level in order to illustrate the family entitlement of the migrant workers.

Family members' entry and residence rights according to EU law Given that the transitional arrangements on the free movement of persons relate only to the ability of new Member State nationals to access work in the EU15 territory, it follows that EU8 and EU2 migrants who gain legitimate access to the labour market of an old Member State are entitled to exercise the same rights of family reunification that applies to EU15 migrants.[2] The starting point for discussing

---

[2] Although, as will be mentioned below, the transitional arrangements do allow for restrictions to be placed on family members' access to the labour market.

the right of family members to install themselves with a migrant worker is now Directive 2004/38 on the free movement rights of citizens and their family members.[3] Prior to this, the position of family members was primarily governed by Articles 10–12 of Regulation 1612/68.[4] Under the updated regime the following family members, regardless of nationality, are entitled to reside with the migrant citizen or, for the purposes of the discussion in this chapter, the migrant worker in the host state:

- the spouse;
- the partner with whom the Union citizen has contracted a registered partnership, on the basis of the legislation of a Member State, if the legislation of the host Member State treats registered partnerships as equivalent to marriage and in accordance with the conditions laid down in the relevant legislation of the host Member State;
- children of the worker who are under the age of twenty one or dependent and those of the spouse or partner (with whom a registered partnership has been conducted); and,
- dependent parents of the worker and those of the spouse or partner (with whom a registered partnership has been conducted).[5]

The definition of family under Directive 2004/38 is wider than it originally was under Article 10 of Regulation 1612/68. First, it applies to children of either the worker or the spouse/partner whereas the previous definition referred to only the children of the worker and the spouse. Secondly, the newer definition extends to partners with whom the worker has conducted a registered partnership (provided such partnerships are legally recognized by the host state) whereas, formerly, only those married to the worker could make use of the family reunification provisions. The definition of family in Regulation 1612/68 had been subject to much criticism on the basis that it was outdated and out of touch with modern society (Stalford 2002; Stalford 2000a; Ackers and Stalford 2004, 69–75; Woods 1999; McGlynn 2001). In particular, commentators criticized the insistence on heterosexual marriage and biological children or, otherwise, relationships of (economic) dependency on the (assumed) breadwinning migrant worker.[6] The more recent definition has attempted to address these concerns.

In addition to the definition in Article 2(2), Article 3(2) of the Directive provides that Member States, in accordance with their own national legislation,

---

3 [2004] OJ L158/77.

4 [1968] OJ L257/2. Note that the ECJ's interpretation of other free movement provisions has also been beneficial for family members, see for example Case 59/85 *Netherlands v Reed* [1987] 2 CMLR 448 were the ECJ interpreted Article 7(2), Regulation 1612/68 to extend a right of residence to the unmarried partner of a migrant worker.

5 Article 2(2), Directive 2004/38.

6 In Case 316/85 *Lebon* [1987] ECR 2811, here the Court asserted that dependency was a matter of fact evident when a worker supported a family member. Economic dependency is discussed below in relation to family members' social entitlement.

shall facilitate the entry and residence of any other family members who are dependents or members of the worker's household, or where serious health grounds strictly require the personal care of the family member. This implies a wider conceptualization of dependency that stretches further than the previous economic construction. Article 3(2) then goes on to stress that Member States shall also facilitate the entry and residence of the partner with whom the worker has a 'durable relationship'. Interestingly, the host Member State is able to undertake an extensive examination of the worker's personal circumstances when assessing the durability of the relationship and must justify any denial of entry or residence. Article 3(2) does not grant an automatic right of residence to these groups of family member. It merely encourages the Member States to examine the position of such individuals on the basis of their own national legislation. The status of the rights granted by this provision is, as Chalmers and colleagues acknowledge (2006, 592), 'nebulous'. Furthermore, they state that:

> The provision anticipates that there are circumstances where dependents and long-term partners may be refused permission to reside in another Member State with the EU citizen. This seems extremely draconian. (Ibid)

Similarly, the inclusion in Article 2(2) of those who have a registered partnership as one of the categories of family member entitled to automatic residence is not unproblematic for those wishing to rely on it. The application of this provision is contingent upon the national law in the host state treating such partnerships as equivalent to marriage. This is essentially an application of the non-discrimination on grounds of nationality principle, one of the key features of free movement law and a general principle of Community law. The origins of this approach can be seen in the reasoning adopted by the Court of Justice in the case of *Reed*.[7] Here, although refusing to interpret the term 'spouse' in the legislation to include unmarried partnerships, the Court was able to extend a right of residence to the unmarried partner of a migrant worker in the Netherlands, on the basis of the right to equal treatment as regards social advantages under Article 7(2), Regulation 1612/68. The ECJ held that, as Dutch law treated those in a stable relationship with a working Dutch national as a spouse, this was a social advantage which could also be enjoyed by an EU migrant worker under the rationale that it would facilitate integration into the host society. Even now that Directive 2004/38 has fortified the status of unmarried partners somewhat, in both Articles 2(2) and 3(2), the *Reed* decision arguably retains its relevance. Article 7(2) of Regulation 1612/68 remains in force alongside the 2004 Directive. Therefore, for migrant workers, it is still possible to use the principle of non-discrimination in respect of social advantages in order to try to secure rights of entry and residence for an unmarried partner (Toner 2006).

It is clear from the above that the Directive does not place unmarried partners on an equal footing with spouses and, as such, the definition of 'family member'

---

7 Case 59/85 *Netherlands v Reed* [1987] 2 CMLR 448.

is still open to criticism on this point.[8] Marriage provides for an automatic and absolute right of entry across the EU.[9] In contrast, the capacity of unmarried partners to qualify as a family member under the free movement provisions depends, for those without a registered partnership, on the discretion of the Member State which is entitled to 'extensively' examine the relationship. For those with a registered partnership, the right of reunification is dependent on the policy of the individual Member State and will, therefore, differ across the EU. The UK's Civil Partnership Act 2004[10] allows only same-sex couples to register their partnerships. It would seem, then, that a migrant worker in the UK is automatically entitled to be joined by a same-sex partner with whom a registered partnership has been conducted. The status of a heterosexual couple in the same situation, however, is not as straightforward as national law does not allow for the possibility of registration of opposite-sex partnerships. The couple would have to rely on the 'nebulous' Article 3 to enforce a right of reunification.

The UK perspective on the entry and residence of family members The UK implemented the provisions of Directive 2004/38 into national law via the Immigration (European Economic Area) Regulations 2006 (which came into force on 30 April 2006).[11] Regulation 7 incorporates the broader definition of family members from Article 2(2) of the Directive, thus importing into national law reunification rights for civil partners. Regulation 8 introduces into national law the category of 'extended family member', this clearly seeks to implement Article 3(2) of the Directive. It provides for rights of entry and residence for extended categories of family member not included in Regulation 7. For example, Regulation 8(3) addresses family members of the EU migrant (and, where applicable, the spouse or civil partner) who, for example, can reside with the migrant on serious health grounds. Furthermore, Regulation 8(5) provides that unmarried partners who 'prove to the decision maker' that they are in a 'durable relationship' with the EU migrant will qualify as an extended family member. This clearly reflects the Directive's insistence that partners must evidence their relationship with the migrant before being granted rights in the host society. As yet, it is unclear how this discretion will be exercised (Toner 2006).

The Immigration (European Economic Area) Regulations also extend the updated definition of family members to EU8 workers, who are registered on the WRS, under the Accession (Immigration and Worker Registration) Regulations 2004.[12] As a result of this amendment, EU8 migrant workers in the UK are now entitled to be joined by the same family members as are EU15 migrant workers. This is a welcome clarification as the original definition of family

---

8 Note that partners of EU nationality are in a privileged position as they can qualify as free movers in their own right by taking up work or simply by virtue of their Union citizenship status. The position of third-country national partners is more precarious.

9 Case 267/83 *Diatta v Land Berlin* [1985] ECR 567.

10 C.33.

11 SI 2006/1003.

12 SI 2004/1219.

members applicable to EU8 workers, contained in Regulation 2(9)(c) of the 2004 Regulations, was narrower even than that in Article 10 of Regulation 1612/68. Specifically, the original definition in the Worker Registration Regulations made no reference to dependents in the ascending line, instead referring only to 'worker's spouse and his children who are under 21 or dependent on him'. Thus, between 2004 and 2006, UK national law denied EU8 workers the right to be joined by their parents in contradiction to the provisions of Community law (even in their narrower, pre-Directive 2004/38 form).

None of the nine unmarried migrant workers interviewed for this research, who had partners also in the UK, had directly attempted to enforce family reunification rights.[13] In the majority of cases, both partners were employed and hence qualified as workers in their own right. In the event of one of the partners becoming unemployed, however, it seems they would be unable to claim an automatic right of residence on the basis of being a family member. This should not, formally speaking, be problematic for those who became involuntarily unemployed, as EU law provides that such workers retain a right of residence in the host state beyond the expiry of the employment relationship.[14] That said, the situation is complicated somewhat, however, by the UK law which attempts to deny those EU8 migrants who are unemployed for thirty days or more, be it voluntarily or involuntarily, a right of residence.[15] If unmarried partners were able to access the status of family member on the basis of their partnership then, should they find themselves unemployed, they would have a strengthened legal status in the UK.

More precarious still is the situation of those unmarried partners of EU8 workers who voluntarily leave a job. Unless such an individual embarks on some vocational training related to the previous employment, they relinquish the worker status.[16] Adding to the insecurity of this group are the Accession Treaties which actually sanction the withdrawal of residence rights from those CEE accession

---

[13] Although at the time of the interviews the Directive's provisions (and, hence, the national regulations) were not in force so, technically, any unmarried partners who did seek to enforce a right of residence at this time would have needed to rely on Case 59/85 *Netherlands v Reed* [1987] 2 CMLR 448. Some spouses did not work and thus did not qualify in their own right as workers. Unless they qualified in their own right under one of the other categories of EU citizen (such as student or financially independent person under Article 7, Directive 2004/38) they were dependent on their status of family member. On the impact of divorce and family separation see Ackers and Stalford 2004; Stalford 2003a; Stalford 2003b. Now see Article 13 of Directive 2004/38 on the right to remain of family members following divorce. Although none of the respondents had a third-country national spouse, such a family member would be more dependent on their derived family status as they cannot qualify in their own right under the rules on citizens' free movement rights.

[14] Previously, case law held that the worker status could continue after the employment has ceased, see Case 39/86 *Lair* [1988] ECR 3161; now, the position is made clear in article 7(3), Directive 2004/38 [2004] OJ L257/13. This is discussed further in Chapter 6.

[15] Regulation 7(2)(b), The Accession (Immigration and Worker Registration) Regulations 2004 SI 1219.

[16] Article 7(3)(d), Directive 2004/38.

migrants who become voluntarily unemployed in one of the older Member States during the transitional period.[17] If one of the members of a partnership gives up work they, therefore, lose the worker status and, unlike a married partner, would not enjoy the automatic protection that flows from qualifying as a family member. Alternatively, such individuals may be able to access some security of residence by qualifying, in their own right, under the more general category of Union citizen entitled to enjoy free movement rights.[18] Although this status is less secure than that of the economically active worker[19] it can still be extremely valuable.[20]

One of the Polish migrant workers who took part in the study had been joined by his pregnant Polish girlfriend in June 2004, a month after he arrived (and thus prior to Directive 2004/38 coming into force).[21] His unmarried partner was not working and, therefore, had an insecure residency status. She did not automatically qualify as a family member, under Community or UK law, and appeared to have no independent citizenship status as she was not a worker,[22] student[23] or, it seemed, financially independent.[24] Such partners who join a worker and who do not formally qualify as a family member may still have difficulty in demonstrating their relationship with the worker, even now Directive 2004/38 is in force, due to the convoluted rules on unmarried partners. In addition, they may have difficulty in enforcing a right to equal treatment in the host state and, consequently, may be denied access to certain benefits and services.[25]

The situation of EU2 family members in the UK differs owing to the imposition of transitional restrictions following the 2007 enlargement. Family members of EU2 nationals who gain entry to the UK by way of qualifying as 'highly skilled' or obtaining a work permit have rights of entry and residence. However, those working in a low-skilled job connected to the SBS or SAWS, or as an au pair, are denied the opportunity to have family members join them in the UK.[26] The fact that work in these sectors is of a temporary nature has

---

17 Treaty of Accession 2003 [2003] OJ L236/17; Article 24, Act of Accession [2003] OJ L236/33, Para 2, Annexes.

18 Article 18 EC; Article 7, Directive 2004/38.

19 For example it is subject to the requirements of having sufficient resources and sickness insurance, Articles 7(1)(b) and 7(1)(c) of Directive 2004/38.

20 See, for example, Case C-85/96 *Martinez Sala* [1998] ECR I-2691; Case C-274/96 *Bickel and Franz* [1998] ECR I-7637; Case C-184/99 *Grzelczyk* [2001] ECR I-6193; Case C-224/98 *D'Hoop* [2002] ECR I-6191; Case C-413/99 *Baumbast* [2002] ECR I-7091; Case C 148/02 *Garcia Avello* [2003] ECR I-11613; Dougan and Spaventa 2003; White 2005; Hailbronner 2005. Citizenship is discussed in Chapter 6.

21 Interview 004.M.

22 Now Article 7(1)(a), Directive 2004/38.

23 Now Article 7(1)(c), Directive 2004/38.

24 In that she did not satisfy the conditions of having sufficient resources and sickness insurance, Article 7(1)(b), Directive 2004/38. For the potential significance of citizenship status for unemployed EU8 nationals in the UK see Chapter 6.

25 On the basis of Article 24, Directive 2004/38.

26 Regulation 7, Accession (Immigration and Worker Authorization) Regulations 2006 SI 2006/3317.

influenced this policy, in that it is assumed family reunification is not a necessity when long-term settlement is not envisaged. It is noteworthy, however, that it is those in lower status, lower paid jobs that are expected to forgo family life during their time in the UK.[27]

The Right of Family Members to Work

The standard position in Community law is that a worker's family members, regardless of nationality, have the right to take up employment in the host Member State.[28] This is likely to be an important consideration when a family is considering a move abroad. If family members are not entitled to work in a host state to help support the family unit, the right to reunification will be rather redundant for many. During the transitional period, however, the implementing Member States have been able to derogate from this provision. Family members who resided with the worker in the host state at the date of accession were granted immediate access to the right to work. However, any family members who joined the worker after the date of accession could be prevented from working for a period of 18 months or until three years after the date of accession (whichever date was, or is in the case of the EU2, earliest).[29] The restriction on the rights of family members to access employment is somewhat peculiar given that under the previous migration regime that governed movement from the CEE to the EU15 – the Europe Agreements[30] – there was no such time delay. This situation is all the more puzzling when considered alongside the standstill clause in the Accession Treaties which specifies that the post-accession conditions should not be more restrictive than those in place prior to the signing of the Accession Treaty.[31] It is unclear why the Accession Treaties themselves have sanctioned harsher conditions than those in place prior to accession in respect of family members' right to work. Indeed, it is paradoxical to grant CEE migrant workers the right to family reunification yet to simultaneously allow Member States to restrict such family members' labour market access. Effectively, such a restriction can render the entitlement to reunification superfluous for many families who could not survive financially on the wage of the single worker. Furthermore, Directive

---

27 Chapter 4 included some discussion on whether those carrying out work as au pairs and domestic workers can qualify as 'migrant workers' under Community law. If such workers can fall within the scope of Article 39 EC, it is arguable that the restricted family reunification rights for low-skilled EU2 migrants are incompatible with Community law. If it is accepted that they have gained lawful access to the labour market, even during the transitional period, surely family members' rights under Community law should apply in full.

28 Article 23, Directive 2004/38; previously Article 11, Regulation 1612/68.

29 Para. 8, Annexes (the relevant date for family members of EU8 nationals was 1 May 2007; for EU2 family members it will be 1 January 2010).

30 Article 37(1), Europe Agreement establishing an association between the European Communities and their Member States, of the one part, and the Republic of Poland, of the other part, Final Act, [1993] OJ L348.

31 Para. 14, Annexes.

2003/86 on the right to family reunification[32] states that Member States must not exclude family members of a third-country national worker from the labour market for a period longer than 12 months. Thus, at EU-level, CEE workers' family members are initially subject to harsher conditions than third-country national migrants' family members, in relation to labour market access, during the transitional period.

In the UK, the operation of the WRS has meant that family members of EU8 nationality have from the outset been able to work in their own capacity subject to fulfilment of the same registration requirements as those applicable to the 'pioneering' worker. What is not clear, however, is whether the UK (lawfully under the Accession Treaty) would have sought to restrict the right to work of a third-country national spouse of an EU8 worker during the three years following accession. As was stated above, amongst the sample of Polish workers the vast majority of married, and also the unmarried but partnered, couples were dual-earning. Therefore each member of the partnership had established their own individual, independent worker-status.

Under the regime applicable to EU2 workers in the UK, family members are only entitled to take up employment if they obtain an independent right to do so. Thus, both EU2 and third-country national family members of Romanians and Bulgarians must first obtain a work permit if they are to take up work in the UK.[33] Between July and September 2007, 195 EU2 national family members of Romanian and Bulgarian migrant workers were granted accession worker cards relating to work permit employment (Home Office Border and Immigration Agency 2007b, 4). The case of *Commission v Luxembourg* really highlights the distinctive nature of family members' rights to work under the transitional arrangements as compared to the standard position under the free movement provisions. Here, Luxembourg was found to be in breach of EU law due a requirement that family members of EU15 migrant workers require a work permit before accessing a labour market.[34]

Emerging Patterns of EU8 Family Reunification in the UK

In order to place the preceding legal detail in a broader social context, it is helpful to make some mention of the relevant qualitative and quantitative data and of the direction of the debate on the extent of EU8 family settlement. Of the 44 Polish migrant workers interviewed for this research, 18 described themselves as single and as living in the UK without any family members or, in the case of return migrants, as having done so for the period they were in the UK. The remaining

---

[32] Directive 2003/86/EC [2003] OJ L251/12. Note that Ireland, the UK and Denmark are not bound by this Directive.

[33] The Accession (Immigration and Worker Authorization) Regulations 2006 SI 2006/3317; The Immigration (European Economic Area) Regulations 2006 SI 2006/1003.

[34] Case C-165/05 *Commission v Luxembourg* (Judgment of 27 October 2005).

26 described themselves as either married or in a serious long-term relationship (17 were married).

With regard to the actual exercise of family reunification rights, five migrant workers had experienced the initial move as a family unit (entire family migration) and three of these had young children (under ten years old) who had moved with them.[35] A further six had been joined by family members some time after making the move to the UK. Of these family followers, one of the six was joined by his fiancée but also had children from a previous marriage who lived with their mother in Poland.[36] Another of the six was joined by his pregnant girlfriend[37] but none had children who joined them in the UK subsequent to the move (instead the 'followers' were partners and spouses).

In respect of those who had not exercised family reunification rights, 15 of the 26 partnered or married respondents were currently separated from their partners or spouses and 14 of these also had children in Poland. It should be acknowledged, however, that a number of those interviewed whilst working in the UK (as opposed to the return migrants in Poland) did express an intention to have their family members join them in the future. In particular, four out of nine male drivers who took part in focus groups appeared to have very concrete plans for their family to join them in the UK.[38]

The statistical data collected from those registering on the WRS does not give any details regarding the partnering patterns of post-accession EU8 migrants, but it does state that 94 per cent of workers who registered between May 2004 and September 2007 had no dependents in the UK at the time of registration (Home Office Border and Immigration Agency 2007, 14). To an extent this may reflect the perception that many of the migrants are young and single at the time of migration (see Chapter 4). Of course, many EU8 migrants may be in a relationship with a partner also based in the UK, who is a registered worker in their own right, or subsequently meet a partner in the UK. The low number of dependents may also indicate, however, that a significant number of EU8 workers in the UK have families (partners and children) at home from whom they are separated (or, at least, this was the case at the date of registration). Such migrant workers are likely to operate a transnational family life. Alternatively, the separated family members may become 'family followers' in the UK and install themselves with the worker at some point subsequent to the initial migration.

Despite evidence in the immediate aftermath of the 2004 enlargement suggesting that family migration was not occurring at a significant rate, in 2006 and 2007 the tone of the debate altered slightly with research suggesting that family settlement in the UK was taking place more frequently as family members, who

35 Interview 007.LR, Interview 307.P, Interview 314.A (this interviewee had her young son with her in the UK but her husband had remained in Poland).

36 Interview 001.JK. This illustrates that the issues to be discussed later on relating to transnational families can still be relevant to those who have been joined by family members in the host state.

37 Interview 004.M.

38 FG 201, FG 202.

had initially remained at home, made the decision to join the worker (Robinson 2007; Pemberton and Stevens 2007; Pemberton 2007). Exercise of the right to family reunification, therefore, would appear to be increasing in relevance to EU8 migrants.

EU8 family 'followers': trailing wives? The research certainly corroborates the view that family mobility is frequently highly complex in nature, 'necessitating the temporary dislocation of family relationships as pressures to move are re-negotiated and family arrangements re-configured' (Ackers and Stalford 2004, 55). It would appear that separated or 'staged' migration is a common strategy adopted by families involved in the migration process. For example, Ackers and Stalford (2004, 146) draw attention to it in their sample of intra-EU family-movers and make the point that the temporary family separation was often as a result of the father's employment situation. Thus, in the main, it was the male partner who 'pioneered' the move and was later joined by his partner/spouse and children. This tendency is reflected clearly in the sample generated for this study. Indeed, all of those who were joined at a later date by their partners and/or children were male. The drivers mentioned above also had future plans to bring their families to the UK, thus fitting into the classification of male pioneers.[39] This would seem to bear out the stereotypical image of the 'trailing wife' that has been evident in much migration research (Bailey and Boyle 2004). Raghuram (2004, 304) uses the notion of 'tied migration' to explain reunification after one member of the family has migrated because of labour market imperatives and notes that 'just as labour migrants are assumed to be men, so too tied migrants are assumed to be women'. It is true that this image can be criticized for failing to recognize the existence of female 'pioneers' in migration flows and the contribution made by female labour migrants to households and markets (see Phizacklea 2000; Breugal 1996). However, it is also true that women continue to bear the main responsibility for domestic work and childcare within households. In this respect, their own employment is often ancillary to that of their male partner's work. Using Bailey and Boyle's (2004, 230) analysis, women are expected to make certain sacrifices and move as tied migrants as 'the family as a whole is expected to benefit from migration by maximising net household economic gain'.

One of the female respondents interviewed had joined her husband, who was working as a bus driver, in August 2004, four months after he arrived in the UK. Initially, they had planned to live transnationally for a number of years but she had found the separation difficult:

> It was very hard. I was thinking every day what is happening there? How is he doing? I felt ill all of the time. (Interview 005.S)

Her husband was able to arrange a job for her working for the same company. Thus, upon arrival the respondent became a migrant worker in her own right

39 Although clearly bus drivers as a group are disproportionately male and hence this skews the gender balance somewhat.

rather than a dependent family member. Clearly, as is apparent from the discussion above, this had important implications for her legal status.

The trailing wife, therefore, does seem to be a relevant label for some of the Polish migrant families that took part in the study. Furthermore, some of the sample clearly anticipated that their female partners would become family followers in the near future. Other research supports the view that the norm, when an international partnership requires mobility, is for the woman to move to be near the man (Ackers and Stalford 2004, 55). At the opposite end of the spectrum, some of the respondents had no plans for reunification and instead had opted to conduct a transnational family life. Significantly, one of the given reasons for doing so in a number of instances was a reluctance on the part of the male migrant worker to ask a female partner to leave her own employment in Poland. Certainly, and especially given the high incidence of de-skilling identified in Chapter 4, a number of male respondents described their partners as having secure and successful jobs in Poland which neither partner wanted to risk the loss of.[40] A consequence of this, however, is that the women who do stay at home will often effectively be single parents with the double burden of work and childcare to contend with.[41]

Reunification in the UK … but with which family and kin? One common aspect of the migration experience that came across in the empirical work was a reliance on extended family members, and sometimes friends, to help facilitate the move to the UK. Many respondents made reference to, for example, aunties, uncles and cousins who were already in the UK and, in many cases, these extended family and kinship networks helped them to settle upon arrival (Boyd 1989). New arrivals would frequently rely on these extended family members, and in some instances (family) friends, for a place to stay when they first arrived, some subsistence until they 'got on their feet' and perhaps some contacts who could arrange work. In addition to other post-accession migrants, the established Polish diaspora in the UK – at least in cities with a tradition of post-war Polish migration such as London and Glasgow – also provided a forum within which recent arrivals could receive valuable assistance. Polish centres and social groups were particularly significant in this respect.

These extended family members and diaspora communities, although not recognized by the EU model of family reunification, nevertheless fulfil a vital integrative function for migrants. For example:

> My uncle was here before and he was working here. Then there was a time when he said 'in a few weeks I'm leaving so if you want to come now I'll give you help and then leave', so that's why I decided to come when I did. He helped me a lot when I first arrived. (Interview 012.GP)

---

40 Interviews 002.PZ, 010.JF and 302.P.

41 Given the significant lack of available childcare facilities in Poland it appears that this may be quite a burden to cope with. In many instances it seems that it will be impossible for lone women with children to continue to work (unless there is informal childcare provided by family members). See Heinen and Wator 2006.

This was particularly true of the younger migrants (aged 20–29) who moved to the UK alone. Although these migrants are not traditional family followers, in the sense that they were not moving to be with immediate family members in a manner envisaged by the free movement provisions, they did move to join some wider kin who had a beneficial impact on their migration experience and general wellbeing. Therefore, although it would not seem that EU8 migrants have made extensive use of their family reunification rights as of yet, this is not a reflection of the importance they place on family life. While some workers move immediately with their family, or are joined by them soon after, many are young and do not (yet) have their own immediate family. Alternatively, some workers plan to stay in the UK for only a temporary period of time and make a positive decision to sustain a transnational family life as reunification or entire family migration is simply not a practical option. As was noted above, other families decide to live separately 'for the time-being' whilst the worker tries to establish him or herself in the UK and, if necessary, arrange for suitable family housing.

The premise upon which Community law initially extended rights to family members[42] was to encourage workers, as factors of production, to exercise their economic right to free movement (Lundsröm 1996; Ackers and Stalford 2004; Ackers 2004; Stalford 2000a). The ECJ has consistently extended benefits to the immediate family members of workers on the basis that such assistance has an indirect benefit for the worker him or herself; the Court has asserted that such an approach was necessary in order to 'facilitate the migrant workers' migration to and integration in the host Member State' (Stalford 2000a).[43] Importantly, in the absence of such immediate family members, it would appear that the majority of workers in the sample gained valuable assistance from other extended kin. Thus it would seem that such parties, although not recognized in the formal legal provisions, can also play an essential role in facilitating the mobility of the worker. From this perspective, the reality of kinship ties for many EU8 migrants, which relies on wider kinship networks, is not accommodated by the family reunification model in the free movement provisions.

Sustaining the Family Unit in the UK: Engagement with Welfare Provision

The above discussion clarified which family members are entitled to exercise the right to reunification and speculated on its relevance to those EU8 migrant workers in the UK. This section moves on to explore the welfare rights accessible to those workers who are joined by their (qualifying) family members and, in doing so, examines some of the methods of sustaining the family in the host state. Again, the extent to which the legal provisions are accessed by, or impact upon, post-accession migrants in the UK is considered.

42 More detail on the nature of the social rights granted to family members is provided below.

43 See, for example, Case 32/75 *Cristini* [1975] ECR 1085; Case 63/76 *Inzirillo* [1976] ECR 2057; Case 207/78 *Even* [1979] ECR 2019.

Workers and Family Members' Social Entitlement

Once a family unit is established, or (re)unified, in a host state an issue that may become important, as a means of facilitating family life, is the ability of the family members to access certain social benefits. At Community level one of the most useful provisions has been Article 7(2) of Regulation 1612/68 which extends to the worker and their accompanying family the right to access the same 'social and tax advantages' which are available to nationals. The Court of Justice has given the notion of social advantages an extremely wide remit and, as a result, it has come to be understood as referring to almost any form of social welfare available to the state's own nationals. In the early case of *Even*, for example, the ECJ defined social advantages to mean any benefits:

> … which, whether or not linked to a contract of employment, are generally granted to national workers primarily because of their objective status as workers or by virtue of the mere fact of their residence in the national territory and the extension of which to workers who are not nationals of other Member States therefore seems suitable to facilitate their mobility within the Community.[44]

Workers have relied on Article 7(2) to gain access to numerous benefits while working in other Member States, and the ability to do so has clearly enabled them to enjoy a 'consolidated economic and social status' (Stalford 2005, 366) which, in turn, benefits their families as well as themselves.[45] In addition to benefits for the worker, it was the use of this functional 'facilitating mobility' reasoning which enabled the Court also to extend access to various social benefits to the family members of workers; the Court's logic has been that by granting family members social advantages the worker indirectly reaps a benefit, thus becoming more integrated into the host society.[46] The rationale can be seen in the early case of *Inzirillo.*[47] Here, the ECJ held that the son of an Italian migrant worker in France was entitled to claim disability benefit from the French authorities:

---

44 Case 207/78 *Ministère Public v Even* [1979] ECR 2019, para. 22.

45 On 'social advantages' see Ellis 2003. In terms of case law see, *inter alia*, Cases 65/81 *Reina* [1982] ECR 33 (subsidized childbirth loans); C-57/96 *Meints* [1997] ECR I-6689 (payment to agricultural workers); C-35/97 *Commission v France* [1998] ECR I-5325 (supplementary retirement pension points); 137/84 *Criminal proceedings against Mutsch* [1985] ECR 2681 (criminal proceedings in defendant's own language); C-237/94 *O'Flynn v Adjudication Officer* [1996] ECR I-2617 (social security payments to help cover the cost of funeral expenses).

46 See, for example, Cases 32/75 *Fiorini v SNCF* [1975] ECR 1085 (family discount rail card); C-278/94 *Commission v Belgium* [1996] ECR I-4307 (tideover benefits); C-185/96 *Commission v Greece* [1998] I-6601 (attribution of large family status). This later line of case law is in contrast to the early decision in Case 76/72 *Michel S* [1973] ECR 457, where it was held that social advantages were available to workers only.

47 Case 63/76 *Inzirillo* [1976] ECR 2057.

> If that were not the case, a worker, anxious to ensure for his child the lasting enjoyment of the allowances necessitated by his condition as a handicapped person, would be induced not to remain in the host state where he has established himself and has found his employment, which would run counter to the object sought to be attained by the principle of freedom of movement for workers. (Para. 17)

The corollary of the facilitating mobility test, however, is that it has framed family members' rights within the context of (financial) dependency upon the migrant worker such that entitlement has become parasitic in nature (Ackers and Dwyer 2002, 47):[48]

> The status of family members and workers differs in a fundamental sense, in that the former only have derived entitlement. Families thus gain their wider social entitlement indirectly through the economic contribution of the worker.

The derivative nature of the rights of family members has been criticized on the basis that it places the family in a potentially vulnerable position, essentially at the mercy of the worker's continuing economic status and willingness to keep the family unit together and not divorce.[49] The Court, through the developing case law on citizenship, had gone some way to fortifying the status of family members.[50] Directive 2004/38 has now enshrined many of the principles established by the Court[51] and it would seem that family members now occupy a stronger position. Most notably, family members of Union citizen migrants are explicitly entitled to access the equal treatment principle in Article 24(1) of Directive 2004/38. Therefore, family members do now enjoy an individual right not to be discriminated against in the host Member State rather than simply a parasitic one.

Article 7(2) of Regulation 1612/68 remains in force alongside Directive 2004/38.[52] At this stage it is not entirely clear what sort of relationship the social

---

48 See, *inter alia,* Case 316/85 *Lebon* [1987] ECR 2811. Of course, the case law is pre-Directive 2004/38.

49 For more information and critique of derivative family rights see Ackers and Dwyer 2002; Ackers and Stalford 1999, 987; Ackers 2004; Stalford, 2000a.

50 For example Case C-413/99 *Baumbast and R* [2002] ECR I-7091 where the Court held that the former spouse of a Community migrant worker (who was a third-country national) could continue to reside in the host society on the basis of her status as 'primary carer' of the migrant worker's child who was continuing to access educational rights in the host Member State (see Reich 2003). Note also the Court's consistent reliance on Article 8 of the ECHR to stress the fundamental principle of family life, see Case C-109/01 *Akrich* [2003] ECR I-9607.

51 For example Article 13, Directive 2004/38 deals with retention of the right of residence by family members in the event of divorce, annulment or termination of registered partnership

52 Although Directive 2004/38 repeals a lot of the secondary legislation in the area (including the three residency Directives: Directive 90/365 [1990] OJ L180/28; Directive 93/96 [1993] OJ L317/59; Directive 90/364 [1990] OJ L180/26) it only repeals Article 10 and 11, Regulation 1612/68 (which governed family rights to join the worker and access employment).

advantages provision, which applies only to workers and their families, will have with the wider equal treatment provision in Article 24(1) of the 2004 Directive which applies to all EU migrant citizens. Article 24(2), however, provides that the principle in Article 24(1) does not apply as regards entitlement to social assistance for the first three months of residence. This would suggest, then, that initially the worker must gain entitlement solely from Article 7(2) which, in turn, means that the family members cannot gain any individual rights and must instead rely on their derived entitlement during this period. In this respect, the parasitic nature of family rights has not been completely eradicated.[53]

Post-accession migrants working lawfully in the UK, and their families, are entitled to rely on these Community law rights to facilitate the enjoyment of their family life in the UK. Of course, as the 'free movement of persons' provisions are based firmly on an ethic of non-discrimination' migrants are effectively entitled to 'national treatment' and thus can access the same family rights as nationals (Stalford 2005, 366).[54] In the UK, however, the early evidence suggested that only a limited number of post-accession EU8 migrants (and their families) had relied on their equal treatment rights to gain access to social benefits. The Accession Monitoring report (Home Office Border and Immigration Agency 2007, 4) has concluded that:

> The numbers applying for tax-funded income-related benefits and housing support remain low. For example, only 2,341 applications for Income Support and Jobseeker's Allowance were processed in quarter 3 of 2007, of which 582 were allowed to proceed for further consideration.[55]

Of course, jobseekers' allowance is an 'out of work' benefit and so does not give an indication of how many of those in work have sought access to certain social benefits. The report does, however, also point out that in 2006, a year which

---

[53] Of course, family members that are also Member State nationals may be able to rely on residence and/or equal treatment rights flowing from their own independent citizenship status, see Chapter 6.

[54] The prohibition against nationality discrimination is enshrined in Article 12 EC and is a central feature of the free movement regime, as is demonstrated by its importance to the operation of the free movement of workers (Article 39 EC), establishment (Article 43 EC) and services (Article 49 EC). Under the Treaty of the Functioning of the European Union, should the Treaty of Lisbon enter into force, non-discrimination would be fused together with citizenship under a new part 2 entitled 'Citizenship and Non-discrimination'. This would include the renumbered provisions on citizenship (Articles 20 26 TFEU) and the equal treatment on grounds of nationality that was previously enshrined in Article 12 EC (Article 18 TFEU). This is according to the table of equivalence annexed to the Treaty of Lisbon ([2007] OJ C306/01).

[55] As was noted in Chapter 3, the UK introduced an additional 'legally resident' condition to the already established habitual residence requirement for benefit entitlement in the light of accession. The effect of this is to exclude out of work EU8 migrants from benefit access, thus accounting for the low number of applications for JSA allowed to proceed.

saw 227,865 WRS registrations, there were only 32,803 EU8 claimants of child benefit and 17,889 EU8 claimants of tax credits (ibid., 25–7). Given the detail of the UK regime, claimants of such benefits would need to be in work (and registered on the WRS) to qualify. To put these figures further into context, it is interesting to note that at the end of 2007 there was a total of 7.4 million claimants of child benefit in the UK (HM Revenue and Customs 2007, 1); furthermore, as of 2 December 2006 there were 5.6 million families receiving tax credits (HM Revenue and Customs 2006, 7).

Certainly, the overwhelming sentiment from the respondents who took part in the qualitative study was that claiming benefits had not been a priority at the time the decision to migrate was made:

> No I never thought about it [social benefits] at all, I don't really like the idea of getting them to be honest. (Interview 001.JK)

> I'm not interested in benefits actually. I don't think this is a really nice thing to be interested in. When I work 12 months in England I think Polish people can have the same as other European Union citizens but I don't think I'll need them for anything. (Interview 002.PZ)

None of the respondents had relied on the right to equal treatment to access social benefits at the time of interview. However, this tendency needs to be understood in the context of the UK's position on social welfare entitlement. As emphasized elsewhere in this book, the UK has curtailed the ability of post-accession EU8 migrants to rely on welfare when seeking work either as a new arrival or former worker (see Chapter 6). The ability of EU8 migrants to access social benefits, or 'social advantages', whilst in work has not been tampered with (providing they comply with the WRS requirement of registration), but it does seem that the message espoused by the UK government has impacted, particularly early on, upon EU8 migrants' perception of their entitlement in the UK. Clearly there are other contributing factors to the apparent low take-up of social benefits; for example temporary moves, which appear to be popular amongst EU8 nationals do not usually necessitate reliance on welfare. It does seem, however, that the campaign funded by the UK government entitled 'Not All Roads Lead to Britain' may have obscured some of the issues relating to social welfare entitlement so as to give the impression that EU8 migrants had no rights to access benefits in the UK regardless of employment status. The campaign, implemented in the accession states by the IOM prior to enlargement, had the objective of informing EU8 nationals of the WRS. The IOM representative interviewed in this study who had helped to implement the campaign confirmed the 'tone' of it:

> The message which came across was that only if you can support yourself can you go to the UK and there will be no access to benefits unless you can support yourself. That is funny because actually if you can support yourself then you don't need benefits. The intention of the campaign was to prevent social tourism or to stop people going to the UK with no work and accessing benefits. (Interview 102.INFO)

Many of the migrant respondents had picked up on this tone and were aware of the UK's attempt to restrict their benefit entitlements. However, the majority of them were also under the mistaken impression that the prohibition on accessing benefits applied even when they were in work:

> Here we are supposed to be equal with English workers but we can't get any social benefits. (Interview 004.M)

> To Polish people and people from the new countries they just say no they don't even ask why they need it [social benefit] even if you are working really hard they still say no. (Interview 012.GP)

Given the added financial security that the availability of benefits can grant to a family unit in a host state, it is possible that a widespread perception of benefit unavailability, circulated in the EU8 states by methods such as the 'Not All Roads Lead to Britain' campaign, had the effect of discouraging family members from moving with a worker to the UK. Access to benefits may have been particularly conducive to the facilitation of family life in the aftermath of enlargement considering the low-paid and insecure nature of many of the sectors in which EU8 migrants are concentrated.

One of the Polish respondents in the UK was herself working in a Human Resources department for a company that had hired Polish workers through an organized migration schemes. She recognized the concern of the workers to ensure their families access to benefits and services, such as health care, in the UK. She was also, despite occupying a position which required her to advise Polish migrants about their status, under a false impression about the extent of the UK's welfare restrictions:

> When Polish people think about settling here and want to bring their family over they think much more about children and about support they can have and health centres and things like that. They can go to the family doctor but here the father of the family or the mother, whoever is the worker, if he or she is sick and can't work they will not get any money from the government for the first (two or three) years so this is very difficult … These are the main questions they ask me all the time. (Interview 013.EM)

It was quite common in the interviews for respondents to link the notion of family reunification in the UK with the need to seek advice about welfare entitlement, reinforcing the potential importance of benefits to the facilitation of family life after migration:

> I haven't really thought about benefits before because I didn't think about staying here that long but now, because my boyfriend is planning to stay here and we are together, we will have to think about it, especially if we start a family. Maybe I would if I was entitled, I mean I have registered but I'm not really sure how it works to be honest. Probably I would have to get some advice. (Interview 019.KS)

I know nothing about benefits or help we can get in the future but my girlfriend wants to find out about this for when the baby comes. (Interview 004.M)

One married couple had spent time in Edinburgh in the months following Poland's accession to the EU (June 2004–January 2005) with their one-year-old son.[56] The husband worked as a kitchen porter and later a waiter but his wife did not take up paid employment in the UK as she cared for the baby. Although the family would have been entitled to claim work-related benefits, they were not aware of ancillary benefits such as Child Tax Credit until later on when they had decided to return to Poland. The woman explained the impact of this:

We went to an office, like a social or council office or something like that, and we were asking about everything. We thought he was very nice and he told us things but he didn't tell us about tax credits. This is a big regret for us because if we'd had tax credits we could have sent our son to a nursery and I could have gone to work, but I had to stay at home with him. It was the end of our visit when we found out about it. (Interview 307.O)

Therefore, had they been aware of the right to equal treatment as regards wider social advantages this would have enabled the woman to exercise her own right to work in the UK; this, in turn, would have added to the financial security of the family unit and elevated her own status to the more secure and individuated one of worker. Overall, it seems that a lack of accessible information, combined with administrative obstacles, has colluded to restrict EU8 migrant workers' access to such welfare entitlement despite those in work being *formally* entitled to claim.

It was mentioned above that there is some evidence that family settlement is increasing amongst EU8 migrants as family members move in order to join the initial 'pioneer' (Pemberton and Stevens 2007). In addition, there have been reports of a so-called 'migrant baby boom' in the British media following the release of statistics which demonstrate that the number of babies born to foreign parents has increased in recent years. CEE migrants have been especially singled out in the reports (Easton 2008). The data released by the Office for National Statistics does show that in 2006 the number of babies born to parents with nationality of one of the EU25 Member States (excluding the UK) was 25,999. In 1996, the figure was significantly lower at 11,527 (ONS 2007).[57] It may well be that those EU8 migrants who moved to the UK around the time of accession have now started to partner and parent; in turn, it is reasonable to suggest that as family life becomes more important so too will the need for support by way of gaining access to various benefits.

Before moving on to examine the migrants' engagement with wider welfare services, attention should be drawn briefly to another mechanism of EU law that can be utilized by EU8 migrants to access financial benefits and potentially

[56] They were interviewed in Krakow in July 2005.

[57] There is no further breakdown between individual countries.

to facilitate family life. Regulation 1408/71[58] attempts to make benefits portable throughout the Member States and, therefore, enables the worker and his or her family members[59] to export certain benefits from their home state on the basis that the right to receive a benefit attaches to the individuals regardless of national boundaries.[60] Examples of benefits covered by the scheme include *inter alia* sickness and maternity benefits,[61] invalidity benefits,[62] old-age benefits,[63] unemployment benefits[64] and family benefits.[65] The ability of EU migrants to export benefits can clearly be a very valuable tool.[66] However, as the legislation is based on the principle of coordination rather than harmonization of national systems there may be significant inequalities in the monetary value of certain benefits at the national level (Ackers and Dwyer 2002, 125). This can mean that transported benefits hold less value in comparison to the host state's national benefit standards than they would if utilized in the state of origin.[67] This would seem to be the case for the majority of CEE migrants who choose to export, given the lower cost of living in CEE when compared to the UK. In any event, none of the respondents that took part in the research had utilized the exportability provisions. Indeed, there was very little awareness of this legal framework amongst the sample.

One guise under which the coordination of social security did come up in the qualitative empirical work, however, was in relation to the aggregation of pension rights which some workers had concerns about. Pensions are clearly of great significance in later life when employment ceases and may fulfil a vital role in sustaining family life post-retirement. Regulation 1408/71, in addition to

---

58 Last consolidated version published [1997] OJ L28/1. Note that a new regulation has been adopted which overhauls the coordination system somewhat: Regulation 883/2004 [2004] OJ L200/1. This will enter into force when a new implementing regulation is finalized. See Pennings 2001; 2005.

59 The ECJ confirmed that family members can rely on Regulation 1408/71 in Case C-308/93 *Cabanis-Issarte* [1996] ECR I-2097. Note, however, that family members is defined by reference to national rather than Community law (Article 1(f)).

60 Article 42 EC, which urges the Community to facilitate free movement by securing for migrant workers and their dependents 'aggregation, for the purpose of acquiring and retaining the right to benefit and of calculating the amount of benefit of all periods taken into account under the laws of the several countries', provides the legal basis for this legislation (This will be re-housed in Article 48 TFEU if the Treaty of Lisbon enters into force).

61 Article 4(1)(a).

62 Article 4(1)(b).

63 Article 4(1)(c).

64 Article 4(1)(g). The ability to export unemployment benefit is limited to a three month period (Article 69(1)). See Wikeley 1988.

65 Article 4(1)(h).

66 For more information on the coordination of social security see Sakslin 2000; Moore 2002.

67 Alternatively, in some instances the transported benefits can have a very high value in the host state, see Ackers and Dwyer's (2002) work on retirement migration and the exportability of pensions.

allowing migrants to export benefits already accrued, enables the aggregation of contributions made to accrue certain benefit rights. Pensions are covered by the coordination regime as 'old-age benefits' to the effect that when national insurance contributions (or equivalent) are paid in a Member State they are personal to the individual concerned and can, thus, be aggregated alongside periods of contribution made in other Member States and later, if necessary, exported (Articles 44–46). Problematically, occupational or supplementary pension schemes are excluded from the coordination regime which applies only to social security benefits provided by legislation. Efforts have been made, however, to improve the portability of supplementary pensions. A Directive aimed at easing the portability of supplementary pensions was passed in 1998.[68] Currently, there is a proposal for a revised Directive, which aims to improve the system set out in Directive 98/49, on the table (European Commission 2005a; Ferrera 2005).

Access to Welfare 'Services': Education, Childcare and Housing

It is not only access to certain fiscal benefits in the host state that can help to facilitate and sustain family life but also access to wider social and welfare services. As Stalford (2005, 366) acknowledges:

> Access to benefits such as appropriate schooling, child raising allowances, public funding for day care and crèche facilities, concessionary 'family' rates for public services such as transport, and favourable healthcare packages, all enhance the 'value' of the employment in a particular host state and, arguably, attract migrants to specific regions within that host state.

This chapter has already emphasized the Community law principle of 'national treatment' upon which migrant workers' access to forms of social entitlement are based. This is true also of their ability to access the various welfare services mentioned in the extract above, in part this is due to the wide application of 'social advantages', but there are also more specific provisions of secondary Community legislation which deal with, for example, the right of children of migrant workers to access education in the host state under the same conditions as nationals[69] and workers' right to equal treatment as regards matters of housing.[70] The remainder of this section speculates, largely on the basis of the empirical work, on post-accession migrants' engagement with these latter two aspects of welfare in the UK.

Education and childcare With regard to children's access to schools, Article 12 of Regulation 1612/68 provides that children of a migrant worker 'who is or has

[68] Directive 98/49 [1998] OJ L209/46.

[69] Article 12, Regulation 1612/68.

[70] Article 9, Regulation 1612/68.

been employed'[71] in the Member State are entitled to be admitted to 'general educational apprenticeship and vocational training courses' under the same conditions as nationals. The scope of the form of educational provision covered is broad:

> Article 12 covers all types and levels of education from pre-school through compulsory courses to vocational training, higher education and special needs provision. (Ackers and Stalford 2004, 205)

Further, due to the approach of the ECJ, Article 12 has not only been instrumental in according children *access* to various educational establishments but has also been utilized to extend the 'ethic of equal opportunity' to cover various forms of maintenance grant and public assistance.[72] In *Casagrande*, for example, the Court determined that 'conditions' included 'general measures intended to facilitate educational attendance'.[73]

Only one of the respondents who took part in the study had a child of school age with her in the UK (the majority were younger). This respondent had moved to London with her six-year-old son, where she worked as a cleaner in a private household, in August 2004. Her husband had remained in Poland. They remained in the UK only until December 2004 due to the difficulties they had experienced when the family unit was separated, but from September to December the child did attend an English primary school. The respondent explained that her son had found the experience to be quite traumatic and that she had been disappointed with the teacher's attitude towards him. Her overall opinion was that her son had needed greater assistance in settling in and, in particular, that his language needs had been neglected. This perception of events had played quite a prominent role in the decision to return to Poland.[74] This would support the view that:

> Problems of integration and progression at school are inextricably linked to the exercise of free movement and … lack of provision to aid this process potentially impedes mobility. (Stalford 2000c, 248)

---

71 In Cases 389 and 390/87 *Echternach and Moritz* [198] ECR 723 (the child of migrant worker was able to continue his education in the host state following his parent's return to their country of origin).

72 On the educational rights of children of migrant workers see Stalford 2000c, 243. This is also an area that the developing law on citizenship has impacted on, for exmple Case C-413/99 *Baumbast and R* [2002] ECR I-7091 and Case C-209/03 *Bidar* [2005] ECR I-2119.

73 Case 9/74 *Casagrande* [1974] ECR 773, here the son of deceased migrant worker was able to rely on Article 12 to claim a means-tested maintenance grant to continue studying after compulsory education ceased.

74 Interview 314.A. In no way is this experience intended to be representative of the schooling experience of Polish or EU8 nationals in general. It is included solely to illustrate the particular experience of this family.

The provisions of Directive 77/486 could have potentially been useful in these circumstances.[75] This Directive supplements Article 12 of Regulation 1612/68 and requires that Member States encourage the integration of children of migrant workers into the education system. In particular, Article 2 specifies that Member States should ensure that free language tuition is available (in both the host country language and, interestingly, in the child's mother tongue language).[76]

Many of the respondents who did not yet have children suggested that they had begun to think about the possibility of having children in the UK. This perhaps supports the point made above about the apparent increasing number of migrants having children in the UK. However, the majority of opinion, represented by the following extract, suggests that concerns surrounding sending children to a 'foreign' education system may be a hindrance to the exercise of, or continuing exercise of, mobility rights:[77]

> The thing is that apparently the level of education is higher in Poland than here. This is what I have heard from a few people. Schools in Poland cover much more material in the first years of studying. Even in primary school they have more knowledge … it really makes me a bit worried about having children here and I think I would have to go back to Poland. (Interview 017.M)

Two families did have firm plans to educate their children in British schools and were happy to do so,[78] however, the majority of opinion expressed concerns regarding schooling in the UK. A contrast can be drawn with Ackers and Stalford's (2004) findings in relation to EU15 workers. Amongst their sample of EU15 migrants there was a greater propensity to migrate with children and install them in a foreign school. There was also evidence that the British education system was held in high regard. This is likely to be at least partially attributable to cultural differences between the EU8 and EU15. Indeed, more recent research by Ackers and Stalford (2007), which examines migration from the CEE region, confirms the finding that frequently Polish migrants value highly their national education system at primary and secondary level, often believing it to be more rigorous and disciplined.[79]

These findings at the individual level, which suggest that education in the UK is not much utilized or valued by CEE migrants, can be juxtaposed against broader concerns about the impact of recent migration on schools. Local authorities in

---

75 Directive 77/486 on the education of the children of migrant workers [1977] OJ L199/139.

76 Implementation of this Directive has been disappointing across the EU, see Stalford 2000c.

77 For further information on how children's education can be a barrier to mobility, including the problems of enforcing recognition of academic qualifications, see Stalford 2000c.

78 Interviews 004.M (who were expecting their first child) and 007.LR (who had a child under one).

79 By contrast, a western education at *undergraduate* level is perceived to carry reputational capital and is thus valued more highly.

some regions of the UK have reported increased pressure being placed on schools as a consequence of the enrolment of EU8 children (Pemberton and Stevens, 2007; Institute of Community Cohesion 2007). Research by Stenning et al. (2006) also found that schools had felt pressure to act as advice centres due to a lack of other available support services. It does seem, though, that the pressures felt have been a result of migrants settling in areas of the UK that have not previously experienced high levels of in-migration. In other words, it is not only a matter of the number of migrants but also the ability of localities to accommodate their needs. From this perspective, it is not necessarily the case that vast numbers of EU8 migrant children have enrolled in schools as even a small number could pose difficulties (in terms of language support, for example) for schools; especially those with little experience of teaching children whose first language is not English.

Access to childcare, as opposed to formal education, is often also of paramount concern to migrant families. This is particularly true of dual-earner couples when a woman's continuing participation in the labour market, post childbirth, is often dependent on the availability and affordability of childcare facilities (Stalford 2005, 368). Reference has already been made above to the married couple who only became aware of the availability of child tax credit immediately prior to their departure from the UK. It will be recalled that the woman here specifically stated that, had they been able to access benefits, the extra financial support would have been used to pay for childcare so that both parents could work. Childcare in the UK, however, is often extremely expensive and is likely to be beyond the means of many of the recently arrived EU8 migrants given that 72 per cent of the workers who registered on the WRS between October 2006 and September 2007 earned only £4.50-£5.99 per hour (Home Office Border and Immigration Agency 2007, 16). Recent figures show that, the average weekly cost of a private nursery place for a child under two is £159 and in London this figure rises to £200.[80]

Access to formal public childcare provision is available to workers on the basis of the equal treatment principle[81] so, again, availability differs across the Member States. As Stalford (2005, 307) points out:

> While migrants enjoy equality of access to state-provided childcare under the free movement provisions, the extent to which they can actually take advantage of formal childcare depends first and foremost on the actual existence of a reliable system of public childcare.

Research suggests that pre-school childcare provision in the UK is limited.[82] The UK only offers minimum provision to the under three age group and, despite

---

80 Figures taken from the Daycare Trusts 2008 Childcare Costs Survey, available online at <http://www.daycaretrust.org.uk/mod/fileman/files/Cost_survey2008.pdf> (last accessed 6 February 2008).

81 Article 7(2), Regulation 1612/68.

82 According to Papadopoulos (1998) the UK only provided formal childcare for 2 to 3 per cent of children under three; for three- to six-year-olds the figure was 60 per cent in 1998, cited in Ackers and Stalford 2004, 160. More recent statistics indicate this trend is continuing, see Perrons et al. 2005, 51.

the figure being higher in relation to three- to six-year-olds, in comparison to the other EU15 Member States this provision is also poor. This low-level of availability coupled with the common necessity of early registration and long waiting lists for childcare facilities, such as nurseries, suggests that EU8 migrants will not be able to access public childcare in any significant numbers.

One form of childcare often unavailable to migrant families on a day to day basis is the informal kind provided by other family and friends (Drew et al. 1998; Finch and Mason 1993). The following extract is taken from an interview with two return migrants (a couple) who confirmed that, when in the UK, they had missed the support provided in Poland by the maternal grandparents:

> A big problem in Scotland is that there is no grandmother ... It is much easier to have grandmother! In Poland grandmother is a very important institution. Right now we are both working because my parents look after our son. (Interview 307.O)

This couple went so far as to say that, although they would like to return to Scotland and had discussed the possibility extensively, the lack of this informal support was the main disincentive to a return. This corroborates research which has found that migrants, and migrant women in particular, miss the emotional and practical support provided by family networks in the state of origin (Stalford 2005, 368–70). In some instances grandparents themselves may move to the host state, ironically as the supposed 'dependent' family members,[83] with the family unit in an effort to help facilitate family life. Ackers and Dwyer (2002, 145), in their research on retirement migration, found that:

> When parents moved to support their children it usually meant helping them to look after grandchildren and run the home in order to enable their children (especially daughters) to work and develop their careers.

This was not a strategy that any of the respondents in the study had yet utilized in a complete sense. However, there were a few instances of parents spending a period of time in the UK to help out during a particularly busy time such as the initial migration or a move to new accommodation.[84] Further, the respondent who had been joined by his pregnant girlfriend explained how they had plans for her mother to stay with them for a month following the birth of the child.[85] Given the availability of discounted air travel this type of visit is increasingly a viable option for migrant families seeking to rely on informal care from kin, even though such arrangements are temporary in nature and not a substitute for sustained childcare provision (Stalford 2005, 369). CEE migrants in the UK, therefore, are unlikely to access easily either (affordable) formal or informal childcare. This could restrict the ability of the family to receive a dual-income as

---

83 Article 2(2)(d), Directive 2004/38.

84 Stalford (2005, 369) recognizes similar occurrences in a sample of migrant scientists.

85 Interview 004.M.

one parent – most likely the mother – will be required to assume the bulk of the caring responsibilities, thereby limiting her own employment prospects and her ability to re-enter the labour market. This reduction in the economic status of the family is likely to increase their financial insecurity which, in turn, may have consequences for the enjoyment of family life in the UK.

Housing 'National treatment' is, again, the key under Community law when it comes to accessing housing in a host Member State. Equal treatment for migrant workers as regards all the rights and benefits accorded to national workers in matters of housing, including ownership and the right to be placed on housing waiting lists, is enshrined in Article 9 of Regulation 1612/68. The Court has recognized the importance of equal treatment in this area by holding that access to housing 'is the corollary of freedom of movement for workers'.[86]

The UK's post-accession regime towards EU8 migrants (set out in Chapter 3) attempts to place restrictions on the ability of the migrants to obtain various social housing benefits. These restrictions follow a pattern consistent with those that apply to other social benefits, such as jobseekers' allowance, in that they add an additional 'legal residence' requirement to the standard habitual residence test used to determine access to social housing and homelessness assistance.[87] This additional residence requirement serves to exclude EU8 new arrival work seekers, and workers who cease employment during the first year of employment, from entitlement to the benefits by virtue of the fact that EU8 migrants have no right to reside under UK law unless they are in work.[88] This chapter, however, is primarily concerned with those EU8 migrants that are in work and registered on the scheme in order to explore some methods of sustaining and facilitating family life in the UK: engagement with forms of welfare provision and services can be one such method. Registered EU8 workers, and indeed EU2 nationals who find lawful employment by obtaining a work permit, are entitled to full equal treatment in matters of housing and the type of housing available can have consequences for one's ability to exercise family reunification rights.

The non-discrimination principle applies to those migrant workers wishing to buy a property in the UK, to those wishing to rent from a private landlord, and

---

86 Case 305/87 *Commission v Hellenic Republic* [1989] ECR 1461, para. 18.

87 The Allocation of Housing and Homelessness (Amendment) England Regulations 2004 SI 2004/1235 amended the description of persons who are to be treated as persons from abroad.. This in turn excludes out of work EU8 nationals from entitlement to homelessness assistance under the Housing Act 1996, C.52. See Chapter 3. It is these provisions which precluded Mr Putans from accessing homelessness assistance when illness prevented him from working (*Putans v Tower Hamlets BC* [2006] EWHC 1634 (Ch)). The 2004 Regulations have since been revoked by the Allocation of Housing and Homelessness (Eligibility) (England) Restrictions 2006 SI 2006/1294 but the changes to the eligibility test are permanently applicable.

88 EU8 workers who cease to work during first year of employment are only lawfully resident for the remainder of month in which they worked, Regulation 5(4)(b), Accession (Immigration and Worker Registration) Regulations 2004 SI 2004/121.

to those who wish to access social (council) housing.[89] Amongst the respondents who took part in the study, the majority were renting from a private landlord or were living in some form of employer-arranged housing. The overwhelming feeling was that of dissatisfaction with their dwellings and it was very common for groups to live together, even outside the scope of employer-arranged accommodation, to enable them to meet the cost of rent:

> I lived in big house with ten other people. It is very expensive in London for people who first arrive but when you live with lots of people it is better and cheaper. (Interview 302.P)

> Now there are two people staying with me but before it was me and five more. So in total it was six people with one bedroom. (Interview 009.BS)

Housing is one area that particularly demonstrates the limitations of the non-discrimination principle as the basis for the exercise of mobility rights. In itself the right to buy property is intact but, due to the notoriously high house prices in the UK,[90] it appears that many of the predominantly low-paid, post-accession EU8 migrants have not been able to access it in practical terms. The woman quoted in the following extract moved to live with her husband. At first they considered buying a house but later realized it was not something they could afford. At the time of the interview they were living in employer-arranged accommodation with other workers:

> At first we looked for a small house on our own but it was too expensive so we ended up living with other workers. We might look again but on our wages I just don't think it will be possible. (Interview 005.S)

Similarly, social housing, which is often more affordable than renting in the private sector, is in great demand and is very difficult to access due to long waiting lists (known as housing registers). Local authorities frequently operate points systems, whereby applicants for housing accrue points in accordance with the severity of their housing needs and the length of time they have been registered for housing with the council (Holmans et al. 2005). Clearly, this is an obstacle for post-accession migrants as it is unlikely that quite recent arrivals would rank highly on a points system which depends, to a large extent, on time spent registered. The

---

89 In Case 63/96 *Commission v Italy* [1988] ECR 29 discriminatory restrictions on access to social housing were held to be unlawful, and in Case C-302/97 *Klaus Konle v Republik Osterreich* [1999] ECR I-3099 the ECJ the right to equal treatment in relation to administrative procedures associated with the acquisition and lease of housing.

90 The average house price in the UK is £230,474, in London this figure rises to £377,807. These figures are cited in an online BBC news report, 'UK House Prices' and are taken from 2007 statistics produced by the Land Registry of England and Wales, Registers of Scotland Executive Agency and University of Ulster in partnership with Bank of Ireland <http://news.bbc.co.uk/1/shared/spl/hi/in_depth/uk_house_prices/html/houses.stm> (last accessed 7 February 2008).

Accession Monitoring report (Home Office et al. 2005a, 31) states that between May 2004 and March 2005 there were only 43 Local Authority lettings to people of EU8 nationality and only 13 of these had arrived in the UK after May 2004. Clearly, this data relates only to the time period immediately following the 2004 enlargement. Robinson (2007, 107) has researched further the extent to which EU8 migrants have been able to gain access to social housing by analysing data relating to Local Authority and Housing Association lettings for the period 2006/7. Robinson found that EU8 migrants represented only 0.8 per cent of all new social housing tenants (1,544 out of a total of 191, 165). Furthermore:

> Despite allegations of preferential treatment in the allocation process, A8 nationals are moving into less popular property types. Only one-third (35.5 per cent) of A8 nationals moved into a house or bungalow, while 60 per cent moved into a flat or maisonette. (Ibid., 108)

Two of the respondents interviewed mentioned that social housing was something they would consider applying for in the future. Both associated their need for more suitable housing with their family situation: one was expecting a child and another had a young baby. The following respondent lived with his wife and baby above a Polish Social Club (where he also worked) with a number of other Polish migrants:

> At the moment we have a big room and I think we can spend the next year here. Anyway, a young baby always stays with the parents and we have got a kitchen and a toilet to share with others … after that I am going to have to apply to some housing association or something so we can live normally. (Interview 007.LR)

This discussion demonstrates the point made by Ackers and Stalford (2004, 275) that EU law 'only delivers tangible benefits through its engagement with domestic welfare systems'. Of course, the principle of equal treatment is valuable in ensuring that workers and their families are not discriminated against within a national territory. However, the right to non-discrimination effectively results in a 'postcode lottery' both between Member States and between regions within a Member State. Conditions in the host Member State, although not discriminatory in nature, may prevent the realization of the Community free movement rights by migrants. The difficulty of accessing affordable housing in the UK, although not falling foul of Article 9 of Regulation 1612/68, disrupts the ability of migrant workers to exercise their rights to family reunification and, in turn, may be a hindrance to the exercise of mobility rights in general. Seemingly, then, as Ackers and Stalford (2004, 275) point out: '[t]he non-discrimination principle is unlikely to smooth the transition of families moving throughout the EU.'

Earlier in this book the popularity with UK employers of organized migration schemes, which enable them to recruit a number of EU8 workers, was acknowledged. One of the features of these schemes is employer-arranged housing which frequently involves groups of workers sharing accommodation. This can be extremely helpful in terms of cost as the rates are often reduced or subsidised by the employer and, given the preceding discussion on the difficulties of accessing housing, this is likely to appear a particularly attractive option. On the other hand, the conditions of living are often poor and many of the respondents who had moved as part of such a scheme spoke of cramped, unclean housing which was situated in an undesirable area. Such conditions, in particular living with other workers, are not amenable to the functioning of family life, especially when children are involved, and it is arguable that this has discouraged some workers from exercising their right to family reunification.

An employer who had organized such a scheme for his own company confirmed the impression that arranged accommodation was not a privilege extended to the worker's family:

> Well, the company provide accommodation for the drivers but the people with families have to find their own. (Interview 203.RBC)

Similarly, one of the employment agency advisers confirmed that, in her experience, many employers were not family-friendly:

> They [the workers] go on their own and this is what the employers, maybe 'require' is not the right word, but they can't take their family when they go because the employer provides accommodation only for the candidate. If it is a group of, say, maybe five drivers then the employer rents them a house but it is only for them. There is no space for a wife and kids. (Interview 405.N)

Unsurprisingly, another employment agency adviser confirmed that those who were most likely to face this type of obstacle to family reunification were those working in the lower echelons of the labour market. As a result, they were earning lower wages which, in turn, prevented them from breaking away from their employer and paying for their own housing:

> Very highly skilled people usually get a longer contract and their job conditions and wages are very good so they can take family. Less-skilled people on short contracts with less money? In my experience 99 per cent go alone. (Interview 403.I)

This mirrors Raghuram's (2004, 306) findings in relation to migrant domestic workers who are frequently required to live in the employer's household and, by doing so, limit the possibility of family reunification for themselves. This author points out:

> They have to wait until they are able to secure some savings … and no longer have to 'live-in' with their employers.

Some of the migrants in the sample were experiencing a similar predicament at the time of interview. In particular, the bus drivers mentioned earlier who had plans for their wives or partners and children to follow them were waiting until they had sufficient means to afford their own home. Similarly, one man who had recently been joined in the UK by his fiancée had been prevented from doing so previously by his employer, with whom he lived, due to the lack of space in the employer's home. His official job was working in the employer's pub and restaurant but he also carried out numerous 'odd-jobs' around their home.[91] Eventually, they had come to an agreement whereby his fiancée was able to live with him in the employer's accommodation, on the condition that she also carried out some work:

> I have spoken with my employer and I think she will start doing cleaning and then maybe start in the kitchen. (Interview JK.001)

The respondent mentioned earlier, who had been joined by his pregnant girlfriend, had initially been housed in employer-arranged accommodation with other workers. Knowing that his girlfriend would be arriving he had found a flat where they could live alone. However, they were not happy with either the conditions or the price of rent which they were finding difficult to meet:

> When we came here in May we had arranged accommodation from the company but I found it very uncomfortable because it was very small and not suitable. Because I was expecting my girlfriend to come, I decided to move out and find something on my own and I did it. Now we live in a rented flat just the two of us but our accommodation conditions could be better. We have to pay lots of money for rent, you know it is very expensive to live here. I am wondering about moving to another city but for now I have to fulfil my contract with this company because I am obliged to work for two years here. (Interview 004.M)

The empirical examples given here illustrate that employers' preferences for organized schemes effectively restrict the migrants' right to family reunification. Furthermore, such schemes allow employers to control the workforce to a much greater extent than would be possible if the workers did not live in the employer's premises. Not only does such accommodation limit migrant workers' ability to have their family members live with them, it also represents a form of institutionalization whereby the workers have restricted opportunity to have an independent existence away from work.

Prior to the adoption of Directive 2004/38 the issue of housing may have had legal as well as practical implications as, under the old regime, the entry of family members was conditional upon the worker having available for them 'housing considered as normal for national workers in the region where he is employed'.[92] This stipulation, which does not appear in the more recent Directive, applied only at the time of the family's entry. In a case that went before the Court of Justice, the German authorities had made renewal of a residence permit conditional upon continued availability of reasonable housing. In holding this unlawful the ECJ referred to the importance of the principle of ensuring family life, as enshrined in Article 8 of the European Convention on Human Rights, and accordingly

---

91 This may reflect a similar phenomenon to that described in Chapter 4 in relation to female domestic workers being 'part of the family' and, hence, never being 'off-duty'.

92 Article 10(3), Regulation 1612/68.

emphasized the importance of family reunion.[93] Had this provision still been in force it may well have prevented certain EU8 migrants in the UK from having their family members join them. In any event, what this discussion appears to demonstrate is that although the right of family reunification is formally applicable to EU8 migrant workers in the UK, in reality, it may not be accessible due to the propensity of some employers, who are playing a prominent role in the post-accession migration space, to dictate the living arrangements of their EU8 migrant employees.

Living Together Apart

The discussion so far in this chapter has explored the legal framework governing the capacity of EU8 migrants to be joined in the UK by their family members and has sought to juxtapose this formal legal entitlement against EU8 migrants' practical ability to rely on it. Although, clearly, some migrants have moved with their families immediately, or have been joined by them since, it also seems that post-accession migration has initially been characterized by a significant trend of family separation. It will be recalled that out of 26 migrants who described themselves as either married or in a long-term relationship, 15 were separated from their (household) family unit by the migration experience. Separation may occur when the migration experience is intended only to be a temporary venture or where the family engages in staged migration and agree that the worker should be the first 'pioneer' to move.

Spending temporary periods in other countries has been a distinguishing feature of migration from the CEE region in the post-Soviet era (Kofman 2004a, 250; Okolski 2001, 105). This trend was evident in the empirical work conducted for this study, for example, the 16 return migrants interviewed had spent a relatively short period of time in the UK and many of the current workers spoke of an intention to return. In spite of this, it may be that in the future the migrants' degree of integration increases and they decide to stay on a more permanent basis.[94] Of course, family separation may occur even if the migration experience is not intended to be temporary. Commonly, a parent may remain in the home state to avoid disrupting their children's education or to continue their own career (Ackers and Stalford 2004, 57). The discussion above has identified a number of

---

[93] Case 249/86 *Commission v Germany* [1989] ECR 1263, paras. 10-11. The Court has consistently emphasized the significance of respect for private and family life in its case law and has linked this to the exercise of family reunification rights. See, *inter alia*, Case C-413/99 *Baumbast* [2002] ECR I-7091; Case C-60/00 *Carpenter* [2002] ECR I-6279; Case C-109/01 *Akrich* [2003] ECR I 9607. In Case C 291/05 *Eind* (judgment of 11 December 2007) the Court expressly referred to the 'right to family reunification' for EU citizens (para. 23) set out in the secondary legislation (previously Article 10, Regulation 1612/68; now, Articles 2 and 2, Directive 2004/38).

[94] Two of the respondents, for example, described how they initially decided to stay only for a temporary period but had then met their partners in the UK (Interviews 020.H and 017.M).

constraints on the practical reliance of the right to reunification stemming from the peculiarities of the UK system: the confusion surrounding the ability of EU8 workers to access benefits; the (negative) perception of the British education system; and the lack of appropriate 'family' housing are all factors that have contributed to a culture of family separation. Reunification will often not be practical. Additionally, at EU level, the rather inexplicable restriction on the right of family members to work contained in the Accession Treaty may have initially prevented some from joining the worker.

The remainder of this section takes a general look at the issue of family separation in that it does not specifically concentrate on either temporary or permanent separation but, rather, explores some of the methods used by families separated by migration to sustain the family unit and facilitate some form of family life. In examining these issues it applies the concept of the transnational family to the experiences of EU8 migrants in the UK. Bryceson and Vuorela (2002, 3) define transnational families as:

> Families that live some or most of the time separated from each other, yet hold together and create something that can be seen as a feeling of collective welfare and unity, namely 'familyhood', even across national borders.

Elements of transnational family life have already been drawn upon in the preceding sections of this chapter. For example, the propensity of family members (often grandparents) to temporarily join their migrating family member(s) to provide help in times of need demonstrates reliance on a family network that transcends the boundaries of the host state. The concept of the 'transnational family' has emerged from the literature on transnationalism (Glick Shiller et al. 1992; Vertovec and Cohen 1999; Boyle 2002) that emphasizes 'the attachments migrants maintain to people, traditions and causes outside the boundaries of the nation state to which they have moved' (Vertovec 2002, 4). Kofman (2002a, 244) argues that use of the transnationalism as a conceptual framework for the study of migration encompasses the fluidity which stems from the migrants regularly crossing borders and is able to capture the part played by family networks and strategies. Building on this, Silver (2006,41) recognizes that migration, as a transnational phenomenon, impacts not only on the migrant but on those family members that remain in the home state:

> Members of transnational families remain linked to one another and experience the process of migration on both sides of the border.

From this perspective, family members are not 'left behind' as migrants consistently maintain ties and allegiances to their home state. Family members continue to be active influences in the migrants' lives despite the migration process separating them and modern communication technology, such as telephones, email and webcams, 'facilitate the ease of communication among families that span international borders' (ibid., 42). Consequently, the influence of family members is likely to be felt much more keenly by migrants today, in the 'informational society'

(Bryceson and Vuorela, 2002, 7) than previously. This was something recognized and appreciated by the respondents:

> Nowadays things are developed so I have contact with my family all the time. We've got webcams so we can see each other, cheap phone calls and emails so I keep in touch quite regularly and it's not like we're confined to letters'. (Interview 017.M)

Despite the ease of communication, it is unlikely that a family life conducted via means of technology can equally substitute actual physical presence. It would be misguided to use the advent of new means of communication to undermine the reality that family separation during migration can be a stressful life event. Such separation can reduce the support available to both the migrant and the family members in the home state. There were numerous references made during the interviews to the difficult nature of family separation. The following respondent had been separated from his fiancée but she had recently joined him:

> Now we are closer but sometimes I phoned less because I got tired of giving out the same information like 'I'm ok, I have work' and sometimes my fiancée would say 'I need you, you must give me support' ... I felt guilty. As a man I felt we must live together as a family and not be separated. I left Poland because we were struggling ... and I think about making a better life for me and them, but I still felt guilty. (Interview JK.001)

The experience of feeling guilt after leaving family echoes the findings of research carried out on retirement migration by Ackers and Dwyer (2002, 49). Likewise, the following man was separated from his girlfriend who had remained in Poland because of her job. The couple were experiencing some problems in adapting to a transnational relationship:

> A few days ago my girlfriend called me and said that she can't stand not being together ... she is in Poland because she has a secure job but she said it is too difficult and she was crying, it was horrible. I thought about going back and, although it was very difficult to decide, I've decided to stay. I can't return to Poland because there is just market research waiting for me which is not really my thing ... I told my girlfriend this and she is doing better now. She understood and I think it's going to be easier with time. I hope so because I'm going to stay here five years because I think this will help the position of both of us for the future. There is high unemployment in Poland and it's very difficult to get a job and, when you get a job, you can't actually expect that you can earn enough money to live on. (Interview 002.PZ)

These are just two of the many instances of distress caused by separation of the family unit in the sample. Earlier on reference was made to a woman who moved to the UK with her six-year-old son. She found being separated from her husband difficult but it seems that the decision to return to Poland was primarily motivated by the sadness her son felt as a result of being away from his father. This respondent explained how her son used to cry a lot and how, even seven months since they returned to Poland, he often talked about how miserable he had felt in London.[95]

Notwithstanding the stress caused by separation, the overwhelming tendency among the sample of respondents interviewed was for family members to approve of the decision to migrate. In the main, the migrant respondents felt that their family had understood, and agreed with, their reasoning that migration had become a necessary means of enhancing their economic status. Such reasoning was also often placed within the context of frustration about the chances of accessing secure and well-paid employment in Poland. Clearly, a supportive attitude on the part of family members can be extremely important for the migrants' sense of security and wellbeing when away from the family unit (Ackers and Stalford 2004, 140). The following extracts are representative of the views emerging from the data:

> My father is very supportive but he wasn't very supportive when I came back! I think he feels that abroad you get a bigger perspective than you do in Poland and the work market is much better. Anyway, they are both liberal and they don't have anything against me moving, I never came across anything negative from them. (Interview 305.S)

> My girlfriend wasn't happy about me leaving but she knew that it was something that would be good for us. It was a decision we made together. (Interview 010.JF)

Migrants who form part of a transnational family and continue to feel a sense of belonging and obligation to the family unit 'back home' essentially live 'between two worlds' (Morokvasic 2004, 16). The next two sub-sections examine ways in which migrants continue to fulfil an obligation to the 'shadow household' in the state of origin during the migration experience (Boyd 1989, 643). First the issue of remittances is considered and, secondly, the propensity of migrants to return home to care for family is examined.

Remittances

The previous chapter made reference to the 'contradictory class mobility' (Parreńas 2001, 1129) experienced by many EU8 migrants who, although experiencing a form of de-skilling, simultaneously experience an improved financial status due to the higher rate of wages in the UK compared to their country of origin. These comparatively higher wages are often partially remitted to separated family members and, therefore, enable the worker to perform a duty to the family remaining in the home state (Silver 2006, 5). According to Vertovec (2002, 4), remittances are an exemplary form of migrant transnationalism. They come in the form of cheques or money sent to family members in the post, electronic money transfers or benefits in-kind, such as gifts of consumer goods from the host state. Remittances are a way in which migrants link with their country of origin and,

---

95 Interview 314.A. This interview was not recorded at the respondent's request but notes were taken throughout (with the respondent's consent).

paradoxically considering the often de-skilled status occupied in the host state, can improve their class status (or the family's status) in the home state by providing a greater economic capacity (Kofman 2004b, 651). Remitted funds may amount to a form of cross-national support of welfare or education, for example money used to provide health care for a family member or to cover the cost of private schooling. Ironically, in some instances it may be that a worker sends remittances to their home state to enable their partner to pay a migrant (usually a woman) to undertake domestic tasks in the home – primarily, childcare and/or household tasks – so that that the partner can undertake paid work.[96] Thus, a Polish man in the UK may send money home so that his wife is able to go out to work and avoid the double burden of paid and domestic work by hiring a worker of, for example, Ukrainian nationality working in Poland's own secondary labour market (see Koryś 2003, 6).

León-Ledesma and Piracha (2004, 65) have researched remittances within the specific context of eastern Europe and argue that remittances have played an important role in poverty alleviation for migrant households. They cite the statistic that in 1999 the total remittance credit for CEE countries was US$7 billion (ibid., 78). In Poland, figures from 2003, estimate that around US$900 million per year is remitted by nationals working abroad (Koryś 2003, 6). There were numerous examples given in the interviews of remittances being sent to family in Poland:

> Sometimes I send £100 or £200 to Poland which is lot of money but here it's not too much. I try to live here very simple and save to send money but it's my decision to do that... I could also pay for my mother's doctor when she was ill so I think I spend money in a good way. Last month I sent £500 for my daughter because she needed braces and other dental treatment. (Interview 001.JK)

The following respondent had separated from his wife sometime before he arrived in the UK but he still felt an obligation to her as well as his son:

> I have a wife and son in Poland. We are not together anymore but I send money to Poland for them. (Interview 004.M)

In addition to remittances being used to facilitate and sustain family life across borders in the migrant worker's absence there were also a number of instances of migrants using savings upon their return to Poland for family or household uses. This was a popular strategy used by younger migrants who had not yet established any form of family household of their own before the migration experience (León-Ledesma and Piracha 2004, 77). For example, the following respondent had worked in the UK, as had his wife. They used the temporary migration experience to save up and when they returned to Poland the savings were put towards the costs of buying their own home:

---

[96] A situation which exemplifies Ehrenreich and Hochschild's 'global care chain' (2003).

> We saved and we used that money for our house. Just 4 months ago we moved into our house so it was worth it! (Interview 311.D)

Money earned in the host state, then, can help to sustain family life from a distance or, alternatively, can help to establish and facilitate family life later on.

In addition to the impact on the individual household or family, remittances also have certain socio-cultural and structural consequences for the home economy. For example, Koryś (2003, 163) points out that while remittances may lift certain households in a society out of poverty, the corollary of this is that the society as a whole becomes more stratified. The economic gulf between those households with workers abroad and those without becomes greater. In addition, remittances are transferred directly from the worker to the family and, as a result, bypass the national taxation system. From this perspective, they can be seen as representing lost wealth that could have itself been utilized to help strengthen the infrastructure of the home country and its services. A suggestion is that societies become reliant on remittances from migrant workers which, in turn, restricts the development of national business and limits opportunities for growth. Arguments of this nature have been framed largely in the context of developing nations (Hoddinott 1994, 459). In the case of Poland, and indeed the CEE region as a whole, it is expected that EU membership itself will help to strengthen the economies and lead to a gradual alignment of the social structure to a standard more akin to that in the EU15. Therefore it would seem that, although at the present time the trend for remittances is continuing, there is not such a pertinent risk of such long-term dependence on remittances. Indeed, it may be that future trends in relation to remittances fall below the pre-enlargement levels once economic standards in the EU8 and EU2 have improved.

Returning Home to Care

Another key aspect of transnational family life is the phenomenon of caring for family, usually elderly relatives in this context, 'at a distance' (Schunk 1996; Rogerson et al; Ackers and Stalford 2004, 153; Ackers and Dwyer 2002, 150). The focus here, then, is not on the impact of separation within the immediate household family but is slightly wider and encompasses the continuing obligations migrant workers feel towards their parents in particular. The free movement provisions, in enabling dependent ascendant relatives to join the worker, assume that older relatives will move to be with the migrant worker should they require care. This is a valuable right and, as has been shown, it is frequently relied upon so that older relatives, typically parents, can *provide* care to grandchildren. This conceptualization, however, does not appear to fit practically with the experience of some dispersed migrant families when the need to provide care to parents actually arises.[97] Frequently, for example, elderly relatives may not be able, or willing, to leave their country of origin and its familiar infrastructure, such as

[97] For some examples of successful reliance on this provision see Ackers 1998, 297.

the health service with which they are linked,[98] and this feeling is likely to be pronounced during a time of illness and/or of frailty. Elderly relatives, particularly those without knowledge of the host state's language, therefore, may not wish to undergo the disruption of a move to a new country (Schunk 1996; Ackers 1998, 299–301). Rather, research suggests that it is principally the migrant worker, or a member of the migrated family unit, who makes (often temporary) return moves to the home state to fulfil the caring obligation (Ackers and Dwyer 2002; Baldassar and Baldock 2002, 70; Reynolds and Zontini 2006). This, rather than the model of reunification enshrined in the free movement provisions, is often perceived as the most viable option to those that find themselves needing to provide care in a transnational context.

The vast majority of the respondents interviewed for this study emphasized the importance of return visits home, often returning to Poland two or three times a year. Moreover, two of the respondents had made temporary visits home in order to care for parents who were ill. One woman had returned to Poland in order to help her mother look after her father;[99] and one man had made return trips to help his sister with the care of their mother.[100] The latter respondent's mother had subsequently died and he explained how he and his sister, who was also working in the UK, had arranged a timetable of care:

> When my mum was very ill in Poland we looked after her. For two months I would go and stay, then for two months my sister would go and stay. At the end my sister stayed for long time and she did most of the caring then. My father was not a good carer for my mum and even now this makes me angry when I think about it. (Interview 001.JK)

His acknowledgement that his sister shouldered the bulk of the caring responsibility, and his father's apparent unwillingness to engage in any meaningful care-giving, perhaps reflects the gendered nature of caring responsibilities. Of course this should not detract from the valuable contribution the respondent made towards his mother's care needs. It simply makes the point that, typically, female siblings carry out, and are *expected* to carry out, more of the care-giving than male siblings. As Ackers (1998, 302) points out, however, it is not always possible to make return trips as such occurrences may require the migrant to give work up in the host state and/or cause disruption to their immediate family unit who have joined them. Parents, again women in particular, with young children attending school in the host state may be particularly restricted in their ability to 'up and leave' for temporary periods. In such instances it is common for the absent worker to contribute in other ways, such as by remitting funds to cover

---

98 Of course those ascendant relatives that do move to join the worker are entitled to access to the health service of the host state on the basis of family members' rights to equal treatment in Article 24 of Directive 2004/38. Certain healthcare benefits can also be exported from the home state under Regulation 1408/71. See Hervey and McHale 2004, 113–19.

99 Interview 012.GP.

100 Interview 001.JK.

the costs of institutional care or helping to organize support by telephone or the use of online resources.

The obligation to provide care for kin (usually parents) transnationally, either physically or by other methods, is felt keenly by migrant workers (Rogerson et al. 1997). Thus it is not only separation from their own immediate household family members, such as a spouse/partner and children, but also separation from the family in general that can cause distress. Accordingly, those respondents in the sample that described themselves as single also may have suffered as a result of family separation, albeit separation from extended family.

The transnational family model would appear to reflect the way in which many EU8 migrants have conducted their family life in the immediate aftermath of migrating to the UK. This is in effect a continuation of pre-EU membership migration patterns, characterized as short-term and temporary stays, in the CEE region. Earlier parts of the chapter alluded to the desire expressed by a number of respondents to have family members join them and also to the apparent increasing tendency of the migrants to exercise rights of family reunification. This may indicate that post-accession migrants are settling more permanently in the UK and that a family unity model is now (becoming) more relevant. In spite of this, family separation has been, and does remain, a very real part of the migration experience for many. For some this is a personal choice, for others it is simply not a viable option to sustain a family in the UK.

Conclusion

This chapter has sought to explore the various ways in which EU8 migrants have facilitated and sustained family life after exercising a right to mobility and taking up work in the UK. The free movement provisions extend valuable rights of reunification and equal treatment to the worker's family members which, undoubtedly, allow many migrant families to maintain an effective family life after migration. Family reunification, however, is not always a model of family life accessible to all migrants as various constraints, social and legal, can work together to restrict the ability of family to join the worker. In the UK context, for example, it has been shown that the practical reality for many post-accession migrants who are housed in accommodation arranged by their employers is that there is simply not adequate space, or even suitable standards of living, for their family to join them. Again in the UK context, the ambiguities in the post-accession migration regime and confusion surrounding benefit restrictions may have conspired to convince EU8 migrant workers that, should their family join them, they would have no entitlement to access any benefits or welfare services. These can be of crucial concern, particularly for those with children. In this respect, the legal and social climate in the UK challenges the ideology behind the extension of family reunification (and related) rights to EU migrant workers – that of facilitating the mobility of the worker. Despite the benefits of family reunification for a migrant worker's integration into the host society, it is not always realistic for EU8 workers to establish a family life in the UK. The discussion has also shown, however, that often extended 'non-household' family members, although outside the scope of the legal provisions, can fulfil such an integrative function.

Those who do exercise the right to family reunification, on the other hand, live in the host society within the operation of the non-discrimination principle. The right to equal treatment with nationals of the host state is an extremely worthy right and does enable the migrant family to access various services and welfare entitlements which can contribute to the facilitation of family life and the welfare of its members. Arguably, however, on some occasions this principle may not provide migrant families with the resources to fully integrate into the society and maintain a sufficiently high level of family life. Again, housing provides a good example within the UK context as the lack of affordable family housing is a feature of life in the UK and, arguably, EU8 migrants feel the impact of this just as much, if not more, than nationals do due to the apparent de-skilled status many currently occupy.

The various constraints on the ability of people to exercise rights to family reunification may encourage a culture of family separation with family members remaining, initially at least, in the home state. Of course, this is not to deny that many choose to maintain transnational links for reasons not related to the social and practical constraints on the right to reunification. For example, those who plan to stay only temporarily in the UK may have little interest in having family follow them. The qualitative work, however, did clearly evidence a longing on the part of workers for family members to join them which was being frustrated by housing constraints, and (often misguided) perceptions as to their welfare entitlement. Operating a transnational family life does enable migrant workers to sustain relationships with people, contribute financially to the family unit 'at home' and even, in some instances, continue to care for family members. In this respect the obligation felt towards family members does not diminish and with developed communication technology the influence of family in the home state on migrants is felt more than ever before. Physical separation, nevertheless, even for short periods can be a painful and stressful experience both for the migrant and the family who remain at home.

Chapter 6

Citizenship in the Context of EU Enlargement: CEE Migrants as Union Citizens

Introduction: Union Citizenship as a Concept and its Link to Mobility

The concern in this chapter is to take a closer look at the relationship between CEE accession nationals and the evolving status of Union citizenship. Previous chapters have illustrated how mobility rights and contingent social entitlement of workers and their families flow from the free movement of persons provisions. As these provisions constitute a central facet of Union citizenship, one of the main objectives of this chapter is to explore the impact of restricted mobility rights during the transitional period on the citizenship status of nationals from the EU8 and EU2 countries.

It is necessary, first, to determine what is meant by 'citizenship' in the context of the EU. Citizenship in a broad sense, although it remains something of a contested concept (Faist 2001, 40), refers to membership and participation in a community (Marshall 1950); additionally, it denotes both entitlements and responsibilities which attach to the citizens who belong to the said community (usually the nation-state) (Kofman 1995, 122). Citizenship then, formally, is a legal status but 'in its fullest sense it is the culmination of incorporation into a society'. Bellamy has identified rights, participation and solidarity as the key components of contemporary citizenship (Bellamy 2004, 6). More specifically, it is civil rights, particularly those that protect individual autonomy and family life; the right to engage in the political process; and to access social rights, such as education and social assistance, that are most crucial to an understanding of modern citizenship. This understanding, of course, has been established predominantly in the context of national citizenship. The notion of Union citizenship (Shaw 1997; 1998), which has its own distinctive features, complements (rather than replaces) national citizenship[1] and is now formally articulated in Articles 17–22 EC as inserted by the Treaty of Maastricht in 1992.[2] The formal creation of the citizenship provisions was part of an aspiration to increase the legitimacy of the European project and

1 Article 17(2) EC.

2 For more detail on the background behind the inclusion of citizenship see O'Leary 1996; see also, the Tindermans Report on the European Union, produced at the request of the Paris summit in 1974, included a chapter entitled 'Towards a Europe for Citizens' (Bull.EC.(8) 1975 II no. 12, 1).

to further the integration of EU nationals living in Member States other than their own (Chalmers et al. 2006, 566–8; Ackers and Dwyer 2002, 16–18). Essentially, the policy concern of the European Commission in particular was to bring 'Europe closer to its citizens' (Ackers and Dwyer 2002, 17).[3]

Article 17 EC clarifies who is able to access the status of citizenship of the Union. Perhaps it is more appropriate to say this provision makes clear that it is the individual *Member States* that determine which individuals gain access to the status as 'every person holding the nationality of a Member State shall be a citizen of the Union'. This demonstrates the exclusionary nature of Union citizenship, as for the many third-country nationals resident in EU Member States it has been an unattainable status and a community within which they have not been able to attain full membership or participation. By its very nature citizenship lays down boundaries between those who are included and those who are excluded (Kofman 1995, 121). One issue that this chapter seeks to explore is whether CEE accession nationals, despite now being nationals of a Member State, remain excluded from full membership and participation within the EU community.

The citizens' rights established in the 'citizenship chapter' agreed at Maastricht include, in Article 18 EC, the right to move and reside freely within the territory of the Member States, subject to the limitations and conditions laid down by the Treaty and the measures adopted to give it effect. There is also the right to vote in local and European elections in the host state (Article 19 EC);[4] the right to diplomatic and consular protection from the authorities of any Member State in third countries (Article 20 EC); and the right to petition the European Parliament and the right to apply to the ombudsman in any one of the official languages of the EU (Article 21 EC). This constitutionalization of the notion of Union citizenship clearly resonates with the notion of free movement as the majority of the applicable rights, notwithstanding Article 18 EC itself, are exercisable only in the event of some cross-border movement.[5] In addition, Shaw (1997, 554) makes the point that the formalization of Union citizenship at Maastricht:

> Was essentially the beginning of a new stage in an on-going process of development of the status of the individual under Community law which had involved inputs from the Court of Justice, and especially its constitutionalisation of the free movement provisions and the right to non-discrimination on the grounds of nationality.

---

3 It is outside the scope of this chapter to give a detailed overview of the history of Union citizenship but see O'Leary 1996; Wiener 1998.

4 It is not the intention here to discuss aspects of political citizenship. See Lardy 1997, 111; Shaw 2003, 461; Shaw and Smith 2006, 145; Shaw 2007.

5 The Court has confirmed that the citizenship provisions are not applicable in wholly internal situation, see Cases 64/96 and 65/96 *Uecker and Jacquet* [1997] ECR I-3171. Union citizens can, however, enforce citizenship rights against their Member State of origin, provided a cross-border element is present. In the context of Article 18 EC see Case C-224/02 *Pusa* [2004] ECR I-5763; Case C-406/04 *De Cuyper* [2006] ECR I-6947; Case C-192/05 *Tas-Hagen and Tas* [2006] ECR I-10451; Case C-76/05 *Schwarz* judgment of 11 September 2007; Case C-11/06 *Morgan* judgment of 23 October 2007.

Citizenship, therefore, stretches further than the articulation in Articles 17–22 EC *per se*, so as to also incorporate the traditional 'economic' free movement provisions,[6] read alongside the extensive interpretation provided by the ECJ of the social rights of economic migrants. It also finds expression via the equal treatment principle in Article 12 EC and various pieces of secondary legislation.[7]

The Treaty of Lisbon, signed in December 2007, does not make any significant substantive changes to the citizenship provisions but there are some innovations of symbolic importance.[8] If ratification proceeds and the Treaty enters into force, the relevant provisions would be contained in a Part Two of the Treaty on the Functioning of the European entitled Non-discrimination and Citizenship. This suggests a greater fusing together of citizenship with the principle of equal treatment. Both the principle of non-discrimination on grounds of nationality (Article 12 EC; Article 18 TFEU) and the more general legislative power to adopt measures to combat discrimination based on sex, racial or ethnic origin, religion or belief, disability, age or sexual orientation (Article 13 EC; Article 19 TFEU) immediately precede the citizenship provisions (Articles 17–22 EC; Articles 20–26 TFEU).[9] In addition, the definition of who constitutes a Union citizen, as well as finding expression in Article 20 TFEU (in the same terms as Article 17 EC), will also be contained in Article 9 of the amended Treaty on European Union (TEU). Article 9 TEU will be the first provision of the new Title II containing Provisions on Democratic Principles. Thus there is a clear attempt to strengthen the links between citizenship and democracy. This Title is geared to enhance the representative and participatory rights of citizens. Importantly, there is a citizens' initiative which enables citizens to invite the Commission to propose legislation in an area (Article 11 TEU).[10]

Union citizenship thus bestows a series of political, civil and socio-economic rights, which in some respects resembles the national citizenship model, but there can be no doubt that free movement remains the trigger for any meaningful relationship with Union citizenship. Ackers and Dwyer (2002, 3) stress that not only is mobility a right that citizens can access in itself, it also constitutes the trigger to other forms of social entitlement, a 'basket of goods', that come into play whilst that right is being exercised, most notably welfare and family rights.[11] They go on to make the point that the development of citizenship has, essentially, taken place alongside the evolution of mobility rights:

6 Articles 39, 43 and 49 EC.

7 Now most notably Directive 2004/38 [2004] OJ L158/77, and Regulation 1612/68 [1968] OJ L257/2.

8 Further, as the pillar structure will be abolished, the citizenship *acquis* will apply throughout EU law as a whole as opposed to only the first Community pillar.

9 In Article 20 TFEU Union citizenship would be 'additional to' national citizenship (instead of complementary to it) and the reference to duties would be removed.

10 The legal basis for the adoption of related legislation would be found in Article 24 TFEU.

11 For example workers' rights of family reunification under Directive 2004/38 (discussed in Chapter 6), or entitlement to social benefits pursuant to Article 7(2), Regulation 1612/68.

> In the absence of mobility, citizenship of the Union contributes little to the social status and day-to-day experience of Community nationals.

It is this interrelationship between rights of mobility and citizenship that demands some discussion of the extent to which the transitional arrangements, by limiting the ability of CEE accession nationals to rely on Article 39 EC and move as workers, effectively excludes them from full access to the status of Union citizenship. The chapter opens with an examination of the impact of the transitional restrictions on the traditionally privileged category of economic migrant workers who, undoubtedly, occupy a less-privileged status during the transitional period. It then goes on to explore the relationship that CEE nationals have with Article 18 EC and broader free movement rights that flow from it. Given that the Accession Treaty refers specifically to the right of Member States to restrict the free movement rights of *workers*, nationals from the newest Member States are able to rely on the right of EU *citizens* to move freely, albeit subject to the more stringent limitations and conditions. In examining the links between CEE nationals and the different sites of free movement in the EC Treaty there is also scope to trace the development of Union citizenship from a predominantly market-based status (attaching only to those 'worthy' economic migrants connected to the functioning of the internal market) to an arguably more inclusive and social conception of citizenship. The latter understanding of citizenship provides scope for economically inactive migrants to gain a degree of access to the status of citizenship and the valuable rights that append to it.

The final substantive section links with earlier chapters by focussing specifically on the UK as a frame of reference. It considers the potential impact of the developing law on citizenship for EU8 migrants who are not economically active in the context of the UK post-accession rules. In particular, the section speculates on the impact of developments in the case law on citizenship, as well as the 2004 Directive on citizens' free movement rights, for migrant work seekers in the UK. This chapter adopts a more theoretical approach to the subject matter than has been evident in some of the preceding chapters. In doing so, it seeks to complement the earlier empirical discussions in order to contribute to a genuine and balanced socio-legal analysis.

Union citizenship, with its reliance on free movement as a central trigger to entitlement, as opposed to a primary reliance on political rights (Everson 1995, 74), appears to have quite different characteristics to the kind of national citizenship described above with reference to Bellamy's classification of rights, participation and solidarity.[12] However, as earlier parts of this book have demonstrated and as the discussion here will illustrate further, the free movement provisions have provided a fertile site for the development and extension of social rights seen as necessary to facilitate the movement and establishment of migrant workers. Similarly, the European Court's jurisprudence interpreting Article 18 EC in conjunction with Article 12 EC has enabled welfare entitlement to be

---

[12] Although Articles 19–21 EC do provide some 'civil' rights and rights of political participation for those citizens in a Member State other than their own.

extended to non-worker migrants under certain conditions.[13] In this respect there is at least a modicum of 'solidarity' evident in the developing citizenship case law. Indeed, authors have drawn a link between the recent emphasis on a 'social Europe' and Marshall's seminal work on citizenship which highlighted the development of social rights as the maturity of a relationship between the state and the people (Shaw 1997). There is then a degree of social citizenship[14] evident in the evolving or maturing arena of Union citizenship. This chapter will touch upon the extent to which social solidarity under the auspices of free movement is, or may possibly be, extended to CEE migrants. Citizenship, therefore, in the context of this discussion (and, indeed, the book as a whole) is measured in terms of the residence rights extended to migrants and the consequent ability to rely on the principle of non-discrimination in the host state in order to access various social rights and benefits on an equal basis with nationals.[15]

Second-Class Citizenship?

Some of the discussions surrounding the eastern enlargements were couched in quite symbolic terms referring to the post-communist CEE countries' 'return' to their rightful place in Europe (Kengerlinsky 2004, 12). This literature portrays the extension of free movement rights as holding particular significance for the citizens of the new Member States on account of the specific historical and socio-political background of the respective countries; specifically, under communism citizens of the CEE countries were subject to mobility restrictions, even between regions within a single state (Petev 1998, 83). For example, prior to enlargement, Maas (2002, 2) argued that:

> For individual citizens in the candidate accession countries, freedom of movement is without a doubt a key symbol of the 'return to Europe' that EU accession represents. Citizens of applicant Member States regard the freedom of movement that EU citizens enjoy as remarkable when contrasted with the limits to movement they experienced under communism.

Given the symbolic importance of free movement, and the significance of mobility to citizenship, it is not surprising that the consequent failure to extend

---

13 Discussed below. See, for example, Case C-85/96, *Martinez Sala* [1998] ECR I-2691, Case C-184/99 *Grzelczyk* [2001] ECR I-6193.

14 On social citizenship see Everson 1995.

15 Enshrined in Article 12 EC. Note that here the terms 'non-discrimination' and 'equal treatment' are used interchangeably to refer to the principle in Article 12 EC. The author acknowledges the point that, in practice, the right of individuals not to be discriminated against may not necessarily result in them being treated on an equal footing with nationals but there is insufficient scope in this book to consider this in any depth. See the literature on the 'substantive versus formal equality' debate including, *inter alia*, Barnard and Hepple 2000; Fredman 2001. On the notions of equal treatment and non-discrimination in EU law see Numhauser-Henning 2001.

the right of free movement in full has led some to comment that CEE accession nationals are, initially at least, relegated to a status of second class Union citizenship (Maas 2002; Carrera 2005, 699). Reich (2004, 16), for example, comments that a seven-year postponement of free movement rights does not conform to the 'spirit of creating a greater Europe after the fall of the Soviet regime'. The remainder of this section explores this assertion in greater detail.

Migrant Workers under the Transitional Arrangements: Downgraded Citizenship Status

The transitional arrangements on the free movement of persons allow the implementing Member States to derogate from Articles 1–6 of Regulation 1612/68[16] in respect of EU8 and EU2 nationals.[17] It is these provisions which enable nationals of the Member States to access the labour markets of the other Member States and, hence, constitute the main source of an EU migrant worker's mobility and employment rights. By permitting Member States to deny labour market access to CEE accession nationals, the transitional restrictions have the effect of rendering the Community law status of 'worker' inapplicable to many of the new EU citizens. As has been demonstrated in earlier chapters, those who qualify as a worker[18] enjoy extensive citizenship rights in the form of secure residence in the host society[19] and, furthermore, contingent social rights such as family and welfare entitlement.[20] The extensive nature of migrant workers' citizenship standing under Community law is illustrated further by the ability of the status to have continuing effects after the employment relationship has come to an end.[21] Directive 2004/38, for example, now makes clear that the status of worker, which arguably includes the right to reside and the attached social rights, continues to apply in the aftermath of a worker being made (involuntarily) unemployed, not being able to work due to illness or an accident, or embarking

16 [1968] OJ L257/2.

17 See Chapter 3 on the operation of the transitional restrictions on free movement.

18 Pursuant to the test laid down in cases such as Case 66/85 *Lawrie Blum* [1986] ECR 2121 of 'for a certain period of time performing services for and under the direction of another person in return for which remuneration is received'.

19 Pursuant to Article 39 EC. Previously Directive 68/360 [1968] OJ L257/13 articulated the procedural requirements connected to the right to reside, now Directive 2004/38 contains the relevant rules. See Chapter 4 and the discussion on EU8 domestic workers in the UK.

20 Pursuant to the non-discrimination principle enshrined in Article 39 EC (and Article 12 EC) and expressed in specific provisions of the secondary legislation such as Article 7(2), Regulation 1612/68 (and ensuing case law), Case 207/78 *Even* [1979] ECR 2019; Case 32/75 *Fiorini v SNCF* [1975] ECR 1085; Case 65/81 *Reina* [1982] ECR I-33; Case 59/85 *Netherlands v Reed* [1986] ECR 1283. See Chapter 5 for discussion of the family rights accessible to EU8 migrant workers who have entered the UK labour market.

21 Although this is one dimension of the worker status that the UK attempts to restrict during the transitional period, see Chapter 3 and later on in this chapter.

on vocational training.[22] This contrasts with the less secure situation of those migrants who move without any 'economic' link, discussed below, whose rights of residence are much more circumscribed.

Before the discussion examines the impact of the transitional arrangements on the citizenship status of CEE accession nationals, the following subsection details the 'usual' typology of free movement entitlement that applies to the different categories of EU migrant citizen.

Differentiated rights for Union citizens EU law bestows distinct citizenship 'packages' on different categories of migrant citizens and, given the Union's economic origins, this has conventionally been determined by the particular category's degree of connection to the functioning of the Internal Market. Thus, the traditional approach to citizenship attaches primacy to the relationship between the individual and the labour market:

> A Community citizen's access to rights and benefits in the host Member State depends on them demonstrating membership of one or more 'classes' of persons, the membership of which gives rise to a distinctive citizenship status based upon an identifiable body of Community law. (Ackers 1998, 111)

Workers usually stand at the summit of the citizenship hierarchy alongside the other citizens, the self-employed and those providing services, also exercising one of the Community's fundamental freedoms. Also at the summit are those retired citizens exercising their right to remain in a Member State in which they have worked.[23] Citizenship, as mentioned earlier, is usually thought of as conferring rights *and* duties. One way of interpreting the traditionally privileged status of market citizens is to view their economic activity as, essentially, a duty fulfilled. Under this analysis, it is their economic contribution to the host Member State that has granted them the right to claim the various social entitlements including access to the extensive non-discrimination principle.[24] However, the very 'absolute' nature of the worker status which emerges from the ECJ's case law undermines this understanding somewhat. The ECJ has adopted an extremely broad understanding

---

22 Article 7(3), Directive 2004/38. The provision enshrines the decision in Case 39/86 *Lair* [1988] ECR 3161 so that in cases of voluntarily unemployment, were the migrant has enrolled on a vocational course, the training should be related to the previous employment. Note that a provision in the Accession Treaty allows EU15 Member States to withdraw the rights of EU8 and EU2 nationals who become voluntarily unemployed during the transitional period: Article 24 of the Act of Accession [2003] OJ L236/33, para. 2, Annexes. It is not entirely clear how the provisions relate but, in the event of an CEE accession migrant worker leaving a job to take up a vocational course, the Member State may attempt to rely on the Accession Treaty during the transitional period to expel the migrant.

23 Previously pursuant to Regulation 1251/70 [1970] OJ Sp. Ed. L143/24; now Directive 2004/38.

24 Although, as will be demonstrated, more recent developments in the citizenship law has led to those without such economic 'value' gaining access to the principle of equal treatment.

of who will constitute a worker so that those who receive wages lower than the official subsistence level in a Member State,[25] or those who require additional public funds to supplement their wages,[26] still acquire the very privileged status despite the contribution they make, in economic terms, being limited in nature. If a worker is classified as undertaking effective and genuine work, their residence and equal treatment entitlement is (almost) unconditional.[27]

Arguably, the family members of the market citizens described above have occupied the next rung down the ladder. Despite the derivative nature of family members' status, it has been a far-reaching one (as was demonstrated in Chapter 5), thanks often to the ECJ's interpretation of secondary legislation which extended the worker's package of entitlement also to the family under the 'facilitating mobility' test.[28] Directive 2004/38 has also solidified the status of family members somewhat by explicitly extending the right of equal treatment to them.[29]

Under the economic paradigm, the bottom rung has been reserved for those with little, or any, connection to the Internal Market. This includes retired persons who exercise mobility rights after ending their occupational life in their own Member State (and thus have no 'right to remain' in any host Member State), students and the financially independent. The rights of these economically inactive citizens are dealt with in more detail below in relation to the status of EU8 and EU2 non-workers; suffice to say for now that their status is much less secure than that of the market-citizen worker. In particular, their rights of residence have been subject to the twin requirements of possessing sufficient resources so as not to become a burden on the public assistance of the host Member State, and of having taken out a policy of comprehensive sickness insurance in the host state for themselves and their family.[30] Traditionally, the equal treatment rights of such citizens have also been more heavily circumscribed. In relation to students, for example, in *Brown* it was decided that, at that stage in the development of Community law, there was no anti-discrimination protection available in the area of maintenance or training grants.[31] Article 3 of Directive 93/96 confirmed this position. However, as will be demonstrated later, the ECJ was able to interpret the provisions of Community law to enhance the equal treatment rights of

---

[25] Case 53/81 *Levin* [1982] ECR 1035.

[26] Case 139/85 *Kempf* [1986] ECR 1741.

[27] Subject to the, strictly defined, derogations on the grounds of public policy, public security and public health now detailed in Article 27–33, Directive 2004/38; previously the position was dealt with under Directive 64/221 [1964] OJ Sp. Ed. L850/64

[28] For example, Case 207/78 *Even* [1979] ECR 2019. See also Chapter 5.

[29] Article 24, Directive 2004/38.

[30] Retired persons: previously Directive 90/365 [1990] OJ L180/28; Students: previously Directive 93/96 [1993] OJ L317/59; Financially-independent persons: previously Directive 90/364 [1990] OJ L180/26. Now the free movement rights of all citizens are set out in Directive 2004/38.

[31] Case 197/86 *Brown* [1988] ECR 3205.

students (and other non-economically active citizens) following the introduction of Article 18 EC.[32]

One final group of migrants to be situated in the hierarchy are work seekers (this category is also important to the discussion below regarding the citizenship status of EU8 migrants in the UK). Community law has traditionally regarded work seekers as semi-workers. The Court has held that if Member State nationals could only move for purposes of accepting offers of employment, then the free movement of workers would be significantly hindered.[33] EU nationals have, therefore, been afforded the right to move freely to other Member States and reside there for the purpose of seeking employment. The Court in *Antonissen* further secured the position of work seekers by stating that they should be granted a reasonable period in which to find work[34] and that, as long as the work seeker could show he or she was continuing to seek employment and had genuine chances of being engaged, the right of residence could continue.[35] Thus the residence status of work seekers appears relatively secure and one could argue that they sit just beneath workers on the citizenship ladder, especially given that they enjoy a (future) connection to the labour market. The equal treatment rights of this group, however, seem to more mirror those sitting at the bottom of the ladder. In effect, as with students, the approach of the ECJ was initially restrictive, holding that work seekers' rights of equal treatment only applied to accessing employment and not to any 'social advantages'.[36] Again, the Court's more recent jurisprudence on the cumulative impact of Articles 18 and 12 EC has now enabled work seekers to enjoy greater access to the non-discrimination principle, thus enhancing their citizenship status.[37] As will be demonstrated below, however, the current position of this group (along with that of students) is complicated by the provisions of Directive 2004/38 which attempts to deny equal treatment as regards social assistance to work seekers (and as regards maintenance grants for students).[38] In some respects, then, for the time being the position of work seekers is slightly unclear as it is difficult to predict how the Court will interpret the provisions of Directive 2004/38. For now we will place them tentatively at the midway point, just beneath the family members of the market citizens as, although their status as regards the right to non-discrimination is ambivalent, their right to reside while genuinely seeking work is secure and not subject to the 'sufficient resources' requirement.

---

32 For example, Case C-184/99 *Grzelczyk* [2001] ECR I-6193; Case C-209/03 *Bidar* [2005] ECR I-2119.

33 Case C-292/89 *Antonissen* [1991] ECR I-745.

34 Six months was suggested as a reasonable period of grace, *Antonissen,* para. 21.

35 Directive 2004/38, on the whole, confirms this position. Although the general right of residence applies for only 3 months (Article 6) it is made clear in Article 14(4)(b) that a Union citizen cannot be expelled so long as they are continuing to seek employment and have genuine chances of being engaged.

36 Case 316/85 *Lebon* [1987] ECR 2811.

37 Case C-138/02 *Collins* [2004] ECR I-2703.

38 Article 24(2), Directive 2004/38.

The place of CEE nationals in the citizenship hierarchy As a result of the transitional arrangements on free movement, post-accession CEE migrants experience a different kind of citizenship status and an altered, and somewhat more complex, hierarchy emerges. What the transitional restrictions do, essentially, is hamper the capacity of nationals from the CEE accession Member States to migrate under the sponsorship of one of the traditional 'economic' Community provisions – Article 39 EC. Articles 43 and 49 continue to apply so that EU8 nationals are free to move to the EU15 to establish a business or to provide (or receive) services,[39] but there can be no doubt that the denial of worker status dents the citizenship status of CEE nationals; certainly, it reduces their potential to be *market* citizens.

The place of workers, as a category of free movers, is relegated on the citizenship scale during the transitional period(s). Furthermore, due to the particular design of the transitional arrangements, workers do not have a uniform entitlement to residence across the EU Member States. Since it is for individual Member States to determine whether or not they restrict labour market access, the citizenship status of CEE nationals differs between Member States.[40] Furthermore, the transitional arrangements may have a negative impact on the citizenship status of CEE migrants even in those Member States that have not restricted labour market access. The UK, for example, allows (and has arguably encouraged) EU8 migration but simultaneously, under the supposed auspices of the transitional arrangements, attempts to limit the application of the 'worker' status strictly to the period when the migrant is in work and registered on the WRS.

One consequence of the transitional arrangement's focus on workers as a category of migrant is to enhance the importance of the distinction between workers and the self-employed. There may be a 'grey zone' (Adinolfi 2005, 490) in some instances as to whether the work being carried out is under the direction of another, and hence is in the capacity of an employee, or is carried out independently and is thus is carried out as a self-employed person.[41] In any event, those CEE nationals who do exercise a right to establishment (or provide services) are entitled to take their place at the top of the hierarchy.[42] Clearly, these economic mobility rights offer real opportunities for industrious and entrepreneurial migrants to enjoy rights even in a host Member State with transitional arrangements in place. A small number of Polish migrants who took part in the author's empirical work had, at some point since entering the UK, engaged in self-employed work. For example, two Polish men had established (independently) construction firms. One was still working in a self-employed capacity at the time of interview and had a number of Polish employees working for him; the other did not feel the business

39 Although, Austria and Germany are entitled to apply national measures to address serious disturbances or the threat thereof, in specific sensitive sectors of their labour market (para. 13, Annexes).

40 See Chapter 3 for an overview of the EU15 Member States' policies.

41 See, *inter alia*, Case C-268/99, *Aldona Malgorzata Jany* [2001] ECR I-8615.

42 Although it does need to be acknowledged that the position of service providers (and recipients), as *non-residents*, is not completely analogous to that of *resident* workers and self-employed persons (Van Der Mei 2003a).

had been profitable and had later started work as a waiter. In addition, a Polish woman had set up a service providing English tuition to other migrants. She had worked in this capacity for one year before finding a job as an administrator for a travel agency. Other respondents expressed little interest in carrying out self-employed work, often citing reasons such as a lack of knowledge as to how to go about setting up a business. A number of other respondents reported that they would simply not know what type of business to set up, suggesting that their skills were not suited to such work. This is interesting as the vast majority of those interviewed were very highly qualified in terms of academic qualifications; yet, it is likely to be those with more vocational qualifications and practical skills (the construction sector providing a good example) will be more able to offer services suitable to self-employment.

Naturally, self-employment will appear more attractive as an option to those seeking to migrate to a Member State which has imposed transitional restrictions. The UK's more restrictive approach towards EU2 nationals may provide an example of CEE nationals being diverted into self-employment as a consequence of the stricter rules surrounding access to the labour market. It is perhaps noteworthy that between July and September 2007, there were 4,545 applications made by Romanians and Bulgarians for a registration certificate based on a status of self-employment in the UK (this accounted for 56 per cent of all applications) (Home Office Border and Immigration Agency 2007b, 6).

Those CEE workers called upon by certain of the Member States to fill gaps in their labour markets and those who gain access on an individual basis (for example by means of obtaining a work permit) do, in theory at least, sit at the top of the ladder, since once access is secured, the principle of non-discrimination as regards social advantages[43] applies in full under the transitional arrangements.[44] However, the reality of such workers' experience may be quite different, as the UK's stance under the 2004 transitional arrangements demonstrates. The UK attempts to limit the citizenship status of EU8 workers by denying rights of residence and equal treatment should the employment relationship come to an end which, as was mentioned earlier, is a privilege extended to migrant workers under Community law.

CEE migrant students, retired persons and economically self-sufficient individuals enjoy access to a higher position in the hierarchy than do workers not required by the EU15 because the transitional mobility restrictions do not apply to those former groups. This clearly demonstrates the reversal of citizenship fortune experienced by workers during the transitional period who, essentially, are downgraded to the bottom of the hierarchy. There is also an argument that, under Community law, these non-economic migrants are accorded a superior

43 Article 7(2), Regulation 1612/68 [1968] OJ L257/2.

44 Note, however, the continuing application of the safeguard clause which enables the EU15 to resort to transitional measures at any point during the transitional period (Act of Accession [2003] OJ L236/33; para. 7, Annexes). It is unlikely, however, that the invocation of this safeguard would sanction the expulsion of those that had already gained access to the status of worker in the territory.

status to those workers who gain access to an EU15 labour market. After all, those working in an EU15 Member state during the transitional period are ultimately at the mercy of the national law and policy of the individual Member State; their free movement 'rights' are attached only to that national territory and are not transferable to any other Member State. Furthermore, the safeguard clause continues to apply until the expiry of the transitional period. As a corollary of the worker's demotion, the family members of such citizens also occupy a less-privileged status during the transitional period. Indeed, the status of family members has been downgraded to an even greater extent under the Accession Treaty, as the transitional arrangements enable the implementing Member States to prevent family members from working for a period of 18 months or until three years after the date of accession (whichever date is earliest),[45] whereas the standard EU law position is for family members to enjoy immediate labour market access.[46]

EU8 and EU2 work seekers similarly occupy a lower citizenship status than their EU15 counterparts. Interestingly, however, residence rights of work seekers flow directly from Article 39 EC itself rather than from the secondary legislation.[47] Arguably then, work seekers' residence rights fall outside the scope of the permitted derogations in the Accession Treaty, the main focus of which is Articles 1–6 Regulation 1612/68 *not* Article 39 EC itself.[48] On this reasoning it may be appropriate to suggest that EU8 migrants do enjoy a right to reside under EU law to seek work for a reasonable period. Admittedly, this argument appears unconvincing when one considers that, in reality, the majority of EU15 Member States have sought to deny residence to work seekers. Essentially, the very existence of the transitional restrictions renders it unlikely that an EU8 or EU2 work seeker would have genuine chances of finding employment;[49] hence, work seekers sit below workers in the new citizenship hierarchy that emerges under the transitional arrangements.

Clearly CEE migrants' citizenship status is downgraded as a result of the transitional restrictions. For this reason, they are denied full membership and participation in the community that they have (formally) joined and are, accordingly, not fully incorporated into the EU 'society' while restrictions are in place. Stalford (2003c, 11) argues:

> The transition arrangements challenge more general, prevailing theories of citizenship which traditionally denote a common political, geographical, social and civil identity, implying a share in individual and collective rights and responsibilities.

---

45 Para. 8, Annexes.

46 Article 23, Directive 2004/38; previously Article 11, Regulation 1612/68. See Chapter 5.

47 Case C-292/89 *Antonissen* [1991] ECR I-745, para. 13.

48 This is discussed in more detail later on but for now it is sufficient to note that the Commission shares this view: European Commission 2002a, 6.

49 Note that the position of work seekers is likely to be different in those Member States that have opened their labour market, see the discussion of the UK later.

Of course, the transitional restrictions are temporal in nature and are not a new phenomenon. After all, they were imposed following the accessions of Greece, Spain and Portugal (although those were lifted early). One wonders, however, whether the spirit within which nationals of the CEE countries have been introduced to the EU will have any longer-term effects for the newest citizens' experience and perception of Union citizenship. Citizenship as a concept was largely absent from the documents surrounding the enlargement process (Stalford 2003c; Maas 2002); indeed, there is no mention of it in the Accession Treaty's transitional arrangements. This is unusual given the frequent contemporary emphasis placed on the concept of Union citizenship, particularly by the European Commission. Furthermore, the rather discriminate way in which the restrictions are focussed on the ten post-communist states, leaving aside Malta and Cyprus, may be fuelling a perception of inequity in the CEE Member States. It suggests a 'them and us' attitude on behalf of the EU15, with Malta and Cyprus perceived as being more like the old Member States, and thus being immediately entitled to full membership of the community, and the EU8 and EU2 being viewed more suspiciously; accordingly, their nationals are excluded from membership and full participation in the Community. Moreover, the specific symbolic significance of mobility rights to those who have experienced stringent movement restrictions in the past adds weight to the argument that the initial exclusion from full citizenship will be felt particularly keenly by many of the nationals in the CEE Member States and may be interpreted as a form of second class membership.

One particular criticism levelled at the transitional arrangements is articulated by Maas (2002, 15):

> Usually, the concept of citizenship is seen as a status that is unitary; either one is a citizen or one is not. That is not the way to think of citizenship in this case; the current enlargement will feature a gradual process of extending rights to individuals.

Arguably, however, Maas's construction of citizenship is firmly based on a national model and displays a fundamental misunderstanding of the workings of Union citizenship. Despite the Court's, and now also the legislature's,[50] insistence that citizenship is destined to be the fundamental status of the nationals of the Member States,[51] the reality is that Union citizenship is highly differentiated and has never offered a unitary status (Fries and Shaw 1998,; Dougan 2004). The hierarchy of citizenship status sketched above corroborates this viewpoint. Advocate-General Léger's vision that 'every citizen of the Union must, whatever his nationality, enjoy exactly the same rights and be subject to the same obligations'[52] has certainly not yet been realized. As has already been pointed out here, the traditional distinction has been between the economically active groups of migrants 'protected by the Treaty's core provisions and long-established secondary legislation and those who fall into more marginal categories such as the

50 Recital 3, Preamble to Directive 2004/38.

51 Case C-184/99 *Grzelczyk* [2001] ECR I-6193, para. 31.

52 Case C-214/94 *Boukhalfa* [1996] ECR I-2253.

unemployed, the disabled, tourists, students, pensioners and the independently wealthy' (Fries and Shaw 1998, 535). Those either side of the distinction have varying degrees of access to the principles of free movement and equal treatment (Ackers 1998). The entrenchment of differentiated citizenship rights for all Union citizens under Community law leads Dougan (2004, 141) to the conclusion that the downgraded status of CEE migrant workers is simply part of this ongoing trend:

> Even as regards nationals of the existing Member States, free movement rights vary according to distinctions drawn by the Treaty itself, under secondary legislation passed by the Community institutions, and through the case law of the Court – distinctions based on nationality, economic worth and financial status – whereby ... some of the least wealthy and most vulnerable members of society are excluded from rights to free movement and residency across the EU.

The restricted citizenship status of CEE nationals, then, simply adds to the norm of differentiation already inherent in Community law.[53] Presumably under this analysis EU8 nationals are not accorded second class membership or, if they are, it does not amount to any more of a disadvantageous position than that experienced by certain groups of EU15 nationals. Undoubtedly it is true that the citizenship provisions, and this is particularly evidenced by the case law on Article 18 EC, appear to privilege those migrants who have, on the whole, adequate financial resources but have fallen on *temporary* difficulties in fulfilling the terms of the secondary legislation.[54] However, while the less wealthy have been largely excluded from the broader citizens' right to free movement, the Court's inclusive construction 'worker' under Article 39 EC has opened up the fundamental right of mobility to those wanting to move to another Member State in search of economic and/or personal fulfilment. Unlike the free movement enshrined in Article 18 EC, residence under Article 39 EC is not subject to any 'limitations and conditions' and is not, therefore, dependent on the possession of such requirements as adequate resources and sickness insurance. Consequently, this provision has been accessible to the less wealthy nationals of the Member States.[55] With this in mind, it is arguable that the particular downgraded citizenship status imposed on EU8 and EU2 nationals can be distinguished from the Community norm of differentiated free movement rights for all, as the transitional restrictions deny access to one of the most valuable categories of market citizen: that of migrant worker. While it is open to less wealthy EU15 nationals to try to increase their economic status by exercising their right to mobility for the purposes of taking up work, EU8 and EU2 nationals' ability to accomplish the same is significantly

---

53 Directive 2004/38 retains the distinction between market citizens on the one hand and students, the financially independent and retired persons on the other.

54 On students see Case C-184/99 *Grzelczyk* [2001] ECR I-6193; on the independently wealthy see Case C-413/99 *Baumbast* [2002] ECR I-7091. For further detail see Dougan and Spaventa 2003.

55 See Cases 53/81 *Levin* [1982] ECR 1035; 139/85 *Kempf* [1986] ECR 1741; 196/87 *Steymann* [1988] ECR 6159.

more restricted during the transitional period(s). Currently, the right to move as a *worker* is more of a central feature of Union citizenship, certainly it is more valuable to CEE nationals, than the broader right to move as a *citizen*; thus, it is difficult not to conclude that EU8 and EU2 nationals are subject to a second rate conception of citizenship during the transitional period(s). Moreover, whereas the hierarchy involving EU15 nationals has been predicated on the basis of each group's perceived economic capacity and value, the post-enlargement hierarchy involving CEE migrants relies to a greater extent on nationality as a deciding factor. Therefore, the rationalization behind the new typology of free movement is more difficult to defend.

Recent research supports the assertion that the primary motivating factors for migration from the EU8 and EU2 Member States are of an economic nature (Markova and Reilly 2006; Jileva 2007). Certainly, the vast majority of the sample of Polish migrant workers interviewed by the author framed their decision to migrate as a strategy to help enhance their financial status due to the higher rates of pay in the UK; often, the specific aim was to help provide better opportunities for family members (either by moving the family unit as a whole to the UK or, more frequently, by remitting funds home to family members). High levels of unemployment in Poland were also frequently cited as a factor influencing the decision to move to the UK.[56] The following extracts illustrate typical responses given by the author's sample of respondents when describing the decision to move to the UK:

> I decided to move because I was looking for a better life and financial situation. I finished studying 12 years ago and then I opened a small shop in Poland. Two years ago lots of big companies opened up shops near to my business and my shop struggled. I decided to sell everything and move for a better as I have to think about getting a better life for my family. (Interview 001.JK)

> Well the main thing is to provide a better future for my family. I think in London I can improve life for my son. (Interview 009.BS)

> I left Poland because, for now, there are no prospective jobs for me. There are no chances for young people at all right now. (Interview 016.D)

The discussion in the following section turns to the broader impact of the citizenship provisions, access to which is not restricted by the Accession Treaty, on the mobility rights of EU8 and EU2 nationals outside the scope of the free movement of workers. Although, in some circumstances, the rights flowing from Article 18 EC can be valuable for certain migrants, it is not an adequate replacement for access to the fundamental *market* right enshrined in Article 39 EC. There is no doubt that the ability to move to another Member State to work

[56] In 2003 the unemployment rate in the EU15 was 8.1 per cent whereas in the EU8 Member States it was 14.5 per cent. In some Polish regions, however, the unemployment rate was above 20 per cent (in particular, Kujaw sko-Pomorskie, Lubuskie and Zachodniopomorskie), see Mladý 2004.

is an extremely valuable right which is often relied upon by those who wish to further their career, gain greater experience or provide a better standard of living for their family. It is this capability that would be most cherished by many CEE nationals. Therefore, although the capacity of 'citizens' to move is left intact, and despite the fact that differentiated citizenship rights are the norm in Community law, the absence of the right to move as a *worker* is significant for CEE nationals' citizenship status, and for the perception they have of their 'worth' in the eyes of the EU15.

CEe Nationals' Citizenship Entitlement as Migrant Citizens

The current transitional arrangements adopt an approach similar to the restrictions put in place following the accessions of Greece (1981) and Spain and Portugal (1986) in that they permit Member States to discriminate on grounds of nationality as regards access to employment. The focus on workers is an attempt by the EU15 to curb potential labour market flooding. In addition, the transitional restrictions represent a desire to avoid the situation whereby employees on low-wages gain automatic rights to social welfare in the host Member State.[57] What the Accession Treaty does not take into account is the existence of the formal citizenship provisions and the potential impact of the mobility rights enshrined in Article 18 EC (which extends a general right to reside in other Member States to all citizens). The Court's requisite jurisprudence, which often applies the non-discrimination principle in Article 12 EC in conjunction with Article 18 EC, also has implications for the citizenship status of EU8 and EU2 migrants.[58] As a result of such developments, which are elaborated on below, citizenship is 'nested'[59] across various sites in the Treaty and is therefore, at least in some form, accessible to CEE nationals in spite of the transitional arrangements.

At the time of the accessions of Greece, Spain and Portugal, citizenship as a concept had not yet been constitutionalized by insertion into the Treaty. Hence, the 2004 and 2007 enlargements have provided the first opportunity for the broader notion of citizenship to interact with the restricted status of market citizenship offered to accession migrants under the transitional arrangements. Despite the extension of more comprehensive free movement rights to *citizens* generally, the transitional arrangements have persisted with the preoccupation, in line with previous enlargements, with *workers*. Consequently, the ability of the EU15 Member States to prevent the migration of nationals from the newest Member States is more constrained in the aftermath of this enlargement than in previous EU expansions.

---

57 See Cases 53/81 *Levin* [1982] ECR 1035; 139/85 *Kempf* [1986] ECR 1741; 196/87 *Steymann* [1988] ECR 6159.

58 Including Case C-85/96 *Martinez Sala* [1998] ECR I-2691 ; Case C-413/99 *Baumbast* [2002] ECR I-7091; Case C-184/99 *Grzelczyk* [2001] ECR I-6193; Case C-138/02 *Collins* [2004] ECR I-2703; Case C-148/02 *Garcia Avello* [2003] ECR I-11613.

59 On the concepts of 'nested' and 'multiple' citizenships see Faist 2001; Kostakopoulou 2001, 66-67; Kostakopoulou 1999.

First in this section, attention turns to the possibility of CEE nationals relying upon the right to residency enshrined in Article 18 EC. Secondly, there is analysis of access to the principle of non-discrimination in Article 12 EC, which may be extended to those found to have a right to reside in an EU15 Member Stare. These entitlements constitute the two main components of Union citizenship extended to migrant citizens. Although they are interlinked, it is helpful to examine them individually in order that the potential application of both citizenship components to the situation of EU8 and EU2 nationals can be appreciated. This approach also mirrors the logic of the relationship between the entitlements: once it is established that a migrant citizen is resident in a Member State, the right to rely on the equal treatment principle in Article 12 EC becomes active.

Rights of residence in the EU15 CEE nationals are entitled from the outset to access the mobility rights attached to the economically inactive categories of migrant citizen, such as students and financially independent persons.[60] In order to present a complete picture of the residence rights available to CEE nationals under these groupings (and the requisite rights of equal treatment examined below) it is necessary to discuss both the old regime in the form of the residence Directives and their relationship with Article 18 EC as determined in the case law of the Court, and the updated regime established by Directive 2004/38.

Article 18 EC confers on all citizens of the Union the right to move and reside freely within the Member States, subject to the limitations and conditions laid down in the Treaty and the measures adopted to give it effect. It was just prior to the insertion of the citizenship provisions in the Treaty that the Community legislature had adopted the residency Directives which addressed economically inactive migrants: Directive 90/365 (retired persons),[61] Directive 93/96 (students)[62] and Directive 90/364 (those persons able to support themselves).[63] Although this cluster of secondary legislation was intended to 'liberate the Community from its economic preoccupation and to prepare the way for a community of citizens' (Hailbronner 2005, 1245), all three Directives made clear that the right of residence was dependent on: the possession of adequate resources not to become a burden on the social assistance scheme of the host Member State; and, being covered by comprehensive sickness insurance. Hence, the Member States were clearly concerned about the possibility of welfare tourism and sought to exclude from the right to reside those who would be unable to support themselves and

60 The status of retired persons is not discussed specifically here, although the rights (and obligations) of this group is analogous to those of financially independent persons in that the resources requirement is central to the grating of residence in an effort to ensure the host welfare state is not unreasonably burdened. Note also that Directive 2004/38 creates a category of permanent residents who, after lawful residence in a Member State for five years, are no longer subject to the resources requirement and enjoy fully the right to equal treatment: Articles 16 21.

61 [1990] OJ L180/28.

62 [1993] OJ L317/59.

63 [1990] OJ L180/26.

their families in the host state. In the initial period following the insertion of the citizenship provisions by the Treaty of Maastricht, it was not entirely clear what sort of relationship existed between the Directives' requirement of self-sufficiency and the 'limitations and conditions' on the right of free movement referred to in Article 18 EC. On the one hand, there was the argument that Article 18 EC simply codified the existing position under Community law to the effect that only economically active and economically self-sufficient citizens could access mobility rights. On the other hand, there was also a sentiment expressed by some that Article 18 EC may have disentangled the links between the right to move freely and the need to be economically active/self-sufficient to the effect that a separate right to mobility for all Union citizens had been created.[64]

Although there was a period of speculation, the Court began to make important pronouncements on the effect of Article 18 EC and, in relation to the extent of the right of residence (Fries and Shaw 1998). It was in the case of *Baumbast* that the Court first declared the right to reside in Article 18 EC to be directly effective.[65] This was despite the argument, put forward by the German and UK governments, that the 'limitations and conditions' referred to in Article 18 EC prevented the right from being free-standing (para. 78). The Court confirmed that the right of residence in Article 18 EC was sufficiently clear, precise and unconditional and, thus, conferred a right upon individuals (para. 86). In *Grzelczyk*[66] the ECJ made the now celebrated statement that 'Union citizenship is destined to be the fundamental status of nationals of the Member States' (para. 31).[67] This statement has now been codified in Directive 2004/38[68] which would suggest the formulation has been embraced also by the Community's political institutions. Additionally, however, in both of the aforementioned cases, the Court confirmed that the 'limitations and conditions' referred to in Article 18 EC did include the requirements of sufficient resources and sickness insurance found in the residence Directives. Thus, the Court confirmed here that Article 18 EC had not completely detached the right to free movement from economic elements; indeed, in *Baumbast* the ECJ stated that the limitations and conditions set out in the residence Directives recognize:

> ... that the exercise of the right of residence of citizens of the Union can be subordinated to the legitimate interests of Member States. In that regard, according to the fourth recital in the preamble to Directive 90/364 beneficiaries of the right of residence must not become an unreasonable burden on the public finances of the host Member State. (Para. 90)

---

64 For more detail on the uncertainty surrounding the effect of the citizenship provisions see Fries and Shaw 1998.

65 Case C-413/99 *Baumbast* [2002] ECR I-7091.

66 Case C-184/99 *Grzelczyk* [2001] ECR I-6193.

67 This has been restated in numerous other decisions of the ECJ including, *inter alia*, Case C-138/02 *Collins* [2004] ECR I-2703 and Case C-148/02 *Garcia Avello* [2003] ECR I-11613.

68 Recital 3, Preamble, Directive 2004/38 [2004] OJ L158/77.

Before taking a closer look at the details and impact of these judgments on the residence rights of CEE nationals, the position of the law following the adoption of Directive 2004/38 needs to be acknowledged. With regards to residence, the Directive retains the twin requirements of sufficient resources and sickness insurance in respect of economically inactive migrants. Hence, the distinction between the economically active and economically viable, on the one hand, and the economically inactive, on the other, remains. The Directive does, though, provide that all Union citizens have a right of residence for up to three months *without any conditions or any formalities* other than the requirement to hold a valid identity card or passport.[69] Therefore, it is only after this three-month period that the above distinction and the 'limitations and conditions' on the right of residence come into play.[70]

The existence of this three month period in the more recent piece of secondary legislation is interesting when held up against the transitional arrangements in the Accession Treaty. Under the terms of the Directive, EU8 and EU2 nationals, as Union citizens, are entitled to make use of this right that allows them to enter and reside in an EU15 Member State without the necessity of fulfilling the resources requirements. The Directive contains no statement of derogation to the effect that CEE nationals are subject to any different rules as a result of the transitional period. Secondly, the very precise language adopted in the annexes to the Act of Accession,[71] which contain the details of the transitional restrictions, focuses solely on Articles 1–6 of Regulation 1612/68[72] and leaves very little scope for a wider interpretation of the transitional arrangements that includes other provisions of Community law. The restrictions only centre on allowing the implementing Member States to derogate from the provisions that usually require them to provide EU nationals with the opportunity to access their labour markets without experiencing discrimination. This ability to enter and reside for a period of three months may prove to be extremely useful for CEE nationals who wish to seek work in a Member State, despite the imposition of transitional restrictions, as it essentially provides a short period of grace within which they can seek employment (assuming lawful employment is possible at all).[73] Once this initial three-month period comes to a close the right of residence for more than three months, in Article 7 of the Directive, becomes the operable provision

69 Article 6, Directive 2004/38.

70 But note the principle of equal treatment does not apply in full during the first three months as Article 24(2) provides that Member States are not obliged to confer entitlement to social assistance during this period. It is slightly confusing, then, that Article 14(1) specifies that the right to reside for 3 months is dependent on the individual (and family members) not becoming an unreasonable burden on the social assistance system of the host Member State.

71 Article 24 of the Act of Accession [2003] OJ L236/33, para 2, Annexes.

72 [1968] OJ L257/2.

73 Discussed further in the section on work seekers below.

and it is here that the various conditions relating to the different categories of migrant can be found.[74]

It is clear that those CEE accession nationals fulfilling the conditions of residence attached to the categories of economically inactive migrant are able to rely on the right to free movement in Article 18 EC during the transitional period. This is a valuable right in itself and, in particular, it seems that many young EU8 nationals have taken advantage of their post-accession ability to move to the EU15 as students.[75] To gain a right of residence under Article 7 of the Directive, students are required to have comprehensive sickness insurance and must assure the host Member State, by means of declaration,[76] that they have sufficient resources to avoid becoming a burden on the social assistance system. They must also be enrolled at a public or private establishment, accredited or financed by the host Member State, for the principal purpose of following a course of study (this includes vocational training).[77] By analogy with the conditions of the three residence directives under the old regime, the requirements now enshrined in Directive 2004/38 will be included in the 'limitations and conditions' that Article 18 EC is subject to.[78]

In addition to those situations in which an individual complies fully with the requirements in the secondary legislation, the manner in which the ECJ has interpreted the caveat of 'limitations and conditions' (albeit under the old regime) indicates there may be occasions when a CEE national does not comply with the letter of the law, in respect of having sufficient resources and comprehensive sickness insurance, yet is (theoretically at least) entitled to rely on a right to reside flowing from Article 18 EC. To explore this assertion further, it is necessary to take a further look at the cases of *Baumbast* and *Grzelczyk*.

In *Baumbast* the British immigration authorities refused Mr Baumbast's application for an extension of his residence permit on the grounds that he and his family were not insured for emergency medical treatment in the UK and so failed to comply with the requirement of sickness insurance in Directive 90/364 (See Dougan and Spaventa 2003; Van der Mei 2003b). Mr Baumbast, a German national, had originally moved to the UK as a worker but later was employed by a German company that required him to work in Asia and Africa. His family

---

[74] Workers and the self-employed have an automatic right to reside (Article 7(1)(a)) that cannot be withdrawn on the basis that they are an unreasonable burden on the social assistance system of the host Member State (Article 14(4)(a)). Member States can restrict the residence rights of these groups on grounds of public policy, public security or public health subject to the details in Articles 27–33.

[75] For example: in 2004/2005 8,390 Polish students took part in the Erasmus exchange program and 2,200 Polish nationals enrolled in British universities (compared to just 965 in 2003/2004). Further, in 2004/2005 Polish nationals constituted the second largest group of non-German students in Germany (after Chinese nationals). Figures cited in Iglicka 2006, 2.

[76] This was also the position under Directive 93/96.

[77] Article 7(1)(c), Directive 2004/38.

[78] Article 7(1)(c) confirms the twin requirements of sufficient resources and comprehensive sickness insurance continue to apply as regards those who aspire to reside on the basis of being financially independent.

continued to reside in the UK where they owned a house and the children attended school. Although the Baumbasts did not satisfy the requirement of having health insurance in the UK they did have comprehensive medical insurance in Germany, where they returned to when they required treatment, and they had never sought to rely on the British welfare system. The UK court sought guidance from the ECJ as to whether Mr Baumbast could derive a right of residence from Article 18 EC.

After making the pronouncements that Article 18 EC was directly effective, but the Member States were legitimately able to ensure nationals of other Member States did not become an unreasonable burden, the Court went on discuss further the notion of 'limitations and conditions'. Most crucially, the Court noted that:

> Limitations and conditions must be applied in compliance with the limits imposed by Community law and in accordance with the general principles of that law, in particular with the principle of proportionality. (Para. 91)

Given that the Baumbasts had not been a burden on the UK's public finances (indeed Mr Baumbast had made a positive economic contribution in the past), that the family were well integrated after residing in the UK for a number of years, and that insurance was in place in another Member State, the Court concluded that:

> To refuse to allow Mr Baumbast to exercise his right of residence... on the ground that his sickness insurance does not cover the emergency treatment given in the host Member State would amount to a disproportionate interference with the exercise of that right. (Para. 93)

Thus by virtue of the application of the principle of proportionality, Mr Baumbast's right of residence remained intact, despite not complying with the formal requirements of the secondary legislation (Dougan and Spaventa 2003; Dougan 2004).

The decision in *Grzelczyk,* while preceding the decision in *Baumbast*, displays a similar line of reasoning in relation to the requirement of sufficient resources for students in Directive 93/96 (Dougan and Spaventa 2003; Jacqueson 2002; Iliopouou and Toner 2002). Rudy Grzelczyk, a French national, studied in Belgium and in the fourth year of his course he applied for the Belgian *minimex* (a non-contributory minimum subsistence allowance). By applying for such a benefit, of course, he indicated that he did not in fact have sufficient resources as stipulated by the Directive. In his previous years of residence, Grzelczyk had worked part time; however, as he was in his last year, he wished to be able to concentrate just on his academic studies. This case is important also for the discussion of the equal treatment principle, but with regards to residence, the Court stressed that refusal of a residence permit cannot be the automatic consequence of recourse to the host Member State's social assistance system (para. 43).[79] The Court placed significance on the fact that Grzelczyk was merely experiencing 'temporary

[79] This has since been codified in Directive 2004/38, Article 14(3).

difficulties' and, as a result, he was entitled to expect to benefit from a degree of financial solidarity between nationals of the host Member State and nationals of other Member States (para. 44). On the basis of these cases, Dougan and Spaventa (2003, 703) stress that:

> Baumbast ... illustrates the application of proportionality to the 'health insurance' requirement imposed by the three Residency Directives. The earlier case of Grzelcyk illustrates (though more in hindsight than in the explicit reasoning of the judgment itself) the application of the principle of proportionality to the requirement of 'sufficient resources' set out in the Residency Directives.

Therefore, this application of the proportionality principle to the exercise of the Member States' discretion may allow the enforcement of a right to reside by an individual who does not actually meet the legislative requirements. Arguably, this remains so following the adoption of Directive 2004/38. The proportionality principle is not expressly codified; rather, Article 14(2) states that economically inactive migrants retain the right of residence so long as they continue to fulfil the conditions attached to that residence (i.e. sufficient resources and sickness insurance). However, the preamble does refer to the importance of migrants not becoming an unreasonable burden on the social assistance system of the host Member State[80] and this is essentially what the application of the principle of proportionality to the twin requirements in the legislation sought to achieve. On the basis of this analysis the stage seems set for the Court to continue to apply proportionality to the Member States' efforts to enforce their limitations and conditions on a right of residence, the determining factor remaining whether the individual has become an 'unreasonable burden'.[81]

Of course, by no means is the right of residence for the economically inactive unlimited, but the Court's use of proportionality has injected a greater degree of flexibility into the black-letter provisions and allowed it to extend residence (and equal treatment) rights to some individuals who fall outside of the formal legislative regime. As a consequence of this case law, during the transitional periods, EU8 and EU2 nationals with adequate resources can reside in the EU15; furthermore, the right is flexible and may not automatically be rescinded should they fail to fulfil one of the conditions in the secondary legislation.

The application of proportionality, though, clearly cannot assist all those economically inactive migrants who experience hardship and fail to fulfil the requirements of residency. A case which demonstrates this is that of *Trojani*[82]

---

80 Recital 10, Preamble, Directive 2004/38.

81 This concept is not quantified but whether or not an individual constitutes an 'unreasonable burden' is often related to the application of the equal treatment principle (described below) which extends the right to access various welfare benefits to resident Union citizens. This may result in lawful residence activating the right to equal treatment which, in turn, enables the migrant to access social assistance; at this point, the Member State may lawfully conclude the claimant is an unreasonable burden and withdraw the right of residence.

82 Case C-456/02 *Trojani* [2004] ECR I-7573, see further Van Der Mei 2005.

where the Member State's application of limitations and conditions was held to be proportionate. Trojani, a French national, was residing in Belgium in a Salvation Army hostel and had made an application to receive the Belgium *minimex* which had been refused by the national authorities.[83] In relation to the issue of whether or not Trojani could enjoy a right of residence by virtue of the right to free movement in Article 18 EC the ECJ confirmed that the requirement of sufficient resources was subject to the principle of proportionality (para. 34). However, the Court went on to note that, in Trojani's case, a lack of resources was precisely the reason why Mr Trojani sought to receive a benefit such as the minimex (para. 35). In contrast to the situation in *Baumbast*, then, Trojani could not derive a right to reside from Article 18 EC because 'there was no indication that … the failure to recognize that right would go beyond what is necessary to achieve the objective pursued by … Directive [90/364]' (para. 36). It seems then that the application of proportionality would only be useful to those CEE migrants who had previously fulfilled the conditions of the Directive, of having sufficient resources and sickness insurance, but later fell on hard times that were temporary in nature.[84] *Baumbast* and *Grzelzcyk* illustrate that the Court values those with a greater sense of 'belonging' to the host state. Article 18 EC is unlikely to be of great benefit to those wishing to establish in the first instance residence in another Member State (Van Der Mei 2005, 432). Further, despite not fulfilling the requirements in the secondary legislation, it is clear that the Baumbasts, in particular, were portrayed as 'worthy' beneficiaries of the right to reside given their clear financial autonomy and the unlikeliness of the family ever requiring social assistance (paras 88-89). Grzelzcyk, too, is described in terms of having worked hard in the past to finance his studies (paras 10–11). By contrast, those such as Trojani who, as Dougan and Spaventa (2003, 712) claim, are the more 'vulnerable members of society' remain 'alienated' from the same right.

Less wealthy CEE nationals will find it difficult to establish a right to reside in the EU15 longer than the initial three-month period of grace granted to all citizens under Directive 2004/38. Taking Poland as an example, considering the high rates of unemployment and the low rates of pay available in the country (Keune 1998), alongside the assertion that many wish to move in order to *increase* their wealth, it would appear that certainly many Polish nationals would fall into the 'vulnerable' group unable to enforce a right of residence in an EU15 state on the basis of Article 18 EC. The economic gulf between the EU8 and EU2, on the one hand, and the EU15, on the other hand, remains gaping. It is no surprise that levels of gross domestic product per citizen (a measure of economic activity in a country) in Bulgaria and Romania are the lowest in the EU, standing respectively

---

83 Note that part of the judgment discusses whether Trojani can be classed as a worker for the purposes of Community law, in which case he would have the right to equal treatment as regards social advantages (Article 7(2), Regulation 1612/68), as he carried out 'odd jobs' for the Salvation Army. The ECJ, after reiterating the definition of worker, ruled it was for the national court to assess whether Trojani fulfilled the criteria (paras. 13–29).

84 As Grzelczyk did.

at 37 and 38 per cent of the EU27 average according to recent figures (Eurostat 2007). Poland, Latvia, Lithuania, Slovakia, Hungary and Estonia's levels of GDP range from 53 to 67 per cent of the EU27 average (ibid., 1). Analysis of the national gross minimum wages of a number of Member States similarly points to the existence of disparities. For example, Bulgaria's monthly minimum wage stands at €81.8 and in Romania the corresponding figure is €104.94; minimum standards in Poland, Slovakia and the Czech Republic reach €230.78, €204.11 and €280.68 respectively. In comparison, the monthly minimum wage in Spain is €540.90 and in the Netherlands the figure is €1,284.60. Further, the UK and Ireland's hourly minimum wages stand at €7.85 (£5.35) and €7.65 respectively (Carley 2006). Whilst it is important not to over-emphasize similarities in the social and economic conditions of the different EU8 and EU2 Member States,[85] the socio-economic context of the newer CEE Member States remains broadly distinct from that of the EU15 Member States. Jandl (2007, 291) has pointed to 'deplorable social and economic conditions, rapid industrial restructuring of the formally centrally planned economies coupled with low incomes and high unemployment and escalating political and conflicts' as distinguishing features of the climate within which the newest Member States are situated. It would seem that, as a consequence of their comparatively lower levels of 'social and economic capital' (Schuster 2005, 757), far fewer EU8 and EU2 nationals than EU15 nationals would currently satisfy the requirements of self-sufficiency in the secondary legislation and secure a right of residency on the basis of Article 18 EC (even read in the light of proportionality).

Clearly, the fundamental test remains that an economically inactive migrant should not become an unreasonable burden. If this threshold is reached the Member State is entitled to expel the individual. On this note, Dougan (2004, 118–19) raises the example of a further interesting scenario. The right of a Member State to expel an individual who no longer fulfils the residency requirements is, as we know, subject to the application of proportionality *and other general principles of Community law*.[86] Dougan (2004, 118) suggests there is scope for an EU8 national, who does not satisfy the conditions of residence as either a self-employed person or self-sufficient citizen, to argue that expulsion would infringe the right to family and private life under Article 8 of the ECHR. The Court has certainly demonstrated an increasing tendency to draw inspiration from this particular provision. For example, in *Akrich*[87] the UK authorities had taken the decision to expel the third-country national spouse of a Community national.[88] The ECJ stressed that the UK must not violate the Akrichs' right to respect for family life:

---

[85] The experience of Slovenia, with GDP only 15 per cent below average and a monthly minimum wage of €521.99, illustrates this point particularly.

[86] Case C-413/99 *Baumbast* [2002] ECR I-7091.

[87] Case C-109/01 *Akrich* [2003] ECR I-9607.

[88] See also Case C-60/00 *Carpenter* [2002] ECR I-6279 which involved the third-country national spouse of a British national providing services, pursuant to Article 49 EC, in other Member States. The ECJ stated that the UK decision to expel Mrs Carpenter

> Even though the Convention does not as such guarantee the right of an alien to enter or reside in a particular country, the removal of a person from a country where close members of his family are living may amount to an infringement of the right to respect for family life guaranteed by Article 8(1) of the Convention. (Para. 59)[89]

Dougan (2004, 118) argues that this line of argument may prove particularly accessible to those EU8 migrants that have demonstrated a desire for themselves and their family to integrate into the host society:

> If the claimant has lived in the host state for a significant period of time, perhaps with his/her family and children, such that the claimant has few remaining personal ties to the country of origin, and the host state has become his/her home for all purposes save nationality, expulsion might be held to strike an unfair balance between the legitimate interests of the Member State and the private rights of the individual.

This analysis is engaging and details another possible way, in addition to the application of proportionality, whereby an EU8 or EU2 national could enforce a right to reside in an EU15 Member State despite the imposition of transitional restrictions. It is doubtful, however, that this will be applied in practice to any great extent. It has already been suggested in this book that many CEE nationals moved alone initially and, furthermore, that the migrants themselves retain active transnational links with their home society. On this understanding it seems unlikely that, at this stage, many EU8 and EU2 nationals and their families will display sufficient degrees of integration in a host state to justify the protection of a right to reside by Article 8 of the ECHR. Furthermore if a CEE family, despite having moved to an EU15 Member State, could integrate back into the home society relatively easily, then arguably their expulsion would pass the threshold in Article 8(2) of the ECHR of being in 'accordance with the law and necessary in a democratic society'. Article 8 of the ECHR only prevents deportation if it is considered unreasonable to send a family back to their country of origin.

Finally on the issue of fundamental rights, it is clear that the Article 8 right to family and private life enshrined in the ECHR is potentially relevant across all Member States (in that deportation of an individual where his or her family members are situated may constitute an unreasonable interference with that right). Other fundamental rights concerns, however, may be exclusively relevant to the situation of EU8 and EU2 nationals. Currently, the newer Member States' human rights standards and levels of protection, most notably those of Bulgaria and Romania, remain distinct from standards in the EU15. For example, Amnesty International has expressed concern that Article 3 (prohibition against torture and inhuman or degrading treatment) and Article 12 (right to marry or found

ran contrary to *Mr Carpenter's* right to respect for family life in Article 8 of the ECHR which was to be protected in his capacity as service provider (paras. 41–42).

89 See also Case C-1/05 *Jia* [2007] ECR I-0001. In Case C-291/05 *Eind* (judgment of 11 December 2007) the Court expressly referred to the 'right to family reunification' for EU citizens (para. 23) in Article 10 of Regulation 1612/68 (now Articles 2 and 3 of Directive 2004/38).

a family) are not adequately safeguarded in Bulgaria and Romania (Amnesty International 2005). This illustrates how the social context of the newer Member States is distinct from the EU15. Moreover, it leaves open the possibility for arguments based on other provisions of the ECHR to be invoked in order to try and rebut a Member State's expulsion of a CEE national.

This discussion has demonstrated that the right to reside in another Member State is no longer based solely on the carrying out of 'worthwhile' economic activity by virtue of Article 18 EC. All Union citizens enjoy a directly effective right to reside throughout the Union and, although this is subject to the conditions set out in the secondary legislation, the Court has injected some flexibility into the operation of these requirements through the application of the principle of proportionality (and other general principles of Community law). Consequently, there may be occasions where a claimant fails to fulfil the requirements yet still retains the right to reside. Despite the transitional restrictions on their movement rights as workers, then, Article 18 EC may well prove valuable for financially independent EU8 nationals seeking to enforce a right to reside in the EU15; or, thanks to proportionality, the almost financially-independent. Article 18 EC still cannot assist the less wealthy in enforcing a right to reside and, in this respect, will not help those who wish to exercise mobility rights in order to better their living standards (and that of their families) by working. Thus, although it is interesting to speculate on the interplay between the right to reside as a *citizen* and the transitional restrictions on *workers'* residence entitlement, the practical impact of Article 18 EC on the experience of CEE nationals is unlikely to be far-reaching.[90]

In any event, the right to reside under Article 18 EC remains significantly more constrained than that which is extended to workers. Despite the inclusion in Directive 2004/38 of the *Grzelczyk* statement that expulsion should not be the automatic consequence of a citizen's recourse to the social assistance system, the host Member State is entitled to conclude, provided the principle of proportionality is respected, that the citizen no longer satisfies the conditions of having sufficient resources and sickness insurance. Furthermore, as will be discussed in the following section, citizens' rights to equal treatment are not as extensive or secure as those extended to market citizens.

CEE migrants' equal treatment rights Clearly, economically active market citizens have an extensive right to residency which,[91] in turn, provides an all-encompassing right to equal treatment in the host Member State[92] that includes within its

---

[90] Although the discussion here is restricted to those EU8 or EU2 nationals who are not workers, such as students or the financially independent. Dougan (2004, 128–32) puts forward a convincing argument about the potential application of Article 18 EC to those EU8 nationals who work *illegally* but satisfy the criterion of being economically active or financially independent.

[91] For example in relation to workers they flow from Article 39 EC and are articulated in Directive 2004/38 (previously Directive 68/360 [1968] OJ L257/13).

[92] Article 24, Directive 2004/38.

remit the ability to access a plethora of social welfare benefits.[93] Economically inactive migrant citizens have not traditionally had such extensive rights to equal treatment.[94] This section will examine, however, how the Court's interpretation of the citizenship provisions in combination with Article 12 EC has enabled lawfully resident, albeit economically inactive, citizens to claim a greater stake in the right to equal treatment and, as a result, better access to a form of (European) social citizenship. Again, this is discussed within the framework of CEE migration during the transitional period, and the impact of Directive 2004/38 on the rights of equal treatment available to CEE migrants is examined.

Article 17(2) EC provides that citizens of the Union shall enjoy the rights conferred by the Treaty and shall be subject to the duties imposed thereby. One such right conferred by the Treaty is that contained in Article 12 EC – the right to be protected against discrimination on the grounds of nationality. It was the case of *Martinez Sala* which first established that citizens lawfully resident in a Member State could challenge unequal treatment they experienced, in comparison to nationals of the host state, on the basis of Article 12 EC (Tomuschat 2000; O'Leary 1999). Mrs Martinez Sala, a Spanish national, had moved to Germany as a child in 1968. She had been employed there, in a variety of jobs, until 1989 but since then had received social assistance from the city of Nuremberg. Up until 1984, Sala had been granted residence permits but, from then on, she was simply in possession of a series of documents certifying that she had applied for an extension to her residence permit. She was, again, issued with a residence permit in 1994 but in 1993 she had applied for, and been refused, a child-raising allowance. Her application was rejected on the basis that she did not have German nationality, a residence permit or residence entitlement. The Court first held that Sala, as a national of a Member State lawfully residing in the territory of another Member State,[95] came within the scope *ratione personae* of the citizenship provisions in the Treaty (para. 61). Secondly, the ECJ went on to state that such a Union citizen could benefit from the equal treatment principle in Article 12 EC in relation to all matters that fell within the scope *ratione materiae* of the Treaty (para. 63). The child-raising allowance was found to fall 'indisputably' within the material scope of the Treaty by analogy with the benefits available to workers under Article 7(2) of Regulation 1612/68 and those qualifying as 'family benefits' under Article 4(1)(h) of Regulation 1408/71 (para. 57).[96]

Martinez Sala has had significant implications for the status of Union citizenship and its relationship with the principle of non-discrimination. O'Leary (1999, 77) makes the point that:

---

93 Article 7(2), Regulation 1612/68. For example, Cases 249/83 *Hoeckx* [1985] ECR 973; C-237/94 *O'Flynn* [1996] ECR I 2617.

94 For example, Case 197/86 *Brown* [1988] ECR 3205.

95 On the basis of national law as opposed to Article 18 EC, see below.

96 Tomuschat (2000, 452) is critical of the application of principles developed in relation to economically active migrant workers to a non-economically active migrant citizen.

> Martinez Sala confirms that Union citizenship explodes the 'linkages' with EC law previously required for the principle of non-discrimination to apply, namely performance or involvement in an economic activity as workers, established persons or providers and recipients of services, preparation for a future economic activity as a student or stagiaire or some sort of relationship with an economic actor as a family member or dependent.

Lawful residence is thus the key to establishing a right to equal treatment as a Union citizen and, as Dougan and Spaventa (2003, 708) point out:

> Equal treatment not only flows from lawful residency; it also makes the latter status more meaningful in practice.

Grzelczyk demonstrates this point nicely. We have already seen that Grzelczyk had a right to reside in Belgium on the basis of Article 18 EC and therefore he fell within the scope *ratione personae* of the citizenship provisions. With regard to the refusal of the Belgian authorities to grant him the *minimex*, the Court further held that this amounted to direct discrimination, comparable with the discrimination experienced by Martinez Sala, which was strictly prohibited by Article 12 EC:[97]

> It is clear from the documents before the Court that a student of Belgian nationality ... who found himself in exactly the same circumstances as Mr Grzelczyk would satisfy the conditions for obtaining the minimex. The fact that Mr Grzelczyk is not of Belgian nationality is the only bar to it being granted to him. It is not therefore in dispute that the case is one of discrimination solely on the ground of nationality. (Para. 29)

In relation to the scope *ratione materiae*, the ECJ in *Grzelczyk* again drew a parallel with Article 7(2) of Regulation 1612/68 (para. 27). Further, the Court stated that, simply through students' movement and residence in another Member State, provisions of Community law relating to them fall within the material scope (para. 35). The ECJ was of the opinion that the introduction in the EC Treaty of the citizenship provisions and a chapter on education and vocational training,[98] alongside the existence of the Students' Residence Directive 93/96, had altered the position of Community law. In the earlier case of *Brown*[99] it had

---

[97] Indirect discrimination is discussed more specifically below in relation to the status of work seekers in the UK but, for now, it is sufficient to note that the Court does adopt a different approach when dealing with a national measure that is indirectly discriminatory on the grounds of nationality. Indirect discrimination can be justified by reference to objective justification under the doctrine of mandatory requirements. In particular, it appears that a Member State is entitled to require that an individual demonstrate a genuine link to the national territory before he/she is able to claim equal treatment as regards to welfare benefits: Case C-209/03 *Bidar* [2005] ECR I-2119; Case C-224/98 *D'Hoop* [2002] ECR I-6191; Case C-138/02 *Collins* [2004] ECR I-2703; Case C-258/04 *Ioannidis* [2005] ECR I-8275.

[98] Title XI, Chapter 3 of Part III of the EC Treaty.

[99] Case 197/86 *Brown* [1988] ECR 3205.

been decided that there was no anti-discrimination protection available in the area of maintenance or training grants.[100] After *Grzekczyk*, then, *Brown* is no longer regarded as a correct statement of the law[101] and the elevated status of students as Union citizens means that the equal treatment principle can apply as regards social security and assistance benefits available to students under national law.

Moving as a student to an EU15 Member State may be an attractive option to EU8 and EU2 nationals during the operation of the transitional arrangements on the free movement of workers. Furthermore, moving as a student may hold out the possibility of entering to reside via the 'back door' as there is somewhat of a grey area surrounding the right of CEE students to access part time work in a Member State applying transitional restrictions. Students usually are allowed access to the labour market on the basis of the principle of non-discrimination but the position as regards EU8 migrant students in Member States applying transitional restrictions is more ambiguous; arguably, under the terms of the Accession Treaty, Member States are lawfully able to prevent labour market access by this group. Surely it will be in a Member State's interest to allow (genuine) students to access part time employment on their territory, although fears of bogus students using the status as a cover for labour market access may persuade Member States that it is safer to deny access. In any event, the ability to move as a student may tempt some with the notion that labour market access will follow. In addition to this perceived attractiveness of moving as a student, however, the legal status is potentially quite a far-reaching one (Dougan 2005a), although the impact of Directive 2004/38 does need to be considered in this respect.

Following *Grzelczyk*, the extent of students' equal treatment rights was considered further in *Bidar* (Barnard 2005).[102] Mr Bidar, a French national, had resided in and been enrolled at a secondary school in the UK for three years before he entered university there. Whilst he was charged the same tuition fee rate as national students, he was denied financial assistance to cover his maintenance costs in the form of a student loan. First, Bidar was clearly entitled to a right of residence in the UK under Article 18 EC read in conjunction with the general residence Directive 90/364 (not the Students' Directive), the conditions of which he satisfied (para. 36). As a result of his lawful residence, Bidar was entitled to equal treatment as regards social assistance benefits (as in *Grzelczyk*), but the issue then was whether those benefits included assistance for maintenance costs through subsidised loans or grants. Once again the Court referred to the developments in Community law cited in *Grzelczyk* (para. 39) before confirming that social assistance:

> Whether in the form of subsidised loans or of grants, provided to students lawfully resident in the host Member State to cover their maintenance costs falls within the

---

[100] Although pre-*Brown*, in Case 293/83 *Gravier* [1985] ECR 593, the ECJ had held that there was a right to equal treatment in relation to fees for higher education.

[101] Grzelczyk, paras. 34–35.

[102] Case C-209/03 *Bidar* [2005] ECR I-2119

> scope of application of the Treaty for the purposes of the prohibition of discrimination laid down in the first paragraph of Article 12 EC. (Para. 48)

This ruling, therefore, fortified the citizenship status of migrant students by confirming that developments in Community law had extended the scope of benefits they could access by virtue of the equal treatment principle. Despite this extension in the scope of equal treatment rights available to students, the reasoning of the Court suggests it will be by no means easy for EU8 and EU2 nationals who move during the transitional period to benefit from such equal treatment in relation to student loans (and grants). As the UK legislation at issue imposed a requirement of three years prior residency before a student could claim a loan, it did not overtly discriminate directly on the ground of nationality; instead, the requirement was intrinsically liable to impact on more non-nationals than nationals and, hence, amounted to indirect discrimination. Thus, the ECJ confirmed that Member States could legitimately expect the individuals in question to display a degree of integration into the host society before granting them access to assistance covering the maintenance costs of students (para. 57). Therefore, CEE nationals residing lawfully in the territory of an EU15 Member State during the transitional period would have to demonstrate a sufficient degree of integration and prior-residency before being able to access the type of benefits in *Bidar*. This is quite a high hurdle to overcome and, in effect, requires the migrant to reside in the host Member State for a significant period prior to the enrolment on a course. The emphasis in the case law on the importance of integration as a key to unlocking solidaristic rights, may be a particularly high hurdle for EU8 and EU2 migrants to overcome during the transitional period. Those who moved from the EU8 to the EU15 after 1 May 2004 or, more significantly, from the EU2 after 1 January 2007 are unlikely to have built up a period of exclusive residence within that territory before embarking on a course of study. Bidar himself did not gain access to the right of equal treatment by virtue solely of the status of migrant student. He had not moved *in order* to study; rather, his access to university stemmed from a long-term residence in the UK which he fulfilled as a financially independent person (he had lived with his grandmother, as her dependent). The circumstances were somewhat exceptional. In addition, even though the Court in *Bidar* spoke in terms of student 'grants and loans', this was in the context of Directive 90/364 not Directive 93/96, which specifically excluded maintenance grants from the scope of equal treatment.[103]

Those CEE students who are integrated to a sufficiently high extent will probably be entitled to protection against discrimination in the area of maintenance loans or grants for students by analogy with *Bidar*. Furthermore, it should be remembered that those legally residing in a Member State for a year prior to accession are not subject to transitional mobility restrictions. This group,

[103] Article 3, Directive 93/96. Therefore the status of maintenance grants and loans, as opposed to general social assistance, under Directive 93/96 was unclear. For further analysis of the impact of *Bidar* (and *Grzekczyk*) on the exclusion in Directive 93/96, see Dougan 2005a; Barnard 2005.

then, is privileged as compared to those EU8 and EU2 nationals who moved after the date of enlargement. In any event, this discussion may be slightly superfluous following the entry into force of the citizenship Directive in 2006. Directive 2004/38 appears to step back from the decision in *Bidar* and, on a literal interpretation, provides that both maintenance grants and loans are excluded from the principle of equal treatment in Article 24 until the individual claiming entitlement has lawfully resided in the territory for five years and is, consequently, a permanent resident under Article 16 of the Directive.[104] To an extent this can be seen as a codification of the Court's stance in *Bidar,* that an individual should be able to display a sufficient degree of integration into the host society, though five years is clearly a harsher test of integration than the three years specified in *Bidar* itself.

Some commentators expect that the Court will continue to apply the *Baumbast*-style principle of proportionality to the terms of the new Directive so the five year threshold may not have to be met in all circumstances in order for the equal treatment principle to be activated in respect of maintenance grants and loans (Dougan 2005a, 969; 2006a, 627–33; Hailbronner 2005, 1264; Dougan and Spaventa 2005, 181). Hailbronner (2005, 1264), for example, makes reference to the Court's application of proportionality to the requirements in Directives 90/364 and 93/96 and suggests that:

> The principle of proportionality, devoid of any precise content if not applied restrictively and its proper systematic context, may again serve as an almost unlimited instrument to amend secondary Community law.

It would seem that, at the point of five years residence, the right to equal treatment accrues *de jure*, regardless of the level of actual integration. Prior to this point, the *de facto* degree of integration can be examined (via a test of proportionality) and may be held sufficient to invoke the equal treatment principle. Therefore, the notion of proportionality may be used again by the Court to justify a departure from the strict letter of the law. Given the emphasis in the case law, however, on the importance of integration as a key to unlocking the right to solidarity,[105] it is likely to remain the case that those who show insufficient levels of integration into a host state, and/or have resided only for a short period of time, will not be able to claim student maintenance grants or loans even with the principle of proportionality being applied to the new legislative regime. *Post-accession* CEE migrants thus are likely to be excluded from this right. There is a developing consensus in the literature that residence, as a symbol of integration, is not only the key to equal treatment but also the differentiator which determines the *extent* of the application of equal treatment to any one individual (Dougan and Spaventa 2003; Barnard 2005; Golynker 2006). With this in mind Dougan (2005a, 969) argues that:

---

[104] Article 24(2), Directive 2004/38.

[105] Most notably Case C-209/03 *Bidar* [2005] ECR I-2119 and Case C-456/02 *Trojani* [2004] ECR I-7573.

It might still emerge from the case law itself that new or very recent arrivals cannot challenge apparently discriminatory restrictions on access to welfare benefits because they are not in fact in a comparable situation to own nationals or other Union citizens who have actually resided in the host.[106]

From this perspective newer arrivals are entitled to equal treatment as regards access to certain advantages in the host Member State,[107] but often will not be able to rely on the principle with regard to social welfare benefits. Barnard (2005, 172) describes the situation, in terms of solidarity, as such:

> While Article 18(1) EC gives newly arrived migrants the right to move and reside freely in the host state there is insufficient solidarity between the newly arrived migrant and the host state taxpayer to justify requiring full equal treatment in respect of social welfare benefits.

This tendency of the Court, to use previous periods of residence as a means to measure the degree to which an individual citizen can access equal treatment, clearly has implications beyond students as a category of migrant, as it applies also in the realm of financially independent persons and work seekers. The transitional arrangements, although applicable only to workers and restricted to the equal treatment rights contained in the provisions granting labour market access, may have an indirect impact on the longer-term ability of EU nationals in general to benefit from the non-discrimination right in Article 12 EC. By denying CEE nationals the right to reside in a territory to take up employment, the Accession Treaty is denying them the ability to employ one of the main methods citizens have used to build up entitlement to equal treatment – integration into a society.[108]

Moreover, the Court's reliance on residence as the main indicator of integration is by no means immune from criticism. For example, it may be that CEE nationals who have taken up work in an EU15 Member State since accession, despite only having resided there themselves for a short period, have strong family ties to that host state.[109] Furthermore, the notion of real and genuine link from the case law on economically inactive migrants does not generally appear in cases involving the economically active; here, the assumption is that such individuals automatically satisfy a certain level of integration by virtue of their economic

---

106 On this comparability model see Dougan and Spaventa 2003.

107 Case C-274/96 *Bickel and Franz* [1998] ECR I-7637 (the right to have criminal proceedings conducted in the citizen's mother tongue); Case C-148/02 *Garcia Avello* [2003] ECR I-11613 (the right of the children of a Union citizen to take their mother's surname where the national law of the host state specified it had to be the father's surname).

108 Both *Martinez Sala* and *Grzelczyk* had been employed in the respective host Member States, a point that did not go unnoticed by the Court.

109 This would be in keeping with the findings of this research in relation to the role extended families have played in facilitating the integration of Polish workers into the UK (see Chapter 5).

activity.[110] This understanding of integration, however, can be challenged by the findings of empirical research examining the experience of new Member State migrants in the UK. Despite the attainment of the (supposedly privileged) migrant worker status and the economic nature of their position it seems that, in many instances, the *quality* of the integration in a social sense is poor. In particular, research carried out on behalf of the Joseph Rowntree Foundation found that migrants from the 2004 CEE accession states spent little time with British people and did not feel strong links to their local community.[111] In both work and social circumstances, the majority of their time was spent with other migrants (Spencer et al. 2007). The experience of the sample of Polish migrants interviewed by the author corroborates these findings. The following two statements represent the general feeling of those interviewed:

> I don't have any British friends. I know a few people but just to say hello to, not proper friends. I have mostly Polish friends. (Interview 010.JF)

> I know some English people at work but I'm not close to them. When I first came here on the bus this guy said to me 'Don't be surprised that you will never have an English friend' and this is true. (Interview 015.RO)

In any event, EU8 and EU2 migrants who are (almost) financially independent and are lawfully residing in an implementing Member State will have access to the principle of equal treatment in Article 12 EC. It would seem that the longer they have resided lawfully – and the extent to which they demonstrate assimilation into the host society – the more far-reaching this right will be. In particular, social benefits may require a high level of integration which may be difficult for post-accession migrants to attain currently. EU15 Member States troubled by the obligation to extend equal treatment rights to CEE nationals may come to the conclusion that it is mutually beneficial for such individuals to work during the transitional period. In this scenario, the Member State benefits from the economic contribution of the taxpaying worker and the individual gains the more secure status of Community worker with a more protected equal treatment entitlement. At any rate, those CEE nationals that do obtain access to social benefits on the basis of their lawful residence may find themselves particularly at risk of losing

---

110 Although there have been signs that the Court is willing to employ the 'real link' notion in situations involving some economically active migrants. For example in Case 213/05 *Wendy Geven v Land Nordrhein-Westfalen* (judgment of 18 July 2007), involving a frontier worker seeking to claim a benefit from the Member State of employment (Germany), the Court used the integration test to help decipher if the strength of Geven's link to the employment market was sufficient strong to justify the extension of equal treatment. See also Case C-212/05 *Gertraud Hartmann v Freistaat Bayern* (judgment given on same day).

111 In addition, beyond the UK context, research suggests that many EU8 and EU2 migrants who access work in other EU15 Member States do not have a concomitant desire to live in the territory where they are employed. Instead, shuttle mobility is a popular strategy adopted in the CEE area, see Iglicka 2001; Iglicka 2000.

their right of residence. It is only 'a certain degree of financial solidarity' that Member States must show to nationals of other Member States (para. 56) and a host Member State remains entitled to take steps to prevent nationals from other Member States becoming an unreasonable burden on the social assistance system.[112] This illustrates the link between the notions of lawful residence, discussed above, and equal treatment:

> Lawful residency entitles them to equal treatment within the host territory; but exercise of that right to equal treatment might, depending on the circumstances, enable the Member State to consider that the claimant has become an unreasonable financial burden. (Dougan and Spaventa 2003, 708)

When assessing whether an unreasonable burden on the social assistance system of the host Member State exists the Court has, so far, adopted a very individualistic approach, applying the principle of proportionality to the particular circumstances of the claimant at issue.[113] This approach has been criticized by Hailbronner (2005, 1261) as being too narrow:

> In any individual case it will hardly ever be possible to show the unreasonableness of a burden. The social system as such cannot be substantially affected by one additional beneficiary.

Up until this point, the potential cumulative effect of a number of similar cases, in Grzelczyk's position for example, has not been considered within the confines of the unreasonable burden test (Dougan and Spaventa 2003, 707). The 2004 and 2007 enlargements may present the Court with the opportunity to incorporate such an element into to its reasoning, should it wish to and should the chance arise, as 'eastern enlargement clearly has greater *cumulative* implications for the existing Member States than they believed they had assumed' (Dougan 2004, 117). The transitional restrictions were adopted, partly, to prevent the Member States from having to deal with (potential) claims for social benefits by (presumably low-paid) CEE migrant workers. Thus, the Member States are likely to be equally concerned about the potential impact of a large number of claims on the basis of Article 12 EC by (almost) financially independent EU8 and EU2 citizens; conceivably, the transitional arrangements actually encourage reliance on this right thus increasing the potential cumulative impact. Therefore, should a situation come before the Court involving a CEE national in a position similar to that of Baumbast or Grzelczyk, the Court may adopt a wider approach to the consideration of whether there is a threat of an unreasonable burden being imposed on the Member State's social welfare system and reach a different conclusion as to the proportionality of denying access to such benefits.

---

[112] Though expulsion cannot be an automatic consequence of recourse to social assistance, *Grzelczyk*, para. 43; Article 14(3), Directive 2004/38.

[113] Case C-413/99 *Baumbast* [2002] ECR I-7091; Case C-184/99 *Grzelczyk* [2001] ECR I-6193.

One issue not yet mentioned, which relates back to the *Trojani* case, is the possibility for migrants who cannot benefit from a right to reside by virtue of Article 18 EC to derive such a right from the national law of the host Member State and then claim resultant access to the equal treatment principle. Trojani, the Court held, despite not fulfilling the conditions of Directive 90/364 appeared to be lawfully residing on the basis of Belgian national law as he had been issued with a residence permit.[114] The right not to be discriminated against attaches to those lawfully resident as a matter of either Community law, such as *Grzelczyk*, or national law, such as *Trojani*. However, as Van Der Mei (2005, 210) acknowledges, this residence under national law is at the discretion of the Member State:

> The ECJ merely said that if Belgium, for whatever reasons, decided to award Mr Trojani lawful residence status, it must also treat him equally as Belgian nationals.

A Member State in this situation is by no means obliged to continue to grant a right of residence to such an individual who does not meet the requirements of sufficient resources and sickness insurance. This particular method of gaining access to the equal treatment principle is highly unlikely to be a viable option for CEE nationals during the time that the transitional arrangements are in force. During this period, the national law of the EU15 is likely to offer very limited opportunities for CEE accession nationals to establish any form of residence.

The discussion here has demonstrated how the citizenship provisions provided the Court with the foundations to develop the citizenship status of economically inactive migrants by reinforcing the rights of residence and equal treatment available to them. In order to achieve this, the Court has relied on certain notions, such as 'proportionality', 'unreasonable burden' and 'financial solidarity' which have informed the application of the citizenship provisions. These concepts are ubiquitous in the Court's judgments on citizenship, yet their actual meanings are not entirely clear and they largely remain undefined.[115] This may be particularly true for 'financial solidarity', which is historically contingent. Its meaning depends on the Member State under consideration (place) and the particular point in time. 'Proportionality' and 'unreasonable burden' encompass standards which will inevitably be heavily dependent on context rather than pre-determined rules. As a consequence of the vague nature of these notions, the Court has been able to maintain a degree of flexibility in the development and application of citizenship.

Certainly, the Court's interpretation of, and reliance on, these concepts has resulted in non-market migrant citizens enjoying greater access to a form of

---

[114] Case C-456/02 *Trojani* [2004] ECR I-7573, para. 37. The claimant in Case C-85/96, *Martinez Sala* [1998] ECR I-2691 also derived her right to reside from the national law of the host state.

[115] For example, 'unreasonable burden' has never been quantified. As a general principle of Community law, however, the meaning of proportionality as a concept is clearer: Article 5(3) EC; Case C-331/88 *ex parte Fedesa* [1994] ECR I-48663; Case 181/84 *ex parte Man* [1985] 2889.

European social citizenship. Valuable though these mobility rights flowing from Articles 18 and 12 EC are, the distinction between economically active market citizens and the economically inactive remains very much alive, and the difference in each group's access to the equal treatment principle reaffirms this distinction. CEE nationals' inability to access the status of worker in the Member States imposing transitional restrictions clearly places them in a disadvantageous position, although in some circumstances this may be tempered by their ability to move under Article 18 EC (and perhaps claims equal treatment rights on this basis). There is greater potential for EU8 and EU2 migrants to enhance their citizenship potential, or shift between the different (multiple) citizenship statuses (from student to worker for example), than was available to those subject to transitional restrictions after previous enlargements (See Kostakopoulou 1999; 2001; 2005). The Court's reliance on the notion of integration (on the basis of residence), however, is likely to be a major obstacle to access of the equal treatment principle in respect of social welfare benefits.

The following section takes a more specific look at the citizenship status of EU8 nationals in the UK as a host Member State not applying transitional restrictions in the strict sense, but still attempting to restrict the citizenship status of those EU8 nationals working on its territory, so that they too, are unable to access social welfare benefits in certain circumstances.

Consequences of the Developing Citizenship *Acquis* for EU8 Migrants in the UK[116]

It is important to consider citizenship in a national, as opposed to simply a Community, context as the delivery of citizenship rights to individuals is largley dependent on the Member State's national law and interpretation of the said Community rights. In order for citizens to access and experience Union citizenship in a meaningful sense, it must filter through the Community sphere to that of the national. Ackers and Stalford (2004, 19) stress that the study of citizenship requires 'consideration of the interaction of several layers of context'. It is not the EU, for example, that provides citizens with welfare benefits; instead, the EU provides the framework of social rights which Member States must tangibly deliver. This conceptualization of citizenship effectively corroborates a model of 'nested' European citizenship. Faist (2001, 46) has argued:

> [European citizenship is] a multi-tiered membership system consisting of a mixture of rights guaranteed by regional, state, inter-state and genuinely European institutions. [Although] the web of governance networks allows for enshrining a few new rights at the supra-national level these interconnect with and re-adapt social rights and institutions in existing welfare states.

Therefore, Union citizenship is 'nested' in various sites at both the EU level (for example in the different free movement 'sites' in the Treaty and ensuing

[116] An earlier version of part of this section has been published in Currie 2006, 207.

secondary legislation and jurisprudence) and the national level. In order to gain a fuller understanding of EU8 nationals' citizenship status during the transitional period it is helpful to consider the interplay between the supranational and national levels.

The UK has provided an interesting framework within which to study the experience of EU8 nationals, largely as a result of the particular stance it adopted towards migration following the 2004 enlargement.[117] By extending open labour market access to EU8 nationals, the UK, in essence, has not implemented transitional restrictions, certainly not in the style envisaged by the Accession Treaty. The fact that the scheme devised by the UK, the Workers' Registration Scheme, attempts to knit together the issues of employment, legal residence and access to social benefits for EU8 migrant workers, renders it a particularly interesting dynamic.[118] The restrictions imposed post-2007 on EU2 nationals reflect more 'standard' transitional arrangements as they include measures to restrict actual labour market access as opposed to benefits which flow from that access. The effect of the 2004 system is to make legal residence dependent upon being in employment and, in turn, access to social benefits is restricted to those legally resident, in other words, those in work. The aim in this section is to explore the possible impact of the developing law on citizenship, discussed in this chapter, upon those EU8 migrants who operate within the UK regime. A case study on EU8 work seekers will be conducted, first because this is a group particularly targeted by the UK's secondary legislation,[119] and secondly, because the Court of Justice's interpretation of the citizenship provisions has had implications for the status of this group under Community law.

A Case Study on EU8 Migrant Work Seekers

The UK treats new arrival EU8 work seekers in the same way as it does former workers who seek employment after becoming unemployed; it denies both a right of residence (after the expiry of a 30 day period of grace) and, consequently, the ability to receive social welfare benefits. However, Community law draws a legal distinction between new arrivals and former workers who become unemployed and seek new employment.[120] It is interesting, then, to chart the interplay between the rules of the Community law system with those of the UK system, which seeks to restrict the citizenship status of EU8 nationals by making attainment of 'worker' status reliant on continued participation in the labour market.

---

[117] The position of the UK was discussed in Chapter 3.

[118] EU8 nationals fulfilling the requirements of one of the other categories of migrant citizen (such as student, financially independent person or retired person) can, of course, reside in the UK.

[119] Accession (Immigration and Worker Registration) Regulations 2004 SI 2004/121, referred to here as Worker Registration Regulations (WRR); Social Security (Habitual Residence) Amendment Regulations 2004 SI 2004/1232, referred to here as 'Social Security Regulations' (SSR).

[120] Case C-138/02 *Collins* [2004] ECR I-2703.

New arrival work seekers It was mentioned earlier, in relation to the citizenship hierarchy, that Community law has traditionally regarded work seekers as holding the status of semi-worker. Nationals of the Member States have been afforded the right to move freely to other Member States and reside there for the purpose of seeking employment.[121] The Court in *Antonissen* further secured the position of work seekers by stating that they should be granted a reasonable period in which to find work[122] and that, so long as the work seeker could show he or she was continuing to seek employment and had genuine chances of being engaged, the right of residence could continue. Directive 2004/38 confirms work seekers' residency rights, essentially, on the same terms.[123]

The UK unequivocally denies EU8 new arrival work seekers a right of residence.[124] On the surface, this appears to comply with the transitional arrangements, the objective of which is to enable the EU15 to control the mobility of EU8 migrants. However, the transitional arrangements, as derogations to the free movement *acquis*, should be interpreted strictly (Hillion 2004, 583). Furthermore, residence rights of work seekers flow directly from Article 39 EC itself rather than from any secondary legislation (para. 13). Arguably then, work seekers' residence rights fall outside the scope of the permitted derogations in the Accession Treaty, the main focus of which is Articles 1–6 of Regulation 1612/68 *not* Article 39 EC itself. This interpretation seems to be shared by the Commission (2002a, 6): its free movement guide, produced to provide information about the operation of the transitional arrangements, states:

> Discrimination is prevented at the job search stage … Indeed all job-seekers are entitled to search for work in other Member States.

Presumably, in an EU15 Member State with transitional restrictions in place, an EU8 migrant would have no reasonable prospects of becoming engaged and the right to reside would expire.[125] EU8 work seekers in the UK would appear to have more secure rights to reside under Community law, as this is a territory which has opted to open the labour market on the very premise that it has job vacancies to fill. From this perspective, it should not be inherently difficult for an EU8 work seeker to show they have genuine chances of finding employment. It seems, therefore, that as a matter of Community law, EU8 work seekers do enjoy a right of lawful residence and the UK's attempt to deny this is incompatible with the Accession Treaty.

---

121 Case C-292/89 *Antonissen* [1991] ECR I-745.

122 6 months was suggested as a reasonable period of grace, *Antonissen,* para. 21.

123 Article 6 contains the initial three month period for all Union citizens and Article 14(4)(b) confirms that those genuinely seeking work and with genuine chances of becoming engaged can continue to reside.

124 Regulation 4(2), WRR.

125 Of course it also true that many CEE migrants will purposely *not* seek work in a Member State that has transitional restrictions in place because they will not expect to be successful.

Moving on to consider more specifically the denial of social welfare provision to work seekers,[126] the early position under Community law was uncompromising. In *Lebon*[127] the Court decided that work seekers were entitled to equal treatment only as regards taking up employment, not in relation to social and tax advantages. The decision of the ECJ in *Collins*, however, challenges this distinction.

Collins[128] was concerned with the UK rules requiring EU migrant work seekers to establish habitual residence as a precondition for access to social benefits.[129] Collins, who had dual Irish and American nationality, was refused income-based jobseekers' allowance on the grounds that he was not habitually resident in the UK. Collins had spent time in the UK sporadically between 1978–1981, during which he had studied and engaged in part time and casual work. He returned to the UK in 1998 and applied for jobseekers' allowance whilst he sought employment. This was refused on the ground that Collins was not habitually resident. On appeal, the Social Security Commissioner referred questions to the ECJ seeking to establish whether any provisions of Community law demanded payment of jobseekers' allowance to a claimant such as Collins.

The Court relied upon the developing case law on citizenship to strengthen the status of work seekers despite the fact that work seekers' rights of residence flow from Article 39 EC rather than Article 18 EC. The Court, therefore, held that the principle of equal treatment in Article 39(2) EC, which *Lebon* had found only extended to access to employment, itself had to be interpreted in the light of Article 12 EC which, as we know from the above discussion, is much broader and covers a variety of social benefits. The Court overruled *Lebon* to the effect that work seekers are entitled to equal treatment as regards access to certain benefits:

> It is no longer possible to exclude from the scope of Article 39(2) of the Treaty – which expresses the fundamental principle of equal treatment, guaranteed by Article 12 of the Treaty – a benefit of a financial nature intended to facilitate access to employment in another Member State. (Para. 63)

The habitual residence requirement, as a condition that would disadvantage a greater number of non-nationals than nationals, thus constituted indirect discrimination against EU migrant work seekers, as Union citizens, which the UK had to objectively justify.[130] In *Collins*, although the Court did accept that a

---

[126] EU8 work seekers could rely on the coordinating provisions in Article 69 Regulation 1408/71 [1997] OJ L28/1 to export unemployment benefits from their home state.

[127] Case 316/85 *Lebon* [1987] ECR 2811.

[128] Case C-138/02 *Collins* [2004] ECR I-2703. For discussion of *Collins* see Dougan 2005; Golynker 2005; Oosterom-Staples 2005.

[129] Of course this concerned the habitual residence rules as they stood prior to accession without the additional 'lawful residence' requirement.

[130] Indirectly discriminatory treatment can be justified if it is was based on objective considerations independent of the nationality of the person concerned and proportionate to the legitimate aim of the national provisions. See Case C-274/96 *Bickel and Franz* [1998] ECR I-7637, para 27; Case C-224/98 *D'Hoop* [2002] ECR I-6191, para. 36.

person could be required to establish a connection, or 'genuine link' (para. 69), with the employment market in the UK in order to become entitled to the means-tested unemployment benefit, this had to be balanced by certain conditions. In particular, if the connection were to be established through a residence test it must be proportionate, it must rest on clear criteria known in advance, and the determination must be susceptible to legal challenge:

> While a residence requirement is, in principle, appropriate for the purposes of ensuring such a connection, if it is to be proportionate it cannot go beyond what is necessary in order to attain that objective. More specifically, its application by the national authorities must rest on clear criteria known in advance and provision must be made for the possibility of a means of redress of a judicial nature. In any event, if compliance with the requirement demands a period of residence, the period must not exceed what is necessary in order for the national authorities to be able to satisfy themselves that the person concerned is genuinely seeking work in the employment market of the host Member State. (Para. 72)

This logic can be seen also in the Court's reasoning in *Ioannidis.*[131] Belgian law required applicants for a tideover allowance, granted to unemployed young people, to have completed their secondary education in Belgium. After reiterating that it is legitimate for a host Member State to require that there is a real link between such a claimant and the national labour market (para. 30), the Court emphasized the importance of ensuring this link is established in a proportionate manner. This particular condition was held to be disproportionate:

> A single condition concerning the place where the diploma of completion of secondary education was obtained is too general and exclusive in nature. It unduly favours an element which is not necessarily representative of the real and effective degree of connection between the applicant for the tideover allowance and the geographic employment market, to the exclusion of all other representative elements. It therefore goes beyond what is necessary to attain the objective pursued. (Para. 31)

The potential significance of the reasoning in *Collins* and *Ioannidis* for EU8 work seekers is clear. Under EU law EU8 migrants who are seeking their first employment in the UK may be eligible to claim benefits, such as jobseekers' allowance, after a reasonable period of genuine job hunting. This would clearly undermine what the UK post-accession system sets out to achieve. Of course, the points made above in relation to the emphasis placed on an individual's degree of integration remain relevant. An EU8 migrant would have to demonstrate that they had 'for a reasonable period, in fact genuinely sought work' in the UK. The situation of work seekers can possibly be considered in a different way to those whose rights flow solely from Article 18 EC, since work seekers have some future connection to the labour market, a symbol of integration into society; accordingly, they may be entitled to expect a greater degree of solidarity from the Member State than an individual who holds out no such promise of future integration.

131 Case C-258/04 *Ioannidis* [2005] ECR I-8275.

The UK restrictions operate across two 'layers'. First, the habitual residence test has already been classified as indirect discrimination in *Collins*, as it is capable of being met more easily by UK nationals.[132] This discrimination impacts upon EU migrants in general, not simply those from the EU8 Member States, and it can be objectively justified on the basis of ensuring a 'genuine link' to the territory under the *Collins* principle. Secondly, and of more interest, is the legal residence requirement. This requirement, although on the surface applying to *all* applicants, clearly sets out to prevent unemployed EU8 migrants from resorting to benefits. As a result of this test, EU8 migrants are automatically excluded from consideration when UK nationals and EU15 migrants in a comparable situation would not be.[133] This layer, therefore, directly discriminates against EU8 nationals. Given that direct discrimination can only be justified by reference to derogations expressly provided for in the Treaty,[134] in theory this should mean that the UK would not have the opportunity to justify this restriction.

However, the issue is not necessarily so straightforward. Like the UK rules on EU8 workers, the case of *Bidar*[135] was concerned with two layers of restriction which had both an indirectly and directly discriminatory impact. Although this case was concerned with migrant students, it is useful to look analogously at how the Court dealt with the discrimination issue. Applicants for student loans in the UK were required to fulfil a test of being ordinarily resident in the UK for three years as well as an additional test of being 'settled' in the UK. The 'ordinarily resident' limb was more easily satisfied by UK nationals (para. 53); however, the 'settled' limb virtually amounted to a blanket ban on the ability of students from other Member States to obtain student loans and, hence, amounted to direct discrimination on the ground of nationality (paras 60–63). The advantage was reserved exclusively for students of UK nationality. Despite this direct discrimination against students from other EU Member States, the approach of the Court was to take the two layers as a single bundle and subject it, as a whole, to the objective justification test. The Court, therefore, did suggest that the apparent direct discrimination was potentially justifiable, though it concluded in *Bidar* that the 'settled' layer of the requirement was disproportionate:

> It is common ground that the rules at issue in the main proceedings preclude any possibility of a national of another Member State obtaining settled status as a student. Thus they make it impossible for such a national, whatever his actual degree of integration into the society of the host Member State, to satisfy that condition and hence to enjoy the assistance to cover his maintenance costs. Such treatment cannot

---

[132] Case C-237/94 *O'Flynn* [1996] ECR I-2617, para. 18.

[133] EU15 nationals in the UK have a right of 'legal residence' under UK national law, both as work seekers and former workers who are now unemployed: the Immigration (European Economic Area) Regulations 2000 SI 2000/2326; the Immigration (European Economic Area) Regulations 2006 SI 2006/1003.

[134] Such as public security and policy. Note that expulsion/discrimination must be based on personal conduct. Article 39 EC; Articles 27–33, Directive 2004/38; previously the position was dealt with under Directive 64/221 [1964] OJ Sp. Ed. L850/64.

[135] Case C-209/03 *Bidar,* [2005] ECR I-2119.

be regarded as justified by the legitimate objective which these rules seek to secure. (Para. 61)

It is possible that, should it be called upon to review the UK rules on EU8 migrants,[136] the ECJ would adopt the same reasoning towards the 'bundle' of rules on work seekers and regard them as justifiable in principle but disproportionate in effect.

The practice of making legal residence reliant on being employed, before EU8 nationals can access social benefits, certainly seems extreme. On the other hand, it could also be argued that there would be something slightly bizarre about the UK, a country commonly perceived as already being generous towards EU8 nationals by allowing them to work, being urged to go further and grant social benefits to those in its territory but unemployed. If the Court was reluctant to classify the rules as discriminatory, it may be tempted to follow the *Kaba* line of reasoning;[137] essentially the Court could find that the residence situation of EU8 migrants is simply not comparable to that of UK nationals and hence there would be no need for the UK to justify the rules. This reasoning rests on the notion that migrants, unlike nationals, have only a conditional right to reside in a Member State (*Kaba I*, para. 30).[138] The Member States are:

> ... entitled to rely on any objective difference there may be between their own nationals and those of other Member States. (*Kaba I*, para. 31)

This could be a problematic stance, however, as should the Court proceed to reiterate the *Kaba* standpoint as regards the non-comparability of nationals and EU migrants, it may risk encouraging Member States to rely on all manner of so-called 'objective differences'. Ultimately the Court risks undoing gains that have been made in relation to the application of the non-discrimination principle to EU migrants when exercising rights of free movement. For example, surely the sufficient resources requirement which applies to non-workers is such an 'objective difference' between nationals and non-nationals. Taken to its logical and full conclusion, the *Kaba* line of reasoning risks rendering Article 12 EC ineffective.

In any event, there is a further dimension to the issue of discriminatory treatment against EU8 migrants: not only are EU8 migrants treated less favourably than UK nationals by the UK rules, they are also treated less favourably than EU15 nationals. It would therefore be extremely difficult to justify a *Kaba*-style argument in this regard. The Court has previously held that a Member State

---

[136] Either as a result of an Article 234 EC preliminary reference from a national court asked to decide upon the legality of the UK rules, or, as a result of an Article 226 EC Commission enforcement action against the UK's illegality.

[137] Case C-356/98 *Kaba I* [2000] ECR I-2623 and Case C-466/00, *Kaba II* [2003] ECR I-2219.

[138] The *Kaba* decision has been subject to criticism, see Peers 2001, 76.

cannot reserve 'special treatment' for workers from a certain Member State whilst denying the same advantage to workers of other EU nationalities.[139]

Presuming that the Court would not be able to ignore the discriminatory treatment of EU8 migrants in the UK when compared with EU15 migrants, it is likely that the UK would be given the opportunity to provide objective justifications for the requirements as a bundle (as in *Bidar*). As we are already aware, habitual residence can be justified on the basis of ensuring the claimant has a 'real link' to the society from which he or she wishes to claim. The legally resident criterion, on the other hand, is more problematic as it is not clear what role this condition plays in ensuring such a degree of integration exists. Arguably it goes too far.

Before moving on, attention must be paid to the potential impact of Directive 2004/38[140] upon the rights of new arrival work seekers as, like with students, the updated legislative regime attempts to restrict the equal treatment rights available to work seekers. Article 24(2) states that the host Member State is not obliged to confer entitlement to social assistance during the first three months of residence, or during the extended period of residence where the work seeker provides evidence that he or she is continuing to seek employment and has genuine chances of being engaged. This clearly seems to run contrary to the *Collins* ruling and, if accepted literally, will render a lot of the arguments put forward here superfluous now that the Directive is in force. As was stressed in relation to the requirement in the Directive that students build up five years lawful residence before gaining the right to access maintenance grants and loans, it seems likely that the principle of proportionality has a role to play here. Hence, the principle in Article 24(2), as a 'limitation and condition' on free movement rights, may itself be subject to the principle of proportionality and thus should only be applied in so far as it is 'necessary to protect the Member State's legitimate interests' (Dougan 2005b, 21).

One other issue that is worthy of note, for purposes of clarification, is whether a work seeker's right to reside is susceptible to termination on the ground that they have become an 'unreasonable financial burden'. Meulman and de Waele (2004, 287) assume that the 'unreasonable financial burden' rule does apply because, arguing for the potential adoption of a cumulative interpretation of the test, they speak of the financial implications of 'multiple Mr Collins's', suggesting that this would amount to such a burden. This would appear to be a mistaken interpretation of the unreasonable burden notion. Whereas the unreasonable burden test was developed by the Court in the context of Article 18 EC and the requirements contained in the old residence directives, work seekers derive their rights principally from Article 39 EC, having gained benefits from Article

139 Case 235/87 *Matteucci* [1988] ECR 5589 a bilateral agreement between Belgium and Germany reserved the eligibility of training scholarships for workers of either Belgian or German nationality. This was held to be contrary to the principle of equality of treatment as regards social advantages in Article 7(2), Regulation 1612/68.

140 [2004] OJ L158/77.

18 EC in an indirect manner. Thus they fall outside the scope of the test.[141] Following the introduction of Directive 2004/38, this position has become even more unambiguous as the new legislation expressly provides that work seekers cannot be expelled from a Member State on the basis that they constitute an unreasonable burden.[142]

The analysis in this section is very much based on a Community law understanding of the developments in the citizenship case law and attempts to predict the approach the ECJ would take if asked to provide guidance on the issues. What this analysis perhaps masques is the propensity of the national courts to undervalue the ECJ's jurisprudence in the area. It is the national courts within which individuals must attempt to assert their Union citizenship rights; therefore, if a national court fails, or is unwilling to appreciate the intricacies of Community law, the discussion above is likely to be little *tangible* relevance. Arguably, the UK's High Court failed to grasp the full implications of Community law in the case of *R (on the application of H and D) v Secretary of State for Work and Pensions)*,[143] a case heard just days after the 2004 enlargement took place. In this case Collins J had the opportunity to consider the impact of the ECJ's judgment in *Collins* on EU8 migrant work seekers. The argument was presented that, as EU8 nationals had been granted the right to access the UK labour market, it must follow that the judgment in *Collins,* and the opening up of the possibility for those seeking work to rely on the principle of equal treatment as regards access to social benefits, must logically apply to the group. This argument was rejected outright by Collins J without any meaningful consideration of the status of citizenship, the ECJ's case law or the extent of the transitional arrangements in the Accession Treaty:

> The fundamental principle is that the annex [of the transitional arrangements] permits discrimination against access to the labour market of this country and that must include discrimination which relates to the provision of benefits in order to entitle that access to be carried out. It is, quite apart from anything else, a perfectly permissible means of avoiding benefit tourism. Thus, it is clearly proportionate. (Para. 29)

This exemplifies the application of a 'common sense' approach to the problem put before the national Court which negates any in-depth consideration of the various legal provisions and principles. In the absence of such a case finding its way before the ECJ, for example, via the use of the preliminary reference procedure in Article 234 EC, it seems that those individuals who do find themselves in the national courts may find that the full extent of their status under Community law fails to be fully explored.[144]

---

141 For example, in *Collins* it was as a result of the developments in the case law regarding Articles 18 and 12 EC that the Court felt able to overrule *Lebon.* From this perspective, work seekers' citizenship status can now be said to be 'nested' in Article 39 EC in conjunction with Articles 18 and 12 EC.

142 Recital 16; Article 14(4)(b).

143 [2004] 3 CMLR 11.

144 The Court of Appeal affirmed the judgment of Collins J on 11 October 2004 (unreported). Discussed in Toner 2007.

Involuntarily unemployed former workers Workers who become unemployed[145] post migration have enjoyed complete access to worker status in the past, including the right to social advantages under Article 7(2) Regulation 1612/68. Once unemployed, although no longer Community workers in the fullest sense, they retain some of the benefits associated with the status:

> Persons who have previously pursued in the host Member State an effective and genuine activity as an employed person as defined by the Court but who are no longer employed are nevertheless considered to be workers under certain provisions of Community law.[146]

If an EU8 national becomes unemployed in the first year of residence, the UK purports to say that they have relinquished their right to reside after 30 days and cannot claim social welfare entitlement. Essentially, the UK expects EU8 migrants to be self sufficient during periods of unemployment or inability to work. Until they have completed 12 months of uninterrupted and registered employment, they are not entitled to out-of-work benefits such as council tax benefit and housing benefit,[147] income support,[148] jobseekers allowance[149] and state pension credit.[150]

Again, the approach of the UK appears incompatible in the light of broader provisions of Community law. It has already been noted, in an effort to demonstrate the depth of the worker's citizenship status, that Directive 2004/38 reaffirms that workers who become involuntarily unemployed continue to have a right of residence in the host state.[151] It follows that, under Community law, an EU8 worker who loses his or her job should continue to have a right of residence in the UK.

Moving on to consider this group's potential ability to claim entitlement to social welfare, it is clear that these ex-workers are in a different position to new arrival work seekers such as Collins. In *Collins* itself the Court touched upon this issue: Collins had previously worked in the UK but there had been a 17 year lapse since that time, such that he was classed as a new arrival work seeker (*Collins,* para. 30). On this basis Article 7(2) of Regulation 1612/68 did not apply to him. The corollary of this finding is that Article 7(2) *can* indeed apply to those who have recently become unemployed in the host Member State, on the basis that they continue to have a 'sufficiently close connection' to the labour market (para. 30). This confirms the established law that termination of an employment relationship does not automatically put an end to all rights enjoyed by a worker

145 The focus here is on involuntary employment. The Accession Treaty allows the EU15 Member States to withdraw the rights of EU8 nationals who become voluntarily unemployed: para 2, Annexes.

146 Case 39/86 *Lair* [1988] ECR 3161, para. 33.

147 Regulation 2, SSR.

148 Regulation 3, SSR.

149 Regulation 4, SSR.

150 Regulation 5, SSR.

151 Article 7(3).

under Community law.[152] The Court in *Collins* explicitly confirms that those who have worked in a Member State, but are no longer in an employment relationship, continue to be 'workers' and are thus entitled to access the same social advantages as national workers (paras 30–31). Directive 2004/38 enshrines these principles as Article 7(3) provides that the 'status of worker' will continue for no less than six months when a worker becomes involuntarily unemployed.

Following this line of argument EU8 nationals who lose their job in the first year should be entitled to rely on Article 7(2) of Regulation 1612/68 and claim social welfare on the same basis as UK nationals. It seems to be disproportionately inequitable that an EU8 national who works in the UK in compliance with the registration scheme for a period as long as 11 months, and then becomes involuntarily unemployed, will have no ability to claim jobseekers' allowance.[153] Furthermore, the ECJ's decision in *Ninni-Orasche*[154] could have important implications for such EU8 migrants who find themselves out of work. Here, the Court found that the expiry of a fixed-term contract can amount to involuntary unemployment and this has interesting ramifications for EU8 workers whose temporary contract expires. Indeed, this principle may be particularly relevant to EU8 workers, given the high concentration of them in temporary employment in the UK.[155] Stalford (2003c, 4) has emphasized the increasing tendency of western employers to impose short-term employment contracts which provide employers with greater flexibility to meet short-term demands without the longer-term financial commitment to staff.[156] Despite this preference for temporary contracts a migrant whose contract expires can argue that they continue to be entitled to equal treatment as regards social and tax advantages under Article 7(2) of Regulation 1612/68. Thus, there is potential scope for their (market) citizenship status to have a meaningful impact on them, beyond the expiry of the actual exercise of the economic right to free movement.

The caution urged as regards the potential for national courts to remain unconvinced by arguments based on developments in Community law is equally relevant here. There have been two cases before the UK courts, both of which were highlighted in chapter 3, concerning claims by former workers for access to some form of social advantage. First, in *Putans v Tower Hamlets,*[157] a Latvian man had

---

[152] *Collins*, paras. 27-31; Case 39/86 *Lair* [1988] ECR 3161, an ex-worker was entitled to a grant as a social advantage on deciding to enter university education. See also Case C-413/01 *Ninni-Orasche,* [2003] ECR I-13187.

[153] Despite having made tax and national insurance contributions for that 11 month period. See White 2005a, 25.

[154] Case C-413/01 *Ninni-Orasche* [2003] ECR I-13187.

[155] 45 per cent of registered workers are in temporary employment (Home Office Border and Immigration Agency 2007).

[156] Note that Directive 1999/70, which puts into effect the Framework Agreement on fixed-term work, may be important for EU8 temporary workers ([1999] OJ L175/43). The Agreement contains a non-discrimination principle (clause 4) and a provision that requires employers to inform fixed-term workers about permanent positions in the workplace (clause 6).

[157] *Putans v Tower Hamlets BC* [2006] EWHC 1634 (Ch). Discussed in Toner 2007.

been employed as a cleaner of trains for nine months before he became ill and had to cease working (involuntarily). On release from hospital, his application for homelessness assistance was rejected on the basis that, as he had not acquired 12 months of registered employment, he did not fulfil the residence requirement. The case came before the High Court on 20 June 2006. At the time of the hearing, Mr Putans was homeless, 'literally sleeping on the streets' according to Mr Briggs QC who was sitting (para. 2). Mr Matthew Feldman, counsel for Mr Putans, presented arguments based on the continuing applicability of the 'worker' status under Community law, in order to seek to demonstrate that Mr Putans had both a right to remain in the UK and a right to claim homelessness assistance on the basis of the principle of non-discrimination on grounds of nationality. Mr Briggs QC accepted that involuntarily unemployment should not result in an individual's right to residence being withdrawn (para. 71). The refusal to grant homelessness assistance or to provide Mr Putans with accommodation, however, was held to be a legitimate response. Mr Briggs QC, like Collins J in the *H and D* case, based this conclusion on a 'plain' reading of the UK law. The High Court seems to easily accept that, as a consequence of the transitional arrangements in the Accession Treaty, nationality-based discrimination against EU8 nationals is justifiable and proportionate:

> In my judgment it [the refusal of housing and homelessness assistance] plainly is authorised by the Act of Accession which… clearly authorises a derogation from Article 39 of the main Treaty and, by necessary implication, a derogation from Article 12, because it is essentially based upon discrimination on the grounds of nationality. (Para. 73)

There is no recognition that, without any entitlement to homeless benefit or accommodation, Mr Putans' right to reside is unenforceable in any practical sense. Further, there is no emphasis placed on the nine months of lawful work carried out by Mr Putans which had only ceased due to his illness. This could have been a particularly relevant consideration on the issue of proportionality. Instead, the judgment includes reference to the 'reasonably obvious' justification for the UK rules: the concern of the Member States to 'cushion their economies from the economic shock of having a large potential increase in the number of persons entitled to enter their labour markets from the A8 states, many of which have higher unemployment than the existing Member States' (para. 79). This acceptance of the existence of transitional arrangements as whole scale justification for the UK's rules, without any consideration of the implications of developments in the status of Union citizenship, is also apparent in the second case to come before the UK courts concerning a former worker.

In *Zalewska v Department for Social Development*,[158] a Polish woman had worked continuously for a 12-month period in Northern Ireland but, due to a change of employment midway, had only been registered on the WRS for part of this period (six months). Thus, in this case the applicant had surpassed the 12

[158] *Zalewska v Department for Social Development* [2007] NICA 17.

month period stipulated in the domestic legislation, and the only troublesome issue was that not all of the employment had been registered on the WRS. Ms Zalewska had applied for income support after ceasing to work. It is not clear exactly why Ms Zalewska left her employment; in other words, it is not certain that she was *involuntarily* unemployed, but it is clear that she was living in a Woman's Aid hostel with her daughter at the time she sought entitlement to the benefit. The Social Security Commissioner sanctioned the refusal of income support, unsurprisingly, on the basis that Ms Zalewska did not have a right to reside in the UK: she had accumulated only six months of registered employment.

Again, arguments based upon the continuing relevance of the worker status under Community law did not succeed in helping the applicant to fortify her rights in the UK context. It was submitted that Ms Zalewska remained a worker and was thus entitled to claim access to social advantages, such as income support, on the same basis of nationals. Like the Social Security Commissioner, the Court of Appeal in Northern Ireland was not convinced. Lord Justice Girvan recognized that 'had she been a citizen of a non-Accession Member State she may well have qualified' but went on to refer to the UK's post-accession rules and applied the 12 month stipulation of registration strictly:

> The applicant only worked as a registered worker for a six month period and thereafter took unregistered employment. She, therefore, failed to fulfil the condition to be satisfied if she was to be treated as lawfully admitted to the labour market during the relevant period. (Para. 24)

Like Mr Briggs QC, Lord Justice Girvan suggests that *carte blanche* nationality-based discrimination against EU8 nationals is acceptable, despite the transitional arrangements only referring to such treatment in the context of labour market access. Further, there is little rigorous application of the proportionality principle, certainly not in the manner as it is understood under Community law. Arguably, it is a disproportionate response to classify an individual who has changed jobs without complying with the formality of re-registering as being unlawfully resident and, consequently, as being undeserving of any (temporary) assistance. Proportionality, though, is not considered beyond the finding that:

> The Policy behind the Registration Scheme is to allow the Secretary of State to monitor and control those [subject to transitional arrangements]. It has a national legal basis which is consistent with the right conferred on Member States to regulate their own labour market in the context of Accession workers. The applicant is unable to demonstrate that the Scheme lacks rationality or proportionality. (Para. 25)

These cases stand as pertinent reminders that it is through the national context that Community law based rights must filter. It does seem, perhaps particularly given the sensitive nature of transitional mobility restrictions, that there has been a tendency of the UK courts to fail to engage with a full and rigorous application with developments in the free movement and citizenship *acquis* when adjudicating on issues relevant to EU8 migrants. This can undoubtedly have a significant impact on the status of EU8 migrants.

Despite the difficulties in enforcing right in practice, it is undeniable that work seekers – in the form of both new arrivals and former workers – now have a more comprehensive citizenship status under Community law than they did previously, which affords them greater opportunity to access the principle of equal treatment. Undoubtedly, the introduction of the formal citizenship provisions and the ensuing interpretation by the ECJ has been the key to this broadening of entitlement and climbing of the citizenship ladder. These developments could potentially have quite positive implications for the status of work seekers in the UK, where the post-accession regulatory regime clearly attempts to deny out-of-work EU8 migrants their full citizenship entitlement. Of course, in order for Community law as discussed here to have a tangible impact on an individual EU8 migrant they would, first of all, have to be aware of (or seek legal advice on) the disparity between the status of work seekers under national and Community law and, second, have the resources and resolve to make a legal challenge in the UK's national courts as to the legality of the UK provisions. In any event, the national court would have to be persuaded of the significance, and applicability, of the citizenship developments to the consideration of the UK's rules in the area.

Conclusion

Drawing on the established case law and literature on the notion of Union citizenship, this chapter has attempted to incorporate the enlargement process into the discussion, and chart some aspects of the relationship between the developing citizenship *acquis* and the transitional mobility restrictions.

The discussion of Union citizenship, and its application to CEE migrants, would support the assertion put forward by Kofman (1995, 122) that membership of the citizenship community is 'messy' in practice. Everson (1995, 85) argues that the European market citizen is the 'role which nationals of the Member States have been expected to play' to help achieve the 'legal and practical realization of the internal market'. This is not the role assigned to nationals of the CEE Member States, at least in the initial phase of their formal membership of the Union. Instead they are expected to forgo participation in EU15 labour markets to ease the fears of the older Member States. Ironically, although EU8 and EU2 nationals do not have full access to the status of European market citizen by virtue of the transitional mobility restrictions, this is tempered, to some limited extent, by their ability to move simply as Union citizens, whose citizenship status has been fortified in recent years and, in some circumstances, can itself allow access to the equal treatment principle and bestow some aspects of solidarity. The changes made by the Lisbon Treaty to the citizenship provisions, such as the strengthening of the links between the status with both the principles of democracy and non-discrimination, further evidence the loosening of the connection between citizens' rights and the Single Market.[159] There is a further (cruel) irony, however, in that, as the EU is moving away from a citizenship conception construed only in economic terms, and when nationals of the newer Member States can rely on the status of economically inactive Union citizen, the status they appear to most desire, that of active market citizen, is not necessarily accessible to them. It is interesting that the reconfigured citizenship provisions, as they will stand should the Lisbon Treaty enter into force, contain a stipulation that 'the Union shall observe the principle of equality of its citizens'. Transitional mobility restrictions, which will no doubt remain relevant in 2009 when the Treaty should be ratified, stand in direct contrast to the spirit behind this principle.[160]

The domestic context is also important when seeking to explore the citizenship status of a group such as CEE migrants. The very nature of transitional arrangements is that there is frequently little in the way of a domestic environment within which to examine the experience of citizenship. The particular stance of the UK towards EU8 migrants, which has not imposed transitional restrictions in the form envisaged by the Accession Treaty, therefore, provides an interesting extra layer of context to the examination of the citizenship status accorded to EU8 migrants. It certainly would appear that developments in the area of citizenship at Community level could potentially, if accessed by an individual EU8 migrant, counter the UK's attempt to restrict the access of EU8 migrant workers in its territory to residence and social welfare rights. This is, of course, dependent on the UK courts' interpretation of the law (or the ECJ's itself in the event of a reference).

The UK system post-2004 gives with one hand, by opening up the labour market, but takes away with the other, by restricting the residence and welfare entitlement of those who have worked but find themselves unemployed prior to building up a year of legal employment. EU8 migrants are unlikely to attempt to claim benefits whilst in work, but if they do become unemployed in the first year, they are automatically denied any social assistance, despite having made a contribution to the public purse. Surely given that the UK has wished to gain from the labour market activity of EU8 migrants, it follows that the UK should embrace its full responsibilities under Article 39 EC.

Finally, it should not be forgotten that citizenship of the Union, in the sense of the formal provisions, was introduced to increase the EU's legitimacy and bring Europe 'closer to its citizens', but the very existence of transitional arrangements on free movement suggests that Europe does not desire to be close to all of its citizens – or, at least not as close to some as it is to others. After all, it is only through exercising rights of mobility that Member State nationals experience meaningful citizenship. As a consequence of this selective intimacy, the legitimacy of the EU in the eyes of some of its newest citizens may be damaged irrevocably as a result of transitional mobility restrictions.

---

[159] Articles 9–12 of the amended TEU (Provisions on Democratic Principles) and Articles 18–26 TFEU (Non-discrimination and Citizenship).

[160] To be enshrined in Article 9 TEU amongst the provisions on democratic principles.

Chapter 7

Conclusion

The objective of the research which informs this book was to explore the status, entitlement and experience of nationals from the CEE accession states, in particular those who migrated to the UK in order to work while the transitional arrangements on the free movement of persons were in operation across the EU15 Member States.

The book has looked to define and critically analyse the transitional arrangements on free movement in terms of the impact such mobility restrictions have on migrants' overall citizenship status and experiences. It has sought to do so by incorporating migrants' personal migration accounts. The Community law entitlement of CEE migrants is analogous neither to that of EU15 migrants nor to that of third-country nationals migrants. Essentially, during the transitional period, EU8 and EU2 migrants occupy a discrete status as regards mobility rights and citizenship experience.

The methodology developed and implemented throughout the research process combined analysis of the legal framework with in-depth qualitative empirical work (together with some examination of secondary statistical data). By adopting a socio-legal approach, an analysis has emerged which not only offers a critique of the legal framework shaping the status of CEE migrants, but also places it within a specific social, cultural and economic context. For example, the migrants' personal accounts underline the human implications of the transitional mobility restrictions and emphasize the significance placed upon the right to free movement by the newest citizens of the Union. In turn, the apparent importance placed on the right to move as a worker serves to highlight the practical hollowness of the citizenship package extended to CEE nationals during the transitional period.

The various chapters of the book have examined migrants' labour market access (Chapter 3), experience and status when working in the UK (Chapter 4) and methods of sustaining family life subsequent to the exercise of mobility rights (Chapter 5). These are all elements that form constitutive parts of an EU migrant's free movement entitlement; together they provide a more holistic exposition of the specific status occupied by CEE, particularly EU8, migrants in the UK during the transitional period. Chapter 6 built on this analysis by exploring the relationship between nationals of the CEE Member States and the evolving status of Union citizenship. The scope of the discussion in this chapter was somewhat broader, and more theoretical, than that in the preceding chapters as it sought to clarify the position of EU8 and EU2 nationals as migrants *qua* citizens under Article 18 EC (in addition to Article 39 EC).

Analysis of CEE migrants' interaction with the free movement provisions and the contingent social entitlement also provides fresh insight into the development of Union citizenship more generally. Renowned contributions to the literature have already drawn attention to the hierarchical and differentiated nature of Union citizenship which continues to privilege those Community migrants making a traditional economic contribution to the host Member State (O'Leary 1996; Shaw 1997; Shaw 1998; Everson 1995; Ackers 1998; Kostakopoulou 1999; Kostakopoulou 2001; Ackers and Stalford 2004). Building on such work, this research has attempted to advance a critical account of the position of migrants subject to transitional mobility restrictions within the hierarchy. Indeed, such migrants provide a striking example of the unequal application of citizenship entitlement which occurs across the different categories of EU migrant despite the formal definition in Article 17 EC which appears, on the surface, to imply a universality of status.[1]

Previous contributions to the literature have also explored the increasingly meaningful citizenship experience of those Community migrants who do not hold the status of market citizen but reside in a host Member State in an economically inactive capacity pursuant to Article 18 EC (Dougan 2005b; Dougan and Spaventa 2003; Hailbronner 2005). By incorporating an empirical element the research has demonstrated how developments towards a more social construction of citizenship are unlikely to be of great tangible benefit to many migrants from the CEE region who, at least in the initial period following accession, have demonstrated most enthusiasm for the prospect of exercising mobility rights as a migrant worker in an effort to increase their own, and often their family unit's, income. Thus, the formal applicability of Article 18 EC largely appears to contrast with the empirical reality. This finding could be relied on to challenge the perception sometimes portrayed (by the media, for example) of large-scale welfare shopping by the economically inactive. The research has demonstrated however, in particular by applying developments in the ECJ's case law on citizenship to the legal regime adopted in the UK in respect of the EU8, that Article 18 EC (and the Court's interpretation of it in conjunction with Article 12 EC) could theoretically prove very beneficial as a means for an EU8 migrant work seeker to overcome the restrictive effects of the UK regulatory system as regards residence and social benefits. Therefore, the empirical reality does not detract from the theoretical possibility that citizenship can endow rights on those EU nationals subject to transitional mobility restrictions. The 2004 and 2007 enlargements provide the first opportunity for such developments in the law to interact with the provisions of the Accession Treaties.

---

[1] This sentiment of universality will be strengthened if the Treaty of Lisbon enters into force [2007] OJ C306/01. Article 9 of the amended TEU will contain a specific proviso that all Union citizens should be treated equally by the Union.

Reflecting on the Analysis at EU Level

As a result of the nature of the transitional arrangements contained in the Treaty of Accession a complex and differentiated patchwork of free movement rights has emerged across the enlarged EU. The complexity created by a system which enables each implementing Member State to dictate the labour market access of EU8 and EU2 nationals has led to high levels of uncertainty and confusion amongst those towards whom the transitional arrangements are directed.

It has been difficult to access accurate, impartial and up-to-date information about the EU-wide policies on free movement in place, particularly after the 2004 enlargement. NGOs at the European level, such as European Citizen Action Service (ECAS)[2] and Citizens Advice International (CAI),[3] have made concerted efforts to publicize and provide information about free movement rights both generally and in the specific context of enlargement. The free movement 'hotline' set up by ECAS in 2006 to offer free advice to migrants on their rights (referred to in Chapter 3), for example, notably appointed Lithuanian and Polish speaking staff to deal with queries (in addition to English, French, German and Italian speakers). Of course, the ability of a migrant to access such services will depend on their awareness of the relevant programme's existence which, in turn, will be influenced by the availability of facilities (such as Internet access). Inevitably, it is often the most economically privileged and/or those with higher levels of education that are able to 'tap in' to such NGO resources, although awareness is also likely to travel via conduits created by migrant networks. Such schemes are obviously fulfilling a valuable function but it also seems that they have been a later development, partially in response to the evident confusion immediately following the 2004 enlargement.

A well-publicized, EU developed programme earlier on in the process could well have helped CEE nationals, EU8 nationals in particular, to navigate the complexity of the differentiated free movement system. On a positive note, there was much more in the way of mobility promotion, rights awareness raising and general discussion about free movement from the EU institutions (predominantly the Commission) during 2006, the European Year of Workers' Mobility. This initiative and the linked EU-wide events, such as the EU-wide job fair, do suggest a commitment to enhancing the degree of available information on mobility entitlement right across the enlarged EU. Presumably, the existence of these schemes assisted the nationals of the Member States involved in the 2007 round of enlargement. Therefore, Bulgarian and Romanian nationals may have more extensive access to information regarding mobility entitlement than was initially available to EU8 nationals despite the overall patchwork of free movement rights becoming even more intricate after 2007. Such inclusive policy activities, however, contrast markedly with the legal provisions in the Accession Treaties establishing

2 See <http://www.ecas.org/> (last accessed 14 February 2008).

3 See <http://www.citizens-advice-international.org/> (last accessed 14 February 2008).

the seven-year transitional arrangements where it is clear that the balance of power rests with the EU15 Member States to the disadvantage of CEE nationals.

It is not only in the EU arena that levels of uncertainty have thrived in relation to the operation of transitional restrictions. The case study of Polish migrant workers in the UK uncovered confusion surrounding various aspects of the domestic regulatory system. Chapter 3, in particular, acknowledged the ambiguity associated with the operation of the Worker Registration Scheme, particularly in the initial post-accession stages, and misconceptions surrounding it. For example it was pointed out how some migrants were unlawfully charged a fee simply to obtain a copy of the documentation relating to registration despite it being freely available online. Chapter 5 similarly pointed to the existence of such uncertainty with regard to the applicability of the right to access social benefits to those EU8 workers complying with the WRS requirements. Here, the confusion surrounding the system conspired to (mistakenly) convince EU8 workers that they were not entitled to receive in-work benefits which, in turn, left some in a financially vulnerable situation unnecessarily and serves as a disincentive to the exercise of family reunification rights. Another area where the degree of complexity, combined with the absence of sustained and accurate information-provision, has promulgated the degree of misinformation is the recognition of qualifications regime. Migrants, agencies and employers alike on many occasions have struggled to grasp the intricacies of this complicated system and the fallibilities of the system have seemingly contributed to the process of de-skilling that has accompanied the migration experience of many early-stage movers.

The point has been made here that a more robust and timely information campaign on the part of the EU, implemented in the CEE Member States to raise awareness of the operation of the transitional arrangements across the EU15, may have overcome some of these difficulties. Some attempt to disseminate information 'on the ground' in the EU8 countries was made by the UK government under the sponsorship of the 'Not All Roads Lead to Britain' campaign (discussed in Chapters 3 and 5). It is certainly true that this campaign succeeded in increasing awareness of the UK's domestic scheme in certain EU8 Member States. However, the tone and intention of this programme, as the campaign's title suggests, was largely to dissuade migration rather than inform in a neutral sense. This was particularly aimed at those contemplating a move who may have considered applying for social benefits when in the UK. From this perspective, this campaign appears to have contributed to the misinformation about the UK system. For example, Chapter 5 pointed out that after being exposed to the 'Not All Roads Lead to Britain' campaign events in Poland, many migrants were left under the mistaken impression that EU8 migrants had no rights to access benefits in the UK regardless of whether they were working and registered on the WRS. An EU-level campaign would have overcome the problem of individual Member States tailoring such a programme to reflect their own political objectives.

The self-interest of the EU15 in respect of the extension of free movement rights to CEE nationals has in fact been prevalent throughout the course of the enlargement process. The very legal provisions setting out the transitional arrangements, by giving the implementing Member States a virtual free hand to determine how they regulate labour market access, embody this tendency. The implementation of transitional provisions has been governed by each individual Member State's labour market needs and demands. As a result of the 'supply and demand' logic embodied in the transitional arrangements, CEE migrants have effectively been assigned the role of a flexible reserve army of labour for the EU15 when labour shortages so require. The corollary of this is that the work such a reserve army is frequently called upon to do is situated in the secondary labour market and, as such, is characterized by poor working conditions, often resulting in a degree of de-skilling for the migrant workers concerned. Chapter 4 highlighted the contradiction between this reality, evident in the context of enlargement, which appears to accept (and even condone) the occurrence of de-skilling as a means to fill labour market gaps in the EU15, and the wider EU policy of encouraging the circulation of knowledge. Indeed, the initial post-accession employment trends involving CEE migrants appear very far detached from the Lisbon Agenda aim of creating 'more and better' jobs for Union citizens (European Commission 2005b). It seems that many EU8 workers in the UK have, at least in the initial stages of the transitional period, exercised mobility rights within the framework of 'more and worse' jobs.

The reserve army notion also raises the issue of the relationship between third-country nationals and CEE accession nationals in the post-accession climate. Previously, it has been third-country national migrants that have carried out much of the work in the EU15 Member States' secondary labour markets. EU8 and EU2 nationals have made the formal transition from third-country national to EU national (or Union citizen), but the reality is that their employment experience continues to be characterized in a manner similar to that of third-country nationals. This reflects their transitional citizenship status in the immediate aftermath of enlargement; they are not yet full members of the free movement community and, hence, cannot expect their labour market experience to alter to any great extent initially. It would be naïve, however, to assume that this will automatically alter on expiry of the transitional arrangements. Although at this point the formal status of EU8 and EU2 nationals will mirror that of EU15 nationals it may be that longer-term social reconditioning will be necessary before stereotypes of what constitutes 'appropriate work' for CEE migrants, and the linked discrimination, on the part of employers and/or professional organizations in the EU15 for example, are eradicated.

There are further thought provoking issues raised by the research relating to the relationship between third country national migration to the EU15, on the one hand, and CEE accession national migration, on the other. Despite EU8 workers having a similar employment experience to third-country nationals in terms of the work carried out, there are significant differences in the legal statuses accorded to the groups. EU8 and EU2 nationals are officially Member State nationals and hence fall within the definition of Union citizen. Thus, although the rights of this group to work in the EU15 are subject to temporary restrictions, they are entitled to access various other citizenship statuses throughout the duration of the transitional periods. For example they can move as a student, retired person or self-sufficient person and can rely on the concomitant right not to be discriminated against pursuant to Article 12 EC.[4] Theoretically, EU8 and EU2 nationals could shift between statuses to maximise the available migration opportunities. Furthermore, those CEE nationals that are granted access as a worker can, formally at least, claim access to the panoply of social and family rights in the host state that attach to the status. Third-country nationals clearly operate outside of this realm but the book has highlighted some anomalies; for example, Chapter 5 demonstrated that CEE workers' family members are potentially subject to harsher conditions than third-country national migrants' family members in relation to labour market access during the transitional period (in those Member States bound by the Directive on family reunification).[5] Similarly, under the Directive on long-term residents, third-country national migrants with the status of long-term resident in one Member State are entitled to take up subsequent residence in another Member State and enter employment there (subject to certain conditions being satisfied).[6] This contrasts sharply with the policy towards EU8 and EU2 migrants during the transitional period as, even if such a worker obtains complete access to one of the EU15 labour markets, the rights they are accorded relate exclusively to that one particular Member State. Transitional arrangements applicable to CEE migrants, then, are altering the traditional distinction between EU migrant workers and third-country national migrant workers. EU migrant workers are no longer a group with a unitary status, and while the discrepancy between the rights of EU15 workers and third-country national workers remains intact, the relationship between EU8/EU2 nationals and third-country nationals is more complex. The preference rule in the transitional arrangements, however, does stand to remind us of the lower status of third-country nationals in the migrant worker food chain.

Reflecting on the Analysis at National (UK) Level

The UK has promoted its own self interest amidst the implementation of the post-accession regulatory regime in quite a striking fashion. The book has shown how the underlying objective of the UK policy of open labour access after 2004 was to fill labour shortages but, more poignantly, it has exposed the inequitable nature of this approach. From a legal perspective, the UK law purporting to implement the transitional arrangements does not comply with either the terms of the Accession Treaty or broader aspects of free movement and citizenship law. The system operates outside the terms of the Accession Treaty as it seeks to go further than derogate simply from the provisions that enable Community nationals to access work in other Member States. Chapters 3 and 6, for example, have demonstrated the apparent unlawfulness of the UK's approach in relation

4 To be renumbered as Article 18 TFEU assuming the Lisbon Treaty enters into force.

5 Directive 2003/86/EC OJ [2003] L 251/12. Ireland, the UK and Denmark are not bound by this Directive.

6 Directive 2003/109/EC [2004] OJ L16/44. Again, Ireland, the UK and Denmark are not bound by this Directive.

to the denial of lawful residence and the right to equal treatment from those EU8 workers who do not fulfil the conditions of the WRS (although the national courts have not accepted arguments of the UK's incompatibility with Community law). By opening up the labour market to EU8 nationals while simultaneously restricting these workers' rights to social assistance should they become unemployed before the 12-month deadline, the UK has benefited significantly from the presence of EU8 workers without fully embracing its obligations as a host Member State. The UK, which has been classified here as a 'wolf in sheep's clothing', has sought to gain from the presence of EU8 migrant workers without extending to the group the complete package of rights that attach to the status. The particular stance of the UK's domestic law, therefore, has a significant impact on EU8 migrant workers' citizenship status and entitlement – which can only become tangible once it is filtered through the national context – despite the fact that once a job has been secured they are formally entitled to a status analogous to that of EU15 migrant workers.

In its report on the functioning of the transitional arrangements, published in 2006, the Commission did not explicitly criticize the dichotomous approach of the UK (European Commission 2006c). Arguably, it would have been politically difficult to express disapproval of a Member State perceived as having implemented a lenient post-accession regime. A more public rigorous critique and exposure of the incompatibility of UK law with Community law, however, may have served to educate and inform the CEE migrant community (or at least those in a position to advise them) about their potential status under Community law as opposed to simply the narrower one assigned to them by national law. It may also have gone some way to persuading the UK, and other EU Member States, that EU8 migrants admitted to the labour market – and nationals of those countries that accede in the future – should be extended the same level of protection as EU15 migrant workers. Admittedly, however, if the Member States' post-accession regimes faced harsher scrutiny it may have had the reverse effect of acting as a disincentive to the removal of transitional measures.

Throughout the chapters the role played by employers and agencies in both facilitating and shaping the migration experience has been explored. These actors have clearly been prominent players in the migration space and their input links across, and feeds into, many of the research themes that have been mentioned here. Chapter 3 examined how the complex legal framework and the atmosphere of uncertainty surrounding the right to work in the UK has contributed to the popularity of agencies as people looked to such bodies to help them navigate the system. The empirical examples, however, also suggest that agencies and employers have contributed to the misinformation surrounding the legal regime. This has occurred both unintentionally, because the particular adviser did not have a full grasp of the law, or, in a deliberate attempt to take advantage of the migrant's uncertainty. Despite the possibility for EU8 migrants to hold a regular employment status in the UK, therefore, it seems a significant number are prevented from accessing the status of migrant worker due to the preference of some employers and agencies to employ workers without a legal status. This leaves the workers in a position in which they are potentially vulnerable to exploitation.

Furthermore, access to certain rights may be curtailed. This was demonstrated in Chapter 5, for example, which revealed that the tendency of employers to arrange accommodation for the workers has implications for their capacity to exercise family reunification rights.

The issue of family reunification links with the culture of family separation that seems to have been prevalent amongst EU8 migrants that moved to the UK during the initial post-accession phase. The point was made in Chapter 5 that the model of family migration enshrined in the free movement provisions, based on the unification of the immediate family unit, is not one that was reflected in the accounts of many of the respondents in this study. There has been a prevalence, particularly early on in the post-accession phases, of single migrants moving without dependents. This trend is likely to be evident (partially at least) not just because much of the post-accession migration has been temporary in nature but also as a result of migrants' uncertainty of their family rights (as a result of the confusion surrounding the system and the perceived lack of access to social welfare) as well as structural and physical constraints, such as low wages and lack of suitable accommodation, preventing the practical fulfilment of a family life in the UK. As the transitional period has progressed further, there has been stronger evidence emerging which suggests that family reunification, or 'new' partnering and parenting in the host state, has become more relevant to the experience of EU8 migrants.

The UK's stance towards the labour market access rights of Bulgarian and Romanian nationals has clearly been of a more blatantly restrictive nature than that directed at EU8 citizens. The extension of the right to work to EU8 nationals has contributed to the imposition of work permit requirements on those citizens in the next round of enlargement. The perception that very large numbers of EU8 migrants have settled in the UK, and consequent reports of infrastructure-related impacts on services, fed into the debates on the accession of Bulgaria and Romania. Concerns regarding increased admissions in schools, pressures on language schools providing English tuition, and local authorities reporting pressures on the availability of housing have been apparent. Interestingly, these 'impacts' do not correspond to those that were put forward in support of transitional arrangements: labour market disruption and social tourism.

The decision of the UK government to impose transitional mobility restrictions on the nationals of these countries has been accompanied by the reservation of places on the low-skilled migration schemes for this group. This decision, which reflects the preference clause in the Treaty of Accession's transitional provisions (see Chapter 3), undoubtedly demonstrates the potential negative impact of EU enlargement on the position of third-country nationals in the Member States. Moreover, it again highlights the expectation held by some of the Member States about the role the new(est) EU citizens should fulfil; essentially, they are expected to carry out the low-skilled, low-status and (presumably) low-paid work. Currently in the UK, the transitional work-permit measures applicable to Bulgaria and Romania exist alongside the Workers' Registration Scheme (which continues to apply to the EU8).

Reflecting on the Methodological Approach

The empirical work focussed on a concentrated group of migrants and employment agencies and thus sought to achieve an in-depth analysis of the experiences of an indicative sample of Polish migrants. It is hoped that this concentrated qualitative analysis, when combined with critical examination of the legal provisions and policy-framework, contributes to an overall rich and interesting insight to the direction of migration, work and citizenship in the enlarged European Union.

By designing and implementing a socio-legal and qualitative research project to examine the status and experiences of migrants from the CEE Member States, the investigation sought to be innovative. Furthermore, the methodology is also novel as a result of the timing of the research. The research planning began in late 2003, a year before the accession of the EU8 took place, allowing the research to develop and unfold alongside the law that it sought to examine and as the 2004 and 2007 enlargements took place. The area has remained a very active one throughout the entirety of the project's life. As a result, the journey the research has taken has, in many respects, mirrored that of the respondents who took part in the research. Both have had to deal with the law 'as it happened' rather than analyse it retrospectively. This is demonstrated by some of the empirical work findings; for example, the initial confusion surrounding the operation of the registration scheme in the UK came across very prominently in the interviews carried out in the early stages (May to August 2004) whereas in the later interviews this was less of a concern as the detail of the law had filtered through to a greater extent (see Chapter 3).

The accessions of the CEE Member States represent a historical and constitutional turning point in the EU's development and the research has utilized this as an avenue to explore further the issue of free movement. Essentially, the research has scoped the free movement rights and status of CEE migrant workers before, during and post enlargement and the methodology has had to incorporate this dynamism. In line with the grounded approach, the analysis of the qualitative data and the 'theory' developed simultaneously.

Free movement within the context of enlargement is a fertile ground for future research activity. Up until this point the focus has been on the CEE accession countries as a unitary group experiencing a form of downgraded citizenship. Arguably, it would also be interesting to explore if divisions exist (or begin to) between the status of EU8 and EU2 citizens and, further, how those from future accession countries fit into the picture (and hierarchy). Such issues lend themselves to the development of future, potentially longitudinal, research projects.

Looking Forward

Overall, the research that lies behind this book has demonstrated that the citizenship status and tangible experience of CEE migrant workers is not only restricted by the transitional arrangements on free movement but also by the impact of the national law's interpretation of these said provisions and, furthermore, by the engagement and input into the process of various actors and migration facilitators. The restricted access of CEE migrants to economic citizenship may be tempered somewhat by the developing notion of non-economic citizenship which is not subject to any transitional restrictions although, on the whole, the empirical reality suggests that most EU8 and EU2 nationals seeking to exercise mobility rights wish to do so as a worker. Thus, in spite of the immediate extension of the broader free movement rights, the exclusion of CEE workers from the mobility entitlement of primary importance to them means that for many the concept of Union citizenship is rather hollow.

From the point of view of the EU15, the transitional arrangements are no doubt regarded as a success. The older Member States have been able to protect themselves from aspects of free movement deemed less desirable; namely, labour market disruption and benefit tourism. Simultaneously, they have been able to develop a policy to suit their own economic needs, be that open labour market access to counter shortages in the lower echelons of the employment market or 'cherry-picking' of the highly skilled in order to fill positions in the professional sectors. The extent to which the transitional arrangements have reflected the EU15's greater balance of power, however, undermines significantly the concept of 'unity' upon which so much emphasis was placed in the build-up to enlargement (Kengerlinsky 2004; Maas 2002). The symbolic notion of EU enlargement creating a United Europe, bringing together nations which once stood on opposite sides of the Cold War divide, has been weakened by the existence of transitional measures that grant Union citizens different access to the right of free movement as a worker on the basis of nationality. From an equality perspective, therefore, particularly given the significance of the principle of non-discrimination on the grounds of nationality in Community law, transitional arrangements are less justifiable and legitimate. In this regard, it is also noteworthy that the Treaty of Lisbon contains an explicit proviso that the Union shall observe the principle of the equality of its citizens.[7] This fortifies the principle of universality already present in the definition of who constitutes a citizen.[8] Transitional arrangements which are themselves based on the unequal treatment of the newest citizens clearly do not reflect this sentiment. The political reality of transitional free movement restrictions does not correlate with the movements, made by the ECJ and the political institutions, towards a citizenship less dependent on market activity. Indeed, the treatment of the newest citizens blatantly undermines such developments.

From a legal point of view, after the expiry of the transitional periods, the citizenship status of CEE nationals will conform to that of EU15 nationals. The law on the free movement of workers will apply in full to all Member State nationals. What is not so clear is whether this formal equality will be sufficient to achieve a more substantive type of equality as regards the citizenship experience of EU15 citizens, on the one hand, and EU8 and EU2 citizens, on the other. Of course, citizenship has never been a universal status. It has always drawn

7 This would be enshrined in Article 9 of the amended TEU.

8 Presently, in Article 17 EC; post-ratification of the Lisbon Treaty to be Article 20 TFEU.

divisions based on different categories of migrants' perceived economic viability. Similarly, transitional arrangements are not new and it does not seem that they have had any negative, long-term implications for those Member State nationals previously subject to them. However, it does appear there is greater potential for the most recent transitional arrangements to have a more far-reaching impact on the citizenship experience of those they address.

First, by explicitly targeting *en masse* the post-communist CEE Member States the message sent (both to those in the CEE Member States and the EU15, Malta and Cyprus) was that Malta and Cyprus were more akin to the EU15 and, hence, more 'welcome' as members. Secondly, as a result of the mobility restrictions experienced under communism, the right of free movement is of particular poignancy to many in the CEE states; it is not difficult to envisage that restrictions placed on the exercise of this right may be interpreted as a form of second class membership by some. This perception may continue long after the expiry of the transitional arrangements. Thirdly, unlike previous enlargements, the 2004 and 2007 accessions took place after the institution of Union citizenship had developed dramatically by being constitutionalized in the Treaty and interpreted expansively by the Court. Therefore, the exclusion of CEE nationals from the full entitlement of free movement rights is arguably a harsher imposition than in earlier accessions.[9] Fourthly, the manner in which the EU15 have relied on the new EU citizens as a reserve army of labour is likely to have particular repercussions. The tendency for CEE nationals to work in the secondary labour markets of the EU15 (this is certainly the case in the UK) further entrenches the depiction of them as second class citizens. The effect of this portrayal may well have implications for the way in which EU8 and EU2 migrants are perceived in the enlarged EU in the long-term. This research, by incorporating the empirical element, has exposed the low-skilled (and low-status) work-trap that EU8 migrant workers have been caught in. It is doubtful that formal equality, in the light of the extension of full free movement rights, will remedy this situation. Cultural perceptions and stereotypes surrounding EU8 and EU2 migrants are important factors shaping the experience of the group and the formal application of the law cannot alter (certainly not in isolation or over a short-time period) the impact of these social forces. While the transitional arrangements are not the root cause of these implicit assumptions and perceptions regarding the 'appropriate' role of CEE nationals in the labour market, they do entrench a certain attitude, specifically, that migrants from the EU8 and EU2 are not (yet) quite as worthy as those from the EU15 (plus Malta and Cyprus).

In addition to the impact of post-enlargement migration on EU8 and EU2 workers in the EU15, the research also raises questions relating to the implications of the current trends for the sending regions. Clearly, the CEE countries are currently experiencing increased outward flows; national commentary in Poland has expressed concern about the risk of brain, skills and youth drain as a result of post-enlargement migration of the 'young *intelligentsia*' (Euroactiv 2006b). In

---

9 On the other hand, as has been demonstrated, the notion of multiple citizenship also offers greater opportunity to access at least some form of citizenship entitlement.

the longer-term, as conditions in the labour markets of the CEE Member States improve, one would expect the number of those migrating to fall and many of those who left to return to their home state.[10] The discussion of de-skilling in Chapter 4 highlighted how the sample of return migrants had been able to access jobs commensurate with their skills on return to Poland. These findings however, were in relation to a sample that had spent a relatively short time in the UK (between six months and two years). What is not so clear is whether those who spend a longer period of time abroad, and perhaps work in a de-skilled capacity during this time, will be able to integrate so easily back into their profession upon return to the state of origin. Longer periods of absence may have a more damaging impact on a migrant worker's home career.

Following on from the discussion above concerning the possibility that citizenship will not equalize (at least not immediately) after the transitional periods expire, a criticism sometimes directed at research focussing on transitional arrangements is that the temporary nature of the restrictions undermines the significance of the findings. Of course, parts of the analysis carried out for this research are time-specific, but it is anticipated that the investigation also contains elements of broader interest and application. For instance, the findings provide a yardstick against which the future patterns of integration of CEE nationals can be tested. Notably, the examination of de-skilling amongst EU8 migrants, of methods of facilitating family life post-migration, and the broader discussion of the citizenship implications of enlargement, provide a basis for future exploration of whether these trends have continuing relevance. It will be interesting to chart further how patterns of family life develop for post-accession migrants. In addition, it will be possible to explore how the passage of time impacts on the migrants' position in the labour market and whether their reliance on agencies diminishes with time.

Enlargement, and by extension transitional arrangements, are unlikely to disappear from the EU agenda. Analogous arrangements will certainly apply to Croatia and Turkey in the longer term (assuming accession progresses). The Former Yugoslav Republic of Macedonia also holds candidate country status. This research, by undertaking an in-depth investigation of the status and experiences of a group of migrants subject to such mobility restrictions, is a useful tool of analysis for forecasting the potential impact of future transitional arrangements. In addition, this research could prove useful as a method of informing future policy to accompany the implementation of transitory free movement restrictions. For example, a sustained and comprehensive information campaign implemented by the EU in the accession countries could help to overcome the problems associated with the complexity, and consequent confusion of, the legal framework. In addition to targeting potential migrants, employment agencies in the accession countries could be involved in such a campaign as such actors have clearly played a significant part in facilitating the mobility of recent migrants from the CEE region.

---

10 This would be consistent with patterns of mobility in the aftermath of the accessions of Ireland, Spain, Portugal and Greece, see Stalford 2003c.

Recognition of some of the pitfalls associated with agency reliance by migrants could prove useful for informing implementation of future EU programmes.

Finally, this research has raised broader issues relating to the nature and value of EU enlargement itself. Whether the restricted citizenship status of accession-country nationals has any consequences for the policy of enlargement in the longer-term remains to be seen. Currently, and seemingly for some time to come, different tiers of EU membership exist with some Member States granted a more meaningful form of association than others. If the citizenship status of those subject to transitional arrangements does not, or is not felt to, equalize with those in the EU15 in the future, and certain citizens continue to experience a form of devalued citizenship, the potential exists for the value of EU membership to be undermined. In other words, if citizenship continues to be a hollow experience the risk is that Member State relationships become more divided, the benefits of EU enlargement for the nationals of the newer Member States diminish or even disappear and, in conjunction, so too does citizen support in the CEE Member States for European integration.

Appendix

Sample of Respondents

Table A1 Sample of Polish migrants interviewed in UK

Age	Male	Female	Total
20–29	7	10	17
30–39	9	1	10
40–49	1	0	1
50–59	1	0	1
Total	18	11	29

Table A2 Sample of return Polish migrants interviewed in Poland

Age	Male	Female	Total
20–29	4	8	12
30–39	1	2	3
40–49	0	1	1
50–59	0	0	0
Total	5	11	16

Employment agencies based in Poland: 5

Key informants (UK and Poland): 3

Bibliography

Ackers, L. (1998), *Shifting Spaces: Women, Citizenship and Migration within the European Union* (Bristol: The Policy Press)

— (2004), 'Citizenship, Migration and the Valuation of Care in the European Union', *Journal of Ethnic and Migration Studies* 30:2, 373–396

— (2005), 'Moving People and Knowledge: Scientific Mobility in the European Union', *International Migration* 43: 5, 99–131

— and Dwyer, P. (2002), *Senior Citizenship? Retirement, Migration and Welfare in the European Union* (Bristol: The Policy Press)

— and Stalford, H. (1999), 'Children, Migration and Citizenship in the European Union: Intra-Community Mobility and the Status of Children in EC Law', *Children and Youth Services Review* 21:11/12, 987–1010

— and Stalford, H. (2004), *A Community for Children? Children, Citizenship and Internal Migration in the EU* (Aldershot: Ashgate)

— and Stalford, H. (2007), 'Managing Multiple Life-Courses: The Influence of Children on Migration Processes in the European Union', *Social Policy Review* 19, 321–342

Adinolfi, A. (2005), 'Free Movement and Access to Work of Citizens of the New Member States: The Transitional Measures', *Common Market Law Review* 42:2, 469–498

Agozino, B. (ed.) (2002), *Theoretical and Methodological Issues in Migration Research: Interdisciplinary, Intergenerational and International Perspectives* (Aldershot: VR)

Allen, J. and Henry, N. (1996), 'Fragments of Industry and Employment: Contract Service Work and the Shift towards Precarious Employment' in Crompton, R. et al. (eds)

Amnesty International (2005), *Amnesty International's Human Rights Concerns in the EU Accession Countries* (London: Amnesty International)

Anderson, B. (2000), *Doing the Dirty Work? The Global Politics of Domestic Labour* (London: Zed Books)

— and Rogaly, B. (2005), *Forced Labour and Migration to the UK* (Oxford: Study prepared by COMPAS in collaboration with the Trades Union Congress)

— et al. (2006), *Fair Enough? Central and East European Migrants in Low-Wage Employment in the UK* (Oxford: COMPAS)

Ardittis, S. (1992), 'The New Brain Drain from Eastern to Western Europe', *The International Spectator* 27:2, 79–96

— (1994), 'East-West Migration: An Overview of Trends and Issues', in Ardittis, S. (ed.)

— (ed.) (1994), *The Politics of East-West Migration* (New York: St Martins Press)

Arnull, A. et al. (2006), *Wyatt and Dashwood's European Union Law* (London: Sweet and Maxwell)

Arrowsmith, J. (2006), *Temporary Agency Work in an Enlarged European Union* (Dublin: European Foundation for the Improvement of Living and Working Conditions)

Bailey, A.J. and Boyle, P. (2004), 'Untying and Retying Family Migration in the New Europe', *Journal of Ethnic and Migration Studies* 30:2, 229–241

Baldassar, L. and Baldock, C. (2002), 'Linking Migration and Family Studies: Transnational Migrants and the Care of Ageing Parents', in Agozino, B. (ed.)

Baldwin, J. and Davis, G. (2003), 'Empirical Research in Law' in Cane, P. and Tushnet, M. (eds)

Barnard, C. (2005a), 'EU Citizenship and the Principle of Solidarity' in Dougan, M. and Spaventa, E. (eds)

— (2005b), 'Comment on Bidar', *Common Market Law Review* 42:5, 1465–1489

— and Hepple, B. (2000), 'Substantive Equality', *Cambridge Law Journal* 59:3, 562–585

Barratt, G. (2003), 'Family Matters: European Community Law and Third Country Family Members', *Common Market Law Review* 40:2, 369–421

Bauder, H. (2003), '"Brain Abuse", or the Devaluation of Immigrant Labour in Canada', *Antipode* 35:4, 699–717

BBC News Report (2005), '19 Women Rescued from "Brothel"', 30 September. Available online at <http://news.bbc.co.uk/1/hi/england/west_midlands/4296412.stm> (last accessed 20 February 2008)

Beaverstock et al. (1999), 'The Long Arm of the Law: London's Law Firms in a Globalising World Economy', *Environment and Planning A* 31:10, 1857–1876

Bellamy, R. (2004), 'Introduction: The Making of Modern Citizenship' in Bellamy, R. et al. (eds)

— et al. (eds) (2004), *Lineages of European Citizenship: Rights, Belonging and Participation in Eleven Nation States* (Basingstoke: Palgrave Macmillan)

Bercusson, B. (2007), 'The Trade Union Movement and the European Union: Judgment Day', *European Law Journal,* 13:3, 279–308

Boeri, T. and Brücker, H. (2000), *The Impact of Eastern Enlargement on Employment and Wages in the EU Member States* (Berlin: European Integration Consortium)

— (2005), *Migration, Co-ordination Failures and EU Enlargement,* Discussion Paper 1600 (Bonn: Institute for the Study of Labour)

Börzel, T.A. and Cichowski, R.A. (eds) (2003), *The State of the European Union: Law, Politics and Society* (Oxford: Oxford University Press)

Boyd, M. (1989), 'Family and Personal Networks in International Migration: Recent Developments and New Agendas', *International Migration Review* 23:3, 638–670

Boyle, P. (2002), 'Population Geography: Transnational Women on the Move', *Progress in Human Geography* 26:4, 531–543

Bradshaw, A. (1997), 'Sense and Sensibility: Debates and Developments in Socio-Legal Research Methods' in Thomas, P.A. (ed.)

Breugal, I. (1996), 'The Trailing Wife: A Declining Breed?' in Crompton, R. et al. (eds)

Bryceson, D.F. and Vuorela, U. (2002), 'Transnational Families in the Twenty-first Century' in Bryceson, D.F. and Vuorela, U. (eds)

— and Vuorela, U. (eds) (2002), *The Transnational Family: New European Frontiers and Global Networks* (New York: Berg)

Bryman, A. (ed.) (1988), *Doing Research in Organization* (London: Routledge)

Buchan, J. and O'May, F. (1999), 'Globalization and Healthcare Labour Markets: A Case Study from the United Kingdom', *Human Resources for Health Development Journal* 3:3, 199–209

Bulmer, M. (2001), 'The Ethics of Social Research' in Gilbert, N. (ed.)

Campani, G. (1993), 'Labour Markets and Family Networks: Filipino Women in Italy' in Rudolph, H. and Morokvasic, M. (eds)

Cane, P. and Tushnet, M. (eds) (2003), *The Oxford Handbook of Legal Studies* (Oxford: Oxford University Press)

Carrera, S. (2005), 'What Does Free Movement Mean in Theory and Practice in an Enlarged EU?', *European Law Journal* 11:6, 699–721

Chalmers, D. et al. (2006), *European Union Law Text and Materials* (Cambridge: Cambridge University Press)

Charmaz, K. (2003), 'Grounded Theory: Objectivist and Constructivist Methods' in Denzin, N.K. and Lincoln, Y.S. (eds)

Choldin, H.M. (1973), 'Kinship Networks in the Migration Process', *International Migration Review* 7:2, 163–175

Chow, K. (2006), *Report on the Free Movement of Workers in EU-25. The Functioning of Transitional Arrangements – Two Years after Enlargement* (Brussels: European Citizens Action Service)

CIETT (2005), *Agency Work Statistics for 2004*. Available online at <http://www.ciett.org/fileadmin/templates/ciett/docs/CIETT_2004_Statistics.pdf> (last accessed 13 February 2008)

Coe, N.M. et al. (2007), 'Mapping the Globalization of the Temporary Staffing Industry', *The Professional Geographer* 59:4, 503–520

Connelly, K. and Pook, S., 'Charity to Offer Destitute Poles Chance to go Home', *The Daily Telegraph*, 18 August 2006

Cook, S. (1991), 'Ethical Implications' in Judd, C.M. et al. (eds)

Cotterrell, R. (1995), *Law's Community: Legal Theory in Sociological Perspective* (Oxford: Clarendon Press)

Craig, P. and de Burca, G. (2003), *EU Law. Text Cases and Materials* (3rd edn.) (Oxford: Oxford University Press)

Crawley, H. (2001), *Refugees and Gender, Law and Process* (London: Jordans and Refugee Women's Legal Group)

Cremona, M. (ed.) (2003), *The Enlargement of the European Union* (Oxford: Oxford University Press)

Crompton, R. et al. (eds) (1996), *Changing Forms of Employment: Organizations, Skills and Gender* (London: Routledge)

Currie, S. (2006), '"Free" Movers? The Post-Accession Experience of Accession-8 Migrant Workers in the UK', *European Law Review* 31:2 207–229

— (2007), 'De-Skilled and Devalued: The Labour Market Experience of Polish Migrants in the UK Following EU Enlargement', *International Journal of Comparative Labour Law and Industrial Relations* 23:1, 83–116

Daily Mail (2004), 'Passport to the Promised Land', 29 April

Davies, P. (1997), 'Posted Workers: Single Market or Protection of National Labour Law Systems', *Common Market Law Review* 34:3, 571–602

Denzin, N.K. and Lincoln, Y.S. (eds) (2003a), *Strategies of Qualitative Inquiry* (London: Sage)

— and Lincoln, Y.S. (2003), *Collecting and Interpreting Qualitative Materials* (2nd edn) (London: Sage)

— et al. (2006), 'Disciplining Qualitative Research', *International Journal of Qualitative Studies in Education* 19:6, 769–782

De Vaus, D. (2001), *Research Design in Social Research* (London: Sage)

Dickson, D. (2003), 'Mitigating the Brain Drain is a Moral Necessity', *Science and Development Network*, 29 May 2003. Available online at <http://www.scidev.net/en/editorials/mitigating-the-brain-drain-is-a-moral-necessity.html> (last accessed 19 February 2008)

Dougan, M. (2004), 'A Spectre is Haunting Europe … Free Movement of Persons and the Eastern Enlargement' in Hillion, C. (ed.)

— (2005a), 'Fees, Grants, Loans and Dole Cheques: Who Covers the Cost of Migrant Education in the EU?', *Common Market Law Review* 42:4, 943–986

— (2005b), 'The Court Helps Those Who Help Themselves … The Legal Status of Migrant Workseekers Under Community Law in the Light of the Collins Judgment', *European Journal of Social Security* 7, 7–34

— (2006), 'The Constitutional Dimension to the Case Law on Union Citizenship', *European Law Review* 31:5, 613–641

— and Spaventa E (2003), 'Educating Rudy and the (Non-)English Patient: A Double Bill on Residency Rights Under Article 18 EC', *European Law Review* 28:5, 699–712

— and Spaventa, E.(2005), '"Wish You Weren't Here …" New Models of Social Solidarity in the European Union' in Dougan, M. and Spaventa, E. (eds)

— and Spaventa, E. (eds) (2005), *Social Welfare and EU Law* (Oxford: Hart)

Drew, E. et al. (eds) (1998), *Women, Work and the Family in Europe* (London: Routledge)

Düvell, F. (2004), *Polish Undocumented Immigrants, Regular High-skilled Workers and Entrepreneurs in the UK* (Warsaw: Institute for Social Studies Working Paper)

Easton, M. (2008), 'UK Paying for Migrant Baby Boom', *BBC News Online*, 29 January 2008. Available online at <http://news.bbc.co.uk/1/hi/health/7215624.stm> (last accessed 19 February 2008)

Ehrenreich, B. and Hochschild, A.R. (eds) (2003), *Global Woman: Nannies, Maids and Sex Workers in the New Economy* (New York: Granta Books)

EIRO (2004), 'New Labour Market Legislation Adopted', 7 June. Available online at <http://www.eurofound.europa.eu/eiro/2004/05/feature/pl0405105f.htm> (last accessed 13 February 2008)

Ellis, E. (2003), 'Social Advantages: A New Lease of Life', *Common Market Law Review* 40:3, 639–659

Euractiv (2006a), 'Free Movement of Labour in the EU-25', 14 August. Available online at <http://www.euractiv.com/en/enlargement/free-movement-labour-eu-27/article-129648> (last accessed 19 February 2008)

Euractiv (2006b), 'Fear of Brain Drain Makes Poland Drop Double Taxation Scheme', 23 October. Available online at <http://www.euractiv.com/en/mobility/fear-brain-drain-poland-drop-double-taxation-scheme/article-156916> (last accessed 19 February 2008)

Eurobarometer Survey (2006), *Geographic and Labour Market Mobility, Europeans and Mobility: First Results of an EU-Wide Survey* (Brussels: European Commission)

European Citizen Action Service (2006), Press Release: ECAS Hotline on Free Movement Rights, 25 August. Available at <http://www.ecas.org/file_uploads/1179.pdf> (last accessed 17 February 2008)

European Commission (DG Enlargement) (2002a), *Free Movement for Persons – A Practical Guide for an Enlarged European Union* (Brussels: European Commission)

— (2002b), *Directorate-General for Education and Culture, Socrates: European Community Action Programme in the field of education (2000–06), Gateway to Education* (Brussels: European Commission)

— (2002c), *Towards a European Research Area: A New framework Programme for European Research* (Brussels: European Commission)

— (2002d), *Proposal for a Directive on Agency work*, COM (2002)149 final

— (2005a), *Proposal for a Directive on improving the portability of supplementary pension rights*, COM (2005) 507 final

— (2005b), *Working Together for Growth and Jobs A New Start for the Lisbon Strategy*, COM (2005) 24 final

— (2005c), Press Release: MEMO/05/229, '2006 – European Year of Workers' Mobility', Brussels, 30 June 2005

— (2005d), *Proposal for a Regulation of the European Parliament and Council on the Law Applicable to Contractual Obligations (Rome I)*, COM(2005) 650 Final

— (Directorate-General for Economic and Financial Affairs) (2006a), *Enlargement, Two Years After: An Economic Evaluation*, Occasional Paper 24 (Brussels: European Commission)

— (2006b), *Europeans and Mobility: First Results of an EU-Wide Survey*, Eurobarometer Survey on Geographic and Labour Market Mobility, Brussels

— (2006c), *Report on the Functioning of the Transitional Arrangements Set Out in the 2003 Accession Treaty (Period 1 May 2004–30 April 2006)*, COM(2006) 48 final

— (2007), *Job Mobility Action Plan*, COM(2007)773 final

Eurostat (2007), 'GDP per Inhabitant Varied from One to More than Seven across the EU 27 Member States, 28 June (Brussels: European Communities)

Erel, U. (2003), 'Skilled Migrant Women and Citizenship' in Morokvasic, M. et al. (eds)

Everson, M. (1995), 'The Legacy of the Market Citizen' in Shaw, J. and More, G. (eds)

Faist, T. (2000), *The Volume and Dynamics of International Migration and Transnational Social Spaces* (Oxford: Clarendon Press)

— (2001), 'Social Citizenship in the European Union', *Journal of Common Market Studies* 39:1, 37–58

Farkas, O. and Rymkevitch, O. (2004), 'Immigration and the Free Movement of Workers after Enlargement: Contrasting Choices', *International Journal of Comparative Labour Law and Industrial Relations* 20:3, 369–397

Favell, A. and Hansen, R. (2002), 'Markets against Politics: Migration, EU Enlargement and the Idea of Europe', *Journal of Ethnic and Migration Studies* 28:4, 581–601

Fawcett, J.T. (1989), 'Networks, Linkages and Migration Systems', *International Migration Review*, 23:3, 671–680

Ferrera, M. (2005), *The Boundaries of Welfare: European Integration and the New Spatial Politics of Social Protection* (Oxford: Oxford University Press)

Fielding, N. and Thomas, H. (2001), 'Qualitative Interviewing' in Gilbert, N. (ed.)

Finch, J. and Mason, J. (1993), *Negotiating Family Responsibilities* (London: Routledge)

Foggo, D. and Habershon, E. (2006), 'Invasion by Poles Hits Lazy Britain', *Sunday Times,* 14 May. Available online at <http://www.timesonline.co.uk/tol/news/uk/article1083068.ece> (last accessed 19 February 2008)

Fontana, A. and Frey, J.H. (2003), 'The Interview: From Structured Questions to Negotiated Text' in Denzin, N.K. and Lincoln, Y.S. (eds)

Forde, C. (2001), 'Temporary Arrangements: The Activities of Employment Agencies in the UK', *Work, Employment and Society* 15:3, 631–644

Fredman, S. (2001), 'Equality: A New Generation?', *Industrial Law Journal* 30:2, 145–endpage

Fries, S. and Shaw, J. (1998), 'Citizenship of the Union: First Steps in the European Court of Justice', *European Public Law* 4, 533

Friese, M. (1995), 'East European Women as Domestics in Western Europe – New Social Inequality and Division of Labour among Women', *Journal of Area Studies* 6, 194–201

Gilbert, N. (ed.) (2001), *Researching Social Life* (2nd edn) (London: Sage)

Gilpin, N. et al. (2006), *The Impact of Free Movement of Workers from Central and Eastern Europe on the UK Labour Market*, Department for Work and Pensions, Working Paper No. 29 (Leeds: Corporate Document Services)

Glaser, B.G. and Strauss, A.L. (1967), *The Discovery of Grounded Theory: Strategies for Qualitative Research* (Chicago: Aldine)

Glick Schiller et al. (eds) (1992), *Towards a Transnational Perspective on Migration* (New York: New York Academy of Sciences)

Golynker, O. (2005), 'Jobseekers' Rights in the European Union: Challenges of Changing the Paradigm of Social Solidarity', *European Law Review* 30:1, 111–122

— (2006), *Ubiquitous Citizens of Europe: The Paradigm of Partial Migration* (Oxford: Intersentia)

Górny, A. and Ruspini, P. (eds) (2004), *Migration in the New Europe: East-West Revisited* (New York: Palgrave Macmillan)

Gospodinova, Z. (2006), 'Low Qualification Levels an Obstacle to Economic Competitiveness', *European Industrial Relations Online,* 12 December

Grice, A. and Brown, J. (2006), 'How Immigrants Sustain Britain's Economic Growth', *The Independent*, 23 August. Available online at <http://www.independent.co.uk/news/uk/this-britain/how-immigrants-sustain-britains-economic-growth-413016.html> (last accessed 18 February 2008)

Gudykunst, W.B. (2004), *Bridging Differences: Effective Intergroup Communication* (4th edn) (Thousand Oaks, CA: Sage)

Guild, E. and Harlow, C. (eds) (2001), *Implementing Amsterdam: Immigration and Asylum Rights in EC Law* (Oxford: Hart)

Gungwu, W. (ed.) (1997), *Global History and Migrations* (Oxford: Westview)

HM Revenue and Customs (2007), *Child Benefit Statistics, Quarterly Statistics, February 2007* (London: National Statistics)

HM Revenue and Customs (2006), *Child and Working Tax Credits Statistics, December 2006* (London: National Statistics)

Hailbronner, K. (2005), 'Union Citizenship and Access to Social Benefits', *Common Market Law Review* 42:5, 1245–1267

Hall, M. (2006), 'Britain "a Magnet for all Scroungers"', *The Express*, 8 November

Halleskov, L. (2005), 'The Long-Term Residents Directive: A Fulfillment of the Tampere Objective of Near-Equality?', *European Journal of Migration and Law* 7:2, 181–202

Hantrais, L. and Mangen, S. (1996), 'Method and Management of Cross National Social Research' in Hantrais, L. and Mangen S. (eds)

— and Mangen S. (eds) (1996), *Cross-National Research Methods in the Social Sciences* (New York: Pinter)

— and Mangen S. (1999), 'Contextualization in Cross-National Comparative Research', *International Journal of Social Research Methodology* 2:2, 93–108

Hedemann-Robinson, M. (2001), 'An Overview of Recent Legal Developments at Community Level in Relation to Third Country Nationals Resident within the European Union, with Particular Reference to the Case Law of the European Court of Justice', *Common Market Law Review* 38:3, 525–586

Heer, D. (1990), *Undocumented Mexicans in the United States* (Cambridge: Cambridge University Press)

Heinen, J. and Wator, M. (2006), 'Child Care in Poland Before, During, and After the Transition: Still a Women's Business', *Social Politics* 13:2, 189–216

Henderson, K. (2000), 'The Challenges of EU Eastward Enlargement', *International Politics* 37:1, 1–15

Hervey, T.K. and McHale, J.V. (2004), *Health Law and the European Union* (Cambridge: Cambridge University Press)

Hess, S. and Puckhaber, A. (2004), "Big Sisters' are Better Domestic Servants? Comments on the Booming Au Pair Business', *Feminist Review* 77, 65–78

Hillion, C. (ed.) (2004a), *Enlargement of the European Union: A Legal Approach* (Oxford: Hart)

— (2004b), 'The European Union is Dead. Long Live the European Union … A Commentary on the Treaty of Accession 2003', *European Law Review* 29:5, 583–612

Hjarnø, J. (2003), *Illegal Immigrants and Developments in Employment in the Labour Markets of the EU* (Aldershot: Ashgate)

Hoddinott, J. (1994), 'A Model of Migration and Remittances Applied to Western Kenya', *Oxford Economic Papers* 46:3, 459–476

Holmans, A. et al. (2005), *Building for the Future (2005 Update)*, Shelter Housing Investment Project Series (Cambridge Centre for Housing Planning Research). Available online at <http://england.shelter.org.uk/policy/policy-961.cfm> (last accessed 24 February 2008)

Home Office (2003), *Control of Immigration: Statistics United Kingdom 2003* (London: Home Office)

— et al. (2005a), Department for Work and Pensions, the Inland Revenue and the Office of the Deputy Prime Minister, *Accession Monitoring Report, May 2004–March 2005*, 26 May

— et al. (2005b), Department for Work and Pensions, the Inland Revenue and the Office of the Deputy Prime Minister, *Accession Monitoring Report, May 2004–June 2005*, 23 August

— et al. (2006), Department for Work and Pensions, Inland Revenue and the Office of the Deputy Prime Minister, *Accession Monitoring Report, May 2004–June 2006*, 22 August

— Border and Immigration Agency (2007), *Accession Monitoring Report, May 2004–September 2007,* Joint Online Report between the Border and Immigration Agency, Department for Work and Pensions, HM Revenue and Customs and Communities and Local Government <http://www.ukba.homeoffice.gov.uk/sitecontent/documents/aboutus/reports/accession_monitoring_report/> (last accessed 17 February 2008)

— and Department for Work and Pensions (2007a), A Cross-Departmental Submission to the House of Lords Select Committee on Economic Affairs, *The Economic and Fiscal Impact of Immigration*, Cm7237 (London: The Stationary Office)

— Border and Immigration Agency (2007b), *Bulgarian and Romanian Accession Statistics* (July–September 2007), Joint Online Report between the Border and Immigration Agency, Department for Work and Pensions, HM Revenue and Customs and Communities and Local Government <http://www.ukba.homeoffice.gov.uk/sitecontent/documents/aboutus/reports/bulgarianromanian/> (last accessed 19 February 2008)

— et al. (2007c), *Living and Working in the UK: Rights and Responsibilities of Nationals from Bulgaria and Romania from 1 January 2007 (*London: Border and Immigration Agency Communications)

Iglicka, K. (2000), 'Mechanisms of Migration from Poland Before and During The Transition Period', *Journal of Ethnic and Migration Studies* 26:1, 61–73

— (2001), 'Shuttling from the Former Soviet Union to Poland: from "Primitive Mobility" to Migration', *Journal of Ethnic and Migration Studies* 27:3, 505–518

— (2006), K., *Free Movement of Workers Two Years After Enlargement: Myths and Reality* (Warsaw: Centre for International Relations)

Iliopouou, A. and Toner, H. (2002), 'Casenote on Grzelczyk', *Common Market Law Review* 39:3, 609–620

Ingham, J. (2006), 'EU Influx Brings New Menace on our Roads', *The Express,* 4 September

Inglis, K. (2004), 'The Accession Treaty and its Transitional Arrangements: A Twi-Light Zone for the New Member States' in Hillion, C. (ed.)

Institute of Community Cohesion (2007), *Estimating the Scale and Impacts of Migration at the Local Level* (London: Local Government Association)

Iosifides, T. (1997), 'Immigrants in the Athens Labour Market: A Comparative Survey of Albanians, Eqyptians and Filipinos' in King, R. and Black, R. (eds)

Jacqueson, C. (2002), 'Union Citizenship and the Court of Justice: Something New Under the Sun? Towards Social Citizenship', *European Law Review* 27:3, 260–281

Jandl, M. (2007), 'Irregular Migration, Human Smuggling, and the Eastern Enlargement of the European Union', *International Migration Review* 41:2, 291–315

Jileva, E. (2002), 'Visa and Free Movement of Labour: The Uneven Imposition of the EU *Acquis* on the Accession States', *Journal of Ethnic and Migration Studies* 28:4, 683–700

— (2007), Labour Migration from Bulgaria to the European Union', paper presented at conference on 'EU Enlargement and Labour Migration within the EU', Warsaw, Poland 23–24 April

Judd, C.M. et al. (eds) (1991), *Research Methods in Social Relations* (London: Harcourt Brace Jovanovich College Publishers)

Kaczmarczyk, P. (2004), 'Migration in the New Europe: East-West Revisited' in Górny, A. and Ruspini, P. (eds)

— (2007), 'Brains on the Move? Recent Migration from Poland and its Impact on the Polish Labour Market', paper presented at IMISCOE conference on 'EU Enlargement and Labour Migration within the EU', Warsaw, Poland, 23–24 April

Kengerlinsky, M. (2004), 'Restrictions in EU Immigration Policies towards New Member States', *Journal of European Affairs* 2:4, 12–18

Keune, M. (1998), *Youth Unemployment in Hungary and Poland: Action Programme on Youth Unemployment*, International Labour Organization, Employment and Training Paper 20 (Switzerland: ILO)

King, R. and Black, R. (eds) (1997), *Southern Europe and the New Immigrations* (Brighton: Sussex Academic Press)

Kofman, E. (1995), 'Citizenship for Some but not for Others: Spaces of Citizenship in Contemporary Europe', *Political Geography* 14:2, 121–137

— (1999), 'Female "Birds of Passage" a Decade Later: Gender and Immigration in the European Union', *International Migration Review* 33:2, 269–299

— (2000), 'The Invisibility of Skilled Female Migrants and Gender Relations in Studies of Skilled Migration in Europe', *International Journal of Population Geography* 6:1, 45–59

— (2004a), 'Family-Related Migration: A Critical Review of European Studies', *Journal of Ethnic and Migration Studies* 30:2, 243–262

— (2004b), 'Gendered Global Migrations', *International Feminist Journal of Politics* 6:4, 643–664

— et al. (2000), *Gender and International Migration in Europe: Employment, Welfare and Politics* (New York: Routledge)

— et al. (2005), *Gendered Migrations: Towards Gender Sensitive Policies in the UK*, Institute for Public Policy Research, Asylum and Migration Working Paper 6

Koryś, I. (2003), *Migration Trends in Selected EU Applicant Countries: Poland* (Warsaw: Central European Forum for Migration Research)

Kostakopoulou, T. (1999), 'Nested "Old" and "New" Citizenship in the European Union: Bringing Out the Complexity', *Columbia Journal of European Law* 5:3, 389–413

— (2001), *Citizenship, Identity and Immigration in the European Union* (Manchester: Manchester University Press)

— (2002a), '"Integrating" Non-EU Migrants in the European Union: Ambivalent Legacies and Mutating Paradigms', *Columbia Journal of European Law* 8:2, 181–202

— (2002b), 'Long-term Resident Third-Country Nationals in the European Union: Normative Expectations and Institutional Openings', *Journal of Ethnic and Migration Studies* 28:3, 443–462

— (2005), 'Ideas, Norms and European Citizenship: Explaining Institutional Change', *Modern Law Review* 68:2, 233–267

Kraus, M. and Scwager, R. (2003), 'EU Enlargement and Immigration', *Journal of Common Market Studies* 42:2, 165–181

Krieger, H. (2004), *Migration Tends in an Enlarged Europe* (Dublin: European Foundation for the Improvement of Living and Working Conditions)

Kupiszewski, M. (2002), 'How Trustworthy are Forecasts of International Migration between Poland and the European Union?', *Journal of Ethnic and Migration Studies* 28:4, 627–645

Kvist, J. (2004), 'Does EU Enlargement Start a Race to the Bottom? Strategic Interaction among EU Member States in Social Policy', *Journal of European Social Policy* 14:3, 301–318

Lanzieri, G. (2007), *First Demographic Estimates for 2006* (Brussels: Eurostat, European Communities)

Lardy, H. (1997), 'The Political Rights of Union Citizenship', *European Public Law* 2:4, 611–633

La Torre, M. (ed.) (1998), *European Citizenship: An Institutional Challenge* (The Hague: Kluwer)

Lawrence, P. (1988), 'In Another Country' in Bryman, A. (ed.)

León-Ledesma, M. and Piracha, M. (2004), 'International Migration and the Role of Remittances in Eastern Europe', *International Migration* 42:4, 65–83

Levitas, R. and Guy, W. (1996), 'Introduction' in Levitas, R. and Guy, W. (eds)

— and Guy, W. (eds) (1996), *Interpreting Official Statistics* (London and New York: Routledge)

Li, P.S. (2001), 'The Market Worth of Immigrants' Educational Credentials', *Canadian Public Policy* 27:1, 23–38

Lorber, P. (1999), 'Regulating Fixed-Term Work in the United Kingdom: A Positive Step Towards Workers' Protection?', *International Journal of Comparative Labour Law and Industrial Relations* 15:2, 121–136

Lundström, K. (1996), 'Family Life and the Freedom of Movement of Workers in the European Union', *International Journal of Law, Policy and the Family* 10, 250–280

Maas, W. (2002), 'Free Movement and EU Enlargement', Paper prepared for the Fifth Biennial Conference of the European Community Studies Association, Toronto, Canada 31 May-1 June 2002

MacDonald, J.S. and MacDonald, L.D. (1964), 'Chain Migration, Ethnic Neighbourhood Formation and Social Networks', *Milibank Memorial Fund Quarterly* 42:1, 82–97

Mahony, H. (2006), 'Italy Opens Up Labour Market to Eastern Europeans', *EUobserver*, 24 July 2006

Man, G. (2004), 'Gender, Work and Migration: Deskilling Chinese Immigrant Women in Canada', *Women's Studies International Forum* 27:2, 135–148

Maresceau, M. (2003), 'Pre-accession', in Cremona, M. (ed.)

Markova, E. and Reilly, B. (2006), 'Bulgarian Migrant Remittances and Legal Status: Some Micro-level Evidence from Madrid', *Sussex Migration Working Paper no.37* (Sussex: Centre for Migration research)

Marshall, T.H. (1950), *Citizenship and Social Class* (Cambridge: Cambridge University Press)

Matiti, M.R. and Taylor, D. (2005), 'The Cultural Lived Experience of Internationally Recruited Nurses: A Phenomenological Study', *Diversity in Health and Social Care* 2:1, 7–16

Mayhew, A. (1998), *Recreating Europe: The European Union's Policy towards Central and Eastern Europe* (Cambridge: Cambridge University Press)

McGlynn, C. (2001), 'The Europeanization of Family Law', *Child and Family Law Quarterly* 35:1, 35–49

McKenna, E. and Beech, N. (2002), *Human Resource Management: A Concise Analysis* (Harlow: Pearson Education)

McLaughlin, D. (2005), 'Doctors Go West in Polish Brain Drain', *The Observer*, 15 May

Meulman, J. and de Waele, H. (2004), 'Funding the Life of Brian: Jobseekers, Welfare Shopping and the Frontiers of European Citizenship', *Legal Issues of European Integration* 31:4, 275–288

Mladý, M. (2004), 'Regional Unemployment in the European Union and Candidate Countries in 2003', *Statistics in Focus* (Brussels: Eurostat European Communities)

Moore, M. (2002), 'Freedom of Movement and Migrant Workers' Social Security', *Common Market Law Review* 39:4, 807–839

Morawska, E. and Spohn, W. (1997), 'Moving Europeans in the Globalising World: Contemporary Migrations in a Historical-Comparative Perspective (1955–1994 v. 1870–1914)' in Gungwu, W. (ed.)

Morokvasic, M. (2004), 'Settled in Mobility': Engendering Post-wall Migration in Europe', 77 *Feminist Review* 77:1, 7–25

— and de Tinguy, A. (1993), 'Between East and West: A New Migratory Space' in Rudolph, H. and Morokvasic, M. (eds)

— et al. (eds) (2003), *Crossing Borders and Shifting Boundaries. Vol I: Gender on the Move* (Opalden: Leske and Budrich)

National Statistics (2006), *News Release: Over 500 a Day Gained Through Migration to the UK* (London: National Statistics)

Newcombe, E. (2004), *Temporary Migration to the UK as an 'Au Pair': Cultural Exchange or Reproductive Labour?*, Sussex Migration Working Paper No. 2 (Sussex: Centre for Migration Research)

Nicolson, S. (2006), 'GPs Swamped by Migrants', *Daily Mail*, 8 September

Numhauser-Henning, A. (ed.) (2001), *Legal Perspectives on Equal Treatment and Non-Discrimination* (The Hague: Kluwer)

Nyikos, S.A. and Pollack, M.A. (2003), 'Researching the European Union: Qualitative and Quantitative Approaches' in Börzel, T.A. and Cichowski, R.A. (eds)

Office for National Statistics (2007), *Births, Selected Background Data, England and Wales (ONS)*. Available online at <http://www.statistics.gov.uk/STATBASE/Product.asp?vlnk=14408> (last accessed 19 February 2008)

Okólski, M. (2000), 'Recent Trends and Major Issues in International Migration: Central and East European Perspectives', *International Social Science Journal* 52:165, 329–341

— (2001), 'Incomplete Migration: A New Form of Mobility in Central and Eastern Europe. The Case of Polish and Ukrainian Migrants' in Wallace, C. and Stola, D. (eds)

O'Leary, S. (1996), *The Evolving Concept of Community Citizenship: From the Free Movement of Persons to Union Citizenship* (The Hague: Kluwer)

— (1999), 'Putting Flesh on the Bones of European Union Citizenship', *European Law Review* 24:1, 68–79

Oosterom-Staples, H. (2005), 'Annotation of Collins', *Common Market Law Review* 42:1, 205–223

Parreńas, R. (2001), 'Transgressing the Nation-State: The Partial Citizenship and "Imagined (Global) Community" of Migrant Filipina Domestic Workers', *Signs* 26:4, 1129–1154

Paternoster, A. (2004), 'Minimum Wages: EU Member States, Candidate Countries and the US 2004', *Statistics in Focus* (Brussels: Eurostat, European Communities).

Peers, S (2001), 'Dazed and Confused: Family Members' Residence Rights and the Court of Justice', *European Law Review* 26:1, 76–83

Peixoto, J. (2001), 'Migration and Policies in the European Union: Highly Skilled Mobility, Free Movement of Labour and Recognition of Diplomas', *International Migration* 39:1, 33–61

Pemberton, S. and Stevens, C. (2007), 'Economic Migration to Housing Market Renewal Areas in North West England – Opportunity or Threat?', *MSIO Policy Report 4* (Merseyside Social Inclusion Observatory, University of Liverpool)

Pemberton, S. (2007), 'Supporting Economic Migrants in the North West of England: Implications for Economic and Social Policy', *Public Policy and Administration* 23:1, 80–99

Pennings, F. (2001), 'The European Commission Proposal to Simplify Regulation 1408/71', *European Journal of Social Security* 3:1, 45–60

— (2005), 'Inclusion and Exclusion of Persons and Benefits in the New Coordination Regulation' in Dougan, M. and Spaventa, E. (eds)

Perrons et al. (2005), 'Work, Life and Time in the New Economy', *Time and Society* 14:1, 51–64

Pertek, J. (1992), 'Free Movement of Professionals and Recognition of Higher Education Diplomas', *Yearbook of European Law* 12, 293

Petev, V. (1998), 'Citizenship and *Raison D'État.* The Quest for Identity in Central and Eastern Europe' in La Torre, M. (ed.)

Phizacklea, A. (1983), 'In the Front Line', in Phizacklea, A. (ed.)

— (ed.) (1983), *One Way Ticket. Migration and Female Labour* (London: Routledge)

— (2000), 'The Politics of Belonging. Sex Work, Domestic Work: Transnational Household Strategies' in Westwood, S. and Phizacklea, A. (eds)

Pitt, G. (2007), *Employment Law* (6th edn) (London: Thomson, Sweet and Maxwell)

Raghuram, P. (2004), 'The Difference that Skills Make: Gender, Family Migration Strategies and Regulated Labour Markets', *Journal of Ethnic and Migration Studies* 30:2, 303–321

— and Kofman, E. (2004), 'Out of Asia: Skilling, Re-skilling and Deskilling of Female Migrants', *Women's Studies International Forum* 27:2, 95–100

Rees, A. (1966), 'Information Networks in Labour Markets', *The American Economic Review* 56:1/2, 559–566

Reich, N. (2003), 'Citizenship and Family on Trial: A Fairly Optimistic Overview of Recent Court Practice with regard to Free Movement of Persons', *Common Market Law Review* 40:3, 615–638

— (2004), 'The European Constitution and New Member Countries: The Constitutional Relevance of Free Movement and Citizenship', paper presented at the Centre for European, Comparative and International Law's Annual Lecture, University of Sheffield, 26 February

Reinsch, P. (2001), *Measuring Immigrant Integration: Diversity in a European City* (Aldershot: Ashgate)

Rendall, M.S. et al. (2003), 'Estimation of annual International Migration from the Labour Force Surveys of the United Kingdom and the Continental European Union', *Statistical Journal of the United Nations Economic Commission for Europe* 20:3–4, 219–234

Rettman, A. (2006), 'EU Law Leaves New Member State Workers in Third Place', *EU Observer*, 20 January

Reynolds, F. (2006), 'The Status of Agency Workers: A Question of Legal Principle', *Industrial Law Journal* 35:3, 320–323

Reynolds, T. and Zontini, E. (2006), *A Comparative Study of Care and Provision,* Families and Social Capital ESRC Research Group (London). Available online at <http://www.lsbu.ac.uk/families/workingpapers/familieswp16.pdf> (last accessed 19 February 2008).

Righter, R. (2006), 'Britain is Enriched by its Poles of Growth', *The Times*, 28 August

Robinson, D. (2007), 'European Union Accession State Migrants in Social Housing in England', *People, Place and Policy Online* 1:3, 98–111

Robson, C. (2002), *Real World Research* (2nd edn) (Oxford: Blackwell)

Rogerson, P.A. et al. (1997), 'Changes in Geographic Proximity between Parents and their Adult Children', *International Journal of Population Geography* 3, 121–136

Romaniszyn, G.K. (1996), 'The Invisible Community: Undocumented Polish Workers in Athens', *New Community* 22:2, 321–333

Rudolph, H. and Morokvasic, M. (eds) (1993), *Bridging States and Markets. International Migration in the Early 1990s* (Berlin: Sigma)

Sakslin, M. (2000), 'Social Security Coordination: Adapting to Change', *European Journal of Social Security* 2, 169

Salt, J. (1992), 'Migration Processes among the Highly Skilled in Europe', *International Migration Review* 26:2, 484–505

Sassen, S. (2000), 'Women's Burden: Counter-Geographies of Globalization and the Feminization of Survival', *Journal of International Affairs* 53:2, 503–524

Schmid, J. (2000), 'Schröder Seeks Delay for East Bloc Workers', *Herald Tribune*, 19 December, available online at <http://www.iht.com/articles/2000/12/19/east.2.t.php> (last accessed 19 February 2008)

Schunk, M. (1996), 'Constructing Models of the Welfare Mix: Care Options of Frail Elders' in Hantrais, L. and Mangen, S. (eds)

Schuster, L. (2005), 'The Continuing Mobility of Migrants in Italy: Shifting between Places and Statuses', *Journal of Ethnic and Migration Studies* 31:4, 757–774

Schwenken, H. (2005), *"Domestic Slavery" versus "Workers Rights": Political Mobilizations of Migrant Domestic Workers in the European Union*, Centre for Comparative Immigration Studies, University of California, Working Paper 116

Shah, P. and Minski, W. (eds) (2006), *Migration, Diasporas and Legal Systems in Europe* (London: Routledge)

Shaw, J. (1995), 'Introduction', in Shaw, J. and More, G. (eds)
— (1997), 'The Many Pasts and Futures of Citizenship in the European Union', *European Law Review* 22:6, 554–572
— (1998), 'The Interpretation of European Union Citizenship', *Modern Law Review* 61:3, 293–317
— (ed.) (2000), *Social Law and Policy in an Evolving European Union* (Oxford: Hart)
— (2003), 'Sovereignty at the Boundaries of the Polity' in Walker, N. (ed.)
— (2007), *The Transformation of Citizenship in the European Union: Electoral Rights and the Restructuring of Political Space* (Cambridge: Cambridge University Press)
— and More, G. (eds) (1995), *New Legal Dynamics of European Union* (Oxford: Clarendon Press)
— and Smith, M. (2006), 'Changing Polities and Electoral Rights: Lithuania's accession to the EU' in Shah, P and Minski, W. (eds)
Shennan, P. (2005), 'Why Poles Do Jobs We Hate', *Liverpool Echo*, 21 July
Silver, A. (2006), 'Families Across Borders: The Effects of Migration on Family Members Remaining at Home,' paper prepared for the Population Association Meeting of America Annual Meeting, 30 March–1 April
Silverman, D. (2001), *Interpreting Qualitative Data: Methods for Analysing Talk, Text and Interaction* (2nd edn) (London: Sage)
Singleton, A. (1999), 'Combining Quantitative and Qualitative Research methods in the Study of International Migration', *International Journal of Social Research Methodology* 2:2, 151–157
Smith, M.P. and Guarnizo, L.E. (1990), *Transnationalism from Below* (New Brunswick: Transaction)
Smith, S. (2004), 'Immigration Hysteria: What they Said about … Immigration and the EU – Tabloids Threaten "Flood" of Gypsies', *The Guardian*, 21 January
Spencer, S. et al. (2007), *Migrants' Lives Beyond the Workplace: The Experiences of Central and East European in the UK* (London: Jospeh Rowntree Foundation)
Spitzer, D. (2004), 'Britain Strives to Limit Immigrants', *The Prague Post*, 22 April 2004
Stalford, H. (2000a), 'The Citizenship Status of Children in the European Union', *International Journal of Children's Rights* 8:2, 101–131
— (2000b), 'The Developing European Agenda on Children's Rights', *Journal of Social Welfare and Family Law* 22:2, 229–236
— (2000c), 'Transferability of Educational Skills and Qualifications in the European Union. The Case of EU Migrant Children' in Shaw, J. (ed.)
(2002), 'Concepts of Family Under EU Law – Lessons from the ECHR', *International Journal of Law, Policy and the Family* 16:3, 410–434
— (2003a), 'Regulating Family Life in Post-Amsterdam Europe', *European Law Review* 28:1, 39–52

— (2003b), 'Old Problems, New Solutions?: European Union Regulation of Cross-National Child Maintenance', *Child and Family Law Quarterly* 15:3, 269–278

— (2003c), 'The Impact of Enlargement on Free Movement: A Critique of Transitional Periods', paper presented at the Third Meeting of the UACES Study Group on the Evolving EU Migration Law and Policy, University of Liverpool, 5 December

— (2005), 'Parenting, Care and Mobility in the EU: Issues Facing Migrant Scientists', *Innovation* 18:3, 361

Staniewicz, T. (2007), 'A Critical Evaluation of Factors Inhibiting A8 Migrants' Full Participation in Civil Society' (University of Warwick: Centre for Rights, Equality and Diversity). Available online at <http://www2.warwick.ac.uk/fac/soc/sociology/research/cred/publications/cred__launch_polish_research.pdf> (last accessed 14 February 2008)

Stanley, L. and Wise, S. (1993), *Breaking Out Again: Feminist Ontology and Epistemology* (London: Routledge)

Stenning et al. (2006), *Assessing the Local and Regional Impacts of International Migration* (Newcastle: Centre for Urban and Regional Development Studies)

Stewart, D.W. and Shamdasani, P.N. (1992), *Focus Groups: Theory and Practice* (London: Sage)

Tamas, K. and Münz, R. (2006a), 'Labour Migration and Transitional Regimes in the European Union', paper presented at the COMPAS International Conference, 'International Labour Migration: In Whose Interests?', University of Oxford, 5–6 July 2006

— (2006b), *Labour Migrants Unbound? EU Enlargement, Transitional Measures and Labour Market Effects* (Stockholm: Institute for Futures Studies)

TGWU (2006), Press Release: Shop Steward Suspended for Speaking out against Agency Workers' Abuse, 27 June. Available online at <http://www.tgwu.org.uk/Templates/News.asp?NodeID=92616> (last accessed 15 February 2008)

TGWU (2005), Press Release: T&G Polish Members Join Nationwide Tesco Protest, 3 September. Available online at <http://www.tgwu.org.uk/Templates/News.asp?NodeID=91843> (last accessed 15 February 2008)

Thomas, P.A. (ed.) (1997), *Socio-Legal Studies* (Aldershot: Dartmouth)

Thompson, P. (2004), 'Researching Family and Social Mobility with Two Eyes: Some Experiences of the Interaction between Qualitative and Quantitative Data', *International Journal of Social Research Methodology* 7:3, 237–257

Thränhardt, D. (1996), 'European Migration from East to West: Present Patterns and Future Directions', *New Community* 22:2, 227–endpage

Tomuschat, C. (2000), 'Comment on Maria Martinez Sala', *Common Market Law Review* 37: 2, 449–457

Toner, H. (2006), 'Legislative Comment: New Regulations Implementing Directive 2004/38', *Journal of Immigration Asylum and Nationality Law*, 20:3, 158–178

— (2007), 'Citizenship and Transitional Arrangements in the UK Courts – a Failure of Legal Protection?', paper presented at Workshop on 'Interrogating

Transitional Arrangements on Free Movement', University of Liverpool, 17 September.

Traser, J. (2006), *Who's Still Afraid of EU Enlargement* (Brussels: European Citizen Action Service)

— and Venables, T. (2008), *Who's Afraid of the EU's Latest Enlargement? The Impact of Bulgaria and Romania Joining the Union on Free Movement of Persons* (Brussels: European Citizen Action Service).

TUC (2005), News Release: Polish PM Urged to Join Forces with UK to Tackle Bad Employers, 24 November. Available online at <http://www.tuc.org.uk/h_and_s/tuc-11110–f0.cfm> (last accessed 15 February 2008)

Van Der Mei, A.P. (2003a), *Free Movement of Persons Within the European Community: Cross Border Access to Public Benefits* (Oxford: Hart)

— (2003b), 'Comments on Baumbast', *European Journal of Migration and Law* 5:3, 419–433

— (2005), 'Union Citizenship and the 'De-Nationalization' of the Territorial Welfare State', *European Journal of Migration and Law* 7:2, 203–211

Vaughan-Whitehead, D.C. (2003), *EU Enlargement versus Social Europe? The Uncertain Future of the European Social Model* (Cheltenham: Edward Elgar)

Velluti, S. (2005), 'Implementing Gender Equality and Mainstreaming in an Enlarged European Union – Some Thoughts on prospects and Challenges for Central Eastern Europe', *Journal of Social Welfare and Family Law* 27:2, 213–225

Vertovec, S. and Cohen, R. (eds) (1999), *Transnationalism* (Aldershot: Edward Elgar)

— (2002), 'Transnational Networks and Skilled Labour Migration', paper presented at Migration Conference, Ladenburg, 14–15 February

Vizi, E.S. (1993), 'Reversing the Brain Drain from Eastern European Countries: The "Push" and "Pull" Factors', *Technology in Society* 15:1, 101–109

Vlad, I. (2004), 'European Views about Accession', *BMJ Careers*, 6 March

Ward, K. et al. (2005), *The Role of Temporary Staffing Agencies in Facilitating Labour Mobility in Eastern and Central Europe* (Manchester: Vedior)

Waldinger, R. and Lichter, M. (2003), *How the Other Half Works: Immigration and the Social Organization of Labour* (Los Angeles: University of California Press)

Walker, N. (ed.) (2003), *Sovereignty in Transition* (Oxford: Hart)

Wallace, C. (1998), *Migration Potential in Central and Eastern Europe* (Geneva: International Organization for Migration)

— and Stola, D. (eds) (2001), *Patterns of Migration in Central Europe* (New York: Palgrave)

Weil, P. (2005), 'A Flexible Framework for a Plural Europe', discussion paper prepared for the UK Presidency (Paris: Centre National de la Recherche Scientifique). Available online at <http://www.number-10.gov.uk/output/Page8378.asp> (last accessed 10 February 2008)

Westwood, S. and Phizacklea, A. (eds) (2000), *Trans-nationalism and the Politics of Belonging* (London: Routledge)

White, R.C.A (2004), *Workers, Establishment and Services in the European Union* (Oxford: Oxford University Press)

— (2005a), 'Residence, Benefit Entitlement and Community Law', *Journal of Social Security Law* 12:1, 10–25

— (2005b), 'Free Movement, Equal Treatment, and Citizenship of the Union', *International and Comparative Law Quarterly* 54:4, 885–906

Wiener, A. (1998), *'European' Citizenship Practice: Building Institutions of a Non-state* (Boulder, CO: Westview)

Wikeley, N. (1988), 'Migrant Workers and Unemployment Benefit in the European Community', *Journal of Social Welfare and Family Law* 10:5, 300–315

Williams, A.M. and Baláž, V. (2004), 'From Private to Public Sphere, the Commodification of the Au Pair Experience? Returned Migrants from Slovakia to the UK', *Environment and Planning* 36:10, 1813–1833

Woods, L. (1999), 'Family Rights in the EU – Disadvantaging the Disadvantaged', *Child and Family Law Quarterly* 11:1, 17–31

Index